Voices

FROM THE HILL

THE STORY OF

OKLAHOMA MILITARY ACADEMY

JOHN WOOLEY

HAWK
PUBLISHING
GROUP

TULSA

LIBRARY OF CONGRESS CATALOG IN PUBLICATION DATA

Voices from the Hill: The Story of Oklahoma Military Academy/John Wooley

[1. Wooley, John - Non-Fiction United States.]

Copyright © 2005 by Rogers State University Foundation

Cover Design by Mullerhaus Publishing Arts, Inc.
Cover photo used with permission of Col. John E. Horne

ISBN 1-930709-55-2
Library of Congress Control Number: 2005921707
Published in the United States by HAWK Publishing Group.

HAWK Publishing Group
7107 South Yale Avenue #345
Tulsa, OK 74136
918-492-3677
www.hawkpub.com

HAWK and colophon are trademarks belonging to the HAWK Publishing Group. Printed in the United States of America.
9 8 7 6 5 4 3 2 1

FROM THE HILL

THE STORY OF

OKLAHOMA MILITARY

ACADEMY

JOHN WOOLEY

Dedication

This book is dedicated to all those whose lives were touched by the Oklahoma Military Academy—especially to the more than 100 former cadets who gave their lives in the service of our country, to those who were wounded in the line of duty, and to the thousands who otherwise served in the Armed Forces of the United States.

Foreword

Voices from the Hill: The Story of Oklahoma Military Academy records the history of Oklahoma Military Academy and its training of approximately 10,000 young men—and a few women—during its 52-year existence. It was written in order to record the history, camaraderie, tradition, heritage, and legacy of Oklahoma Military Academy, as well as the facts, statistics, myths, and many of the personal stories that helped created the *esprit de corps* so valued by the cadets. Because the number of former OMA students shrinks each year, there was a certain urgency attached to this project.

Writing and publication of *Voices from the Hill* was made possible by the financial support of 125 alumni, their families, and friends of Oklahoma Military Academy. The participation of the Rogers State University development staff and the curator of the OMA Museum was vital to the success of this project as well.

Contributors' names are listed in the appendix, which also includes lists of OMA alumni and former students killed in action and long-serving faculty and administration staff members. Everyone concerned with this book has worked diligently with the information available to insure the accuracy of these lists. Since OMA ceased to exist some 34 years ago, the records we used may be incomplete or contain errors. If you know of any changes that should be made to these lists to ensure their accuracy in the future, please contact the OMA Alumni Association, Rogers State University, 1701 Will Rogers Blvd., Claremore, OK 74017.

All income from the sales of this book will be dedicated to the support and perpetuation of the Oklahoma Military Academy Museum, located in the former Meyer Barracks building on the RSU campus.

Acknowledgements & Notes on Sources

I am indebted to those whose reminiscences, both oral and written, represented the lives and experiences of the thousands who attended the school on the Hill. They include, from the 1930s, Col. John Horne, Col. Robert Lewis, Louis Miller, Lt. Gen. William E. Potts, Lt. Col. Edwin D. Ramsey, A. Blaine Imel Jr., and Donald Ruggles; from the '40s, Alex Adwan, Matthew Braun, Col. Glen Burke, Col. A. Frank Cochran, DeAtley Hampton, Bud Inhofe, Kenneth D. Kirkland, Lt. Col. Harlan G. Koch, Joe McBride, John E. Martin, Anthony Massad, Col. James Morrison, and Col. Harry Poarch; from the '50s, Jim Barker, Charles Cline, Gene Crose, Bill B. Harris, Jon Hines, B.G. Jones, Sam M. Matthews, Bill Ramsay, Dr. Donald Routh, Rob Roy Routh, and Ted Wright; and from the '60s and '70s, James Elder, Phil Goldfarb, Gen. Timothy Malishenko, Wayne McCombs, Alan Phillips, David Raper, John S. Ross, and Tom Seely.

Most of these men graciously consented to interviews; a few sent manuscripts ranging from one handwritten page to near book-length. I am grateful for everything they shared.

For their help and generosity in sending source material, I must also thank Gary J. Dean, OMA alumni Ben Boyd and Lt. Col Walter Price. While not an alumnus, Ray Bingham supplied valuable first-hand information about a period in the school's history, while Steve Gragert at the Will Rogers Memorial made rare material available to me, enriching and illuminating the relationship Claremore's favorite son had with the academy in the 1930s.

OMA Museum curator Gene Little was a great help to this book in a number of ways, as was his predecessor, Norman Shaw. *Tulsa World* researchers Austin Farley, Keith Binning and Hilary Pittman gave me access to most of the dozens of newspaper stories that helped form the backbone of this narrative, and Eddie Kerschen and Barbara Vaughan of Tulsa's downtown QuikPrint were helpful in that area as well. Brian Byrne of radio station KWGS was another important part of the process that saw *Voices from the Hill* go from manuscript to book, as was my editor at the *World*, Cathy Logan.

Finally, if not for William Bernhardt and HAWK Publishing Group, and his kind, smart, and indefatigable HAWK editor, Jodie Nida, this book would probably not exist. It *certainly* would not exist without the wisdom and guidance of the OMA Alumni Board of Directors, including grads DeAtley Hampton and Alex Adwan and Rogers State University's Vice President for Development, Dr. Danette McNamara Boyle. These three were with the project long before even a line was written; they stayed with it through every step of the journey from idea to published book, offering insightful, thoughtful help throughout. Also indispensable were the members of Dr. Boyle's staff at the RSU Foundation and Alumni Center, led by administrative assistant Amanda Hardt. They include Sherry Alexander, Tonni Harrald, Dayna Smith, Kimberly Earickson, Island SpottedBear, and Kristi Hall.

In addition to the sources mentioned above, I must also acknowledge the use of a master's thesis and two doctoral dissertations, all of which are mentioned in the book's text. Don R. Robards' 1947 thesis *A History of the Oklahoma Military Academy* was especially valuable, as was Dr. Larry Dean Rice's 1992 dissertation *Eighty Years of University Preparatory Education on College Hill*. Another dissertation, Homer M. Ledbetter's *A Study of the Oklahoma Military Academy from 1950*, was also useful, giving insight into the man who would become one of OMA's longest-tenured presidents.

For the sake of readability, I have corrected minor spelling and punctuation errors and standardized a few abbreviations and terms that changed, however subtly, over the course of the school's five-plus decades.

~ John Wooley

Table of Contents

Company Formation in front of
Preparatory Hall (The Administration Building) ~ 1921

Introduction

Color Guard ~ 1928

The campus of Rogers State University spreads across the top of a picturesque hill, which slopes gently down to meet the outskirts of the sprawling northeastern Oklahoma city of Claremore. One of the Sooner State's newest universities, RSU offers more than a dozen four-year degree programs to its nearly 4,000 students, boasting its own television and radio stations as well.

The university is named after one of the most prominent families that ever lived in the area, and just across the highway from the school lies the most famous of that clan: Will Rogers, the humorist, vaudeville performer, cowboy philosopher, and major movie star whose life was cut short in an Alaskan plane crash in 1935. Rogers is buried on the grounds of the Will Rogers Memorial, a first-rate museum and tribute to Rogers' life and work that continues to be a major tourist attraction.

One weekend a year, scores of people from all across the country make a pilgrimage to the Rogers State campus as well. These aren't tourists, however. They are men with a deep and almost spiritual connection to the campus, a bond so strong that it pulls hundreds of them periodically back to the place long known as College Hill (or, simply, the Hill), to the place where—as they'll tell you—they did their growing up. Most of them weren't men then, but teenagers. And it wasn't Rogers State University then, nor was it RSU's most immediate predecessors, Rogers State College and Claremore College. Instead, it was a unique institution called Oklahoma Military Academy, where three generations of boys became men. They not only learned, but lived, the three words in the OMA logo—courage, loyalty, and honor—while acquiring skills and codes of behavior that would serve them well for a lifetime.

Even during the rest of the year, when the OMA alumni aren't gathered on the Hill for their weekend reunion, it's easy to see the continued imprint of the academy. The most obvious is the Oklahoma Military Academy Museum, which takes up the entire second story of an RSU administration building named Meyer Hall. Originally the first barracks opened for academy cadets back in 1920, Meyer Hall, like many of the other structures on campus, holds more than a hint of ages past, of the young ghosts who slept in long-ago bunks, jumping up at the sound of reveille and marching out the doors in sharp military style, shoes shined and uniforms spotless. Sometimes, you can feel them around you.

At the very front of the campus stands a statue by Yon Sim Pak that represents every young man who donned an OMA uniform. Known as the Lone Cadet, the handsome figure, rifle shouldered and body snapped to attention, stands on a grassy slope looking down on a tidy shimmering small lake and beyond, to Claremore itself. About 40 feet behind the Lone Cadet, the American flag flies from atop a flagpole, erected by the OMA Parents Association during the wartime fervor of 1943, with a base financed by OMA's class of '37. Years later—two decades, in fact, after the academy graduated its last class in 1971—a monument was added beside the base of the flagpole. Featuring the Cadet Prayer on its left-hand side and the OMA seal in the middle, it includes the following inscription:

> *Oklahoma Military Academy was established in 1919. For 52 years, young cadets developed to their fullest—mentally, morally and physically. They were taught the responsibility of defending the land of the free and the home of the brave. The ones honored by this monument carried the full burden of this responsibility. This is intended to be a hallowed place dedicated to the recognition of all those of College Hill who have served and will serve their country.*

* * * * *

Once a year in that hallowed place, former cadets from all over gather for a morning formation and cadet memorial service. Part of the OMA Alumni Reunion, it features a posting of the colors followed by reports from cadet commanders representing each decade of the academy's existence. Although there's some playfulness in the ceremony, with threats of demerits passed laughingly between the men, it turns serious and solemn when the time comes to recognize those alumni who have died in the year since their last meeting. The adjutant in charge places a red flower on the monument for each one of the fallen cadets, adding a pink flower to represent loved ones. After the names are read, the sad, lonely sound of "Taps" echoes through the morning air on College Hill, as the survivors stand at attention.

They surely know that this ceremony is about the living as well as the dead. They know that there are fewer of them with each year that passes, but they also know that as long as one of them lives he will carry with him the memory of Oklahoma Military Academy, of the friends made and the lessons learned and the young lives lived together on the Hill. It's that shared memory that brings these men back to look again and again at the place where they grew up, to bring wives and sons and daughters to see it, to swap stories once again about being a "rabbit," about teachers and fellow cadets, about demerits, about pranks and practical jokes—about everything they went through as they made the transformation from boys to men.

Much of this book is in their words. There is historical fact here, of course, but there are also lots of good stories, told by the men who lived them. Oklahoma Military Academy wasn't simply a collection of buildings on a scenic hilltop campus. It was a place where thousands of young men lived and worked and learned, and, with this collection of history and reminiscence, we hope to take you there and put you in the midst of them, in the barracks and the classrooms and out on the campus and beyond, to show you what it felt like to be alone and frightened on your first day away from the security of home and family, waiting with trepidation on an unknown future—and then, to gradually gain confidence and discipline and that all-important sense of camaraderie until, finally, you were forever and irrevocably tied to the people and the place. Glen Burke, Class of '53, summed those feelings up nicely in a speech at the 1991 OMA reunion:

We all know there was something special about this place. We're reminded of it when we visit the Hill. It's hard to explain, but we've all experienced that feeling of nostalgia when a thousand memories begin flooding our minds. Remember what it was like when we stood that last formation at the flagpole after graduation? It was something to see young soldiers, many soon to become second lieutenants on active duty, cry like little boys. It was impossible to hold the tears back. We tried at first, but emotion took control as we said goodbye to each other, and to our home for the past four or five years.

Yes, there was something special about OMA. We had *"esprit de corps"*—a deep-rooted loyalty and enthusiasm for the place…

It's the *esprit de corps*, a deep and complex set of emotions still beating in the hearts of those who attended OMA, that pulls so many of the academy's graduates back to College Hill year after year, and it's that spirit that rises from these pages like the young ghosts of the cadets on the Rogers State University campus. Every one of the many thousands of young men who attended Oklahoma Military Academy came away with different personal experiences, unique to themselves; yet, the shared experience and emphasis on courage, loyalty and honor created an *esprit*-fueled bond that forever binds them to one another, and to the place where they suffered together, learned together, felt pride together, and matured together.

"Everyone who attended OMA could probably write a book on memorable incidents," said former cadet Matthew Braun, who went on to distinguish himself as an author of western novels. "But what many of us remember most is that our collective experience taught us the meaning of *esprit de corps*. Teamwork and camaraderie among men are lessons we all learned in our life on the Hill. There is no memory stronger than that of fellowship."

Freshman Class ~ 1920

The Beginning

Attention! ~ 1920

Oklahoma Military Academy officially opened its doors in the fall of 1919, the year after the end of the Great War. At the time, there was exactly one building on campus, Preparatory Hall, with the mess hall and heating plant in the basement, and classrooms and offices in the upper stories. Barracks for the cadets weren't finished until the next spring, so the 40 full-time students who comprised that first class lived in tents on the campus throughout the fall and winter, attending classes in the lone building, Preparatory Hall, and drilling with wooden rifles.

The institution had begun life as the Eastern University Preparatory School, founded in Claremore in 1909. At the time, Oklahoma had only been a state for a couple of years, after two territories—Oklahoma Territory to the west, and Indian Territory to the east—had merged in preparation for statehood. While their respective territories blended into one state, political leaders from each former territory still wanted to take care of their own constituents.

One of the areas where this political partisanship was felt was in the establishment of state schools. Oklahoma A&M College in Stillwater and the University of Oklahoma in Norman had both begun in Oklahoma Territory in 1890; Indian Territory had no colleges at the time. It wasn't until after the merger with Oklahoma Territory and Oklahoma's subsequent statehood that institutions of higher learning were opened in Wilburton (the Oklahoma School of Mines and Metallurgy) and Chickasha (The Industrial Institute and College for Girls), both towns in the former Indian Territory.

A university preparatory school—which was a state-run school with a curriculum that prepared students for college—had been operating in Oklahoma Territory since 1901; again, for various reasons, there were none in pre-statehood Indian Territory. Once the new state of Oklahoma came into being, however, the legislature moved to make the educational opportunities more equitable in both of the former territories. So, Eastern University Preparatory School was born.

At first, however, it wasn't supposed to be in Claremore at all. The house bill that called for the school's establishment initially located it in Holdenville, south and west of Claremore near the center of the state. Rogers County representative C. S. Wortman managed to get the bill amended, fighting off another challenge from an Atoka legislator who wanted the school in his own area. Oklahoma Governor C.N. Haskell signed the bill establishing the institution at Claremore on March 25, 1909.

In his 1992 doctoral thesis on the various colleges and other institutions that have existed on Claremore's College Hill over the years, Larry Dean Rice told of a conversation between Wortman's granddaughter and then-RSU President Dr. Richard Mosier, in which the woman said that her grandfather "loved to tell the story of his return to Claremore by train shortly after disclosure of the location of the new school had been made to the local citizenry. According to his account, he was met by a cheering throng of supporters who by torchlight bore him upon their shoulders to the lobby of the main hotel in Claremore where the celebration lasted into the wee hours of the morning."

In order to meet the requirements of the bill, a tract of land had to be secured for the school. Albert L. Kates, owner and publisher of the *Claremore Progress* newspaper, had been squarely behind getting a new school in Claremore; once the bill establishing the school was passed and signed, he joined other family members and boosters in buying and donating the 40 acres atop the hill that would become the Eastern University Preparatory School campus. The first building was named, naturally enough, Preparatory Hall.

For all the initial excitement about its appearance, however, Eastern University Preparatory School had a relatively brief run, closing its doors in spring of 1917. While enrollment and the number of faculty members continued to rise, politics came into the picture again, with opponents of the school—and, especially, its location—charging that it was little more than a high school for Claremore's students. The February 16, 1913, *Claremore Progress* carried an article by Joseph Hamilton rebutting that claim. He wrote that Eastern University Preparatory School was in Claremore because of the city's "beauty and healthfulness," and further noted that fewer than half of the institution's 214 students were actually Claremore residents. (The others were from out of town, boarding with Claremore families.)

Despite Mr. Hamilton's defense of the school's location, the grumbling continued from other parts of the state, and the challenges turned into a threat when Governor Lee Cruce proposed a plan to cut down the number of state-supported schools—at the time, there were 19, serving a total Oklahoma population of well under 100,000 —in order to save money and improve the quality of those that would remain after the downsizing. Following a consultation with a number of national educators, Cruce proposed abolishing 11 of the 19, including both preparatory schools (the other was located in Tonkawa, in former Oklahoma Territory). A school-abolition bill was quickly drafted in the House of Representatives, but it ran into serious opposition and was ultimately tabled.

It was Cruce's successor, Governor R.L. Williams, who finally drove the nails into Eastern University Preparatory School's coffin, with a simple veto of the state's usual funding for the school. It was 1917, and, he pointed out, there were several regular high schools in Oklahoma, which essentially served the same function as preparatory schools. To him, the two preparatory schools were needless state expenses.

Because of a lack of appropriations, Eastern University Preparatory School ended its run after the spring semester of 1917, with the building and grounds turned over, interestingly enough, to the city of Claremore— to be used as the temporary headquarters of Claremore High School.

* * * * *

In 1918, H. Tom Kight—the man considered the father of Oklahoma Military Academy—was a state representative from Claremore. It was the final year of World War I, and patriotism and love of country swelled in the hearts and minds of Americans. In that environment, Kight began to work on the idea of reopening the former Eastern Oklahoma Preparatory

H. Tom Kight

School as a military school. The idea quickly gained momentum, becoming a part of the platform of the 1918 Democratic nominee for governor, William Durant. While Durant was defeated, Kight achieved his goal, introducing an ultimately successful legislative bill to establish what would become Oklahoma Military Academy in the old Eastern Oklahoma Preparatory School location. Governor J.A.B. Robertson signed the bill on March 10, 1919—only a few months after the armistice was declared and the Great War was, for all practical purposes, history.

Another OMA founding father was S. M. Barrett, who had been the final president of Eastern University Preparatory School and Oklahoma's Director of Vocational Education. A member of a military family, Barrett had been kept out of West Point because of a serious injury, but he'd long held the ambition of organizing a military school. According to a 1947 interview with Barrett, conducted by historian Don R. Robards, Kight and the rest of the committee drafted the bill creating Oklahoma Military Academy in Barrett's Oklahoma City offices.

It was a good time to be opening a military school. The war and America's part in winning it had not only created a new wave of patriotism, but also an appreciation for the value of military training, to help assure the country was ready in case of another international conflict. In addition to receiving state funding for the new academy —including a $75,000 appropriation for the construction of barracks — President Barrett also received help from the federal government. Along with Claremore's C.D. Davis, the secretary of OMA's newly appointed Board of Regents, Barrett made a spring 1919 trip to Washington, D.C., where the two successfully won approval of the as-yet-unopened academy as a Junior Reserve Officer Training Corps (ROTC) center.

Created by the government only three years earlier as a part of the National Defense Act, ROTC provided a system of military training at educational institutions. ROTC cadets were organized into Army-style units of squads, platoons, companies (troops), and battalions (squadrons), with cadet officers in charge. The participating young men were trained in Military Science and Tactics (MS&T) a program of study that included such things as assembly, disassembly, care, use, function and maintenance of their assigned weapons; military history and tactics; recognition of military equipment, both friendly and hostile, and its capabilities; military organization; and use of terrain in combat situations—among other things.

ROTC had two divisions. The beginning two years were the junior division, providing courses that could qualify students as non-commissioned officers. The final two years comprised the senior division, qualifying selected students as second lieutenants upon completion of the ROTC course requirements. The government provided some equipment and regular military personnel to participating schools.

So, Oklahoma Military Academy was born. And the beginning class of 20 high-school-age students, who huddled in tents throughout the fall and winter of 1919 while awaiting the building of Meyer Barracks, became the first in a long line of cadets that wound down through the decades, weathering a Great Depression and three wars and changing times and attitudes, for over half of the 20th Century.

APPLICATION FOR ADMISSION

TO THE
OKLAHOMA MILITARY ACADEMY
Claremore, Oklahoma

Date..................

I hereby apply for the admission of my (son .ward) to the Oklahoma Military Academy at Claremore, Oklahoma, for the school year commencing September .... and ending May .... Subject to the provisions of the Academy catalogue and regulations of the institution and agree to abide by the decisions of the authorities of tthe Military Academy in matters of discipline and conduct.

I further certify that he is of good moral character and that I will assume the necessary financial obligations.

Name of Applicant ....

                 Last Name   First Name   Initial

Age .... Date of Birth .... Height .... Weight ....

School last attended .... Has he ever been dismissed from any school? ....

Has he been vaccinated for Small Pox. .... Typhoid? .... (State year in each case). He is ready for the (underscore) Freshman, Sophomore, Junior, Senior year, High School; Freshman, Sophomore year in College.

REFERENCE AS TO APPLICANT'S CHARACTER

  1. Name ....

        Address ....

                    (A Former Teacher)

  2. Name ....

        Address ....

Remarks: (Confidential) ....

....

....

Upon enrollment of my (son or ward) as a cadet in the Oklahoma Military Academy, I hereby agree that if he should be dismissed, or leave the Academy without authority or without an honorable discharge that I will forfeit any balance due, except the allowance for spending money.

WITH THIS APPLICATION should be mailed a check for $30.00, as Registration fee. This is not an extra charge, but is merely an evidence of good faith. The amount will be placed to your credit and DEDUCTED from the first payment due at the opening of the September term. It is agreed that this reservation fee will be forfeited to the Oklahoma Military Academy if the cadet does not enter school by September 15, 1929.

Signed:—

....
Signature of parent or guardian.

....
Address

OKLAHOMA MILITARY ACADEMY

THE DAILY ROUTINE OF DUTIES

	School Days	Saturday	Sunday
Reveille	6:00 A. M.	6:00 A. M.	7:00 A. M.
Mess	6:45 A. M.	6:45 A. M.	7:45 A. M.
Sick Call	7:15 A. M.	7:15 A. M.	8:15 A. M.
School	7:45 A. M.		
Inspection		8:40 A. M.	
Church Call			8:50 A. M.
Mess	12:10 P. M.	12:20 P. M.	12:55 P. M.
Guard Mount	12:45 P. M.	12:45 P. M.	1:45 P. M.
School	1:05 P. M.		
Fatigue	3:10 P. M	12:55 P. M.	
Retreat	5:40 P. M.	5:05 P. M.	5:05 P. M.
Mess	6:20 P. M.	5:20 P. M.	5:20 P. M.
Call to Quarters	7:30 P. M.	7:30 P. M.	8:00 P. M.
Tattoo	9:30 P. M.	9:30 P. M.	9:30 P. M.
Taps	10:00 P. M.	10:00 P.M.	10:00 P. M.

Colonel S.M. Barrett
President 1920–1925

Colonel Walter E. Downs
President 1925–1940

The 1920s

By Old Claremore's western border
Reared against the sky
Proudly stands our Alma Mater
As the years roll by.
Forward ever be our watchword
Conquer and prevail.
Hail to thee! Our Alma Mater
OMA — All hail!

OMA — OMA — OMA forever,
Sing to me once again,
Sing praise to our Alma Mater
Rah! Rah! Rah! for OMA!

— Oklahoma Military Academy school song
as published in the 1928 *Guidon*

In February of 1920, a famous acquaintance of OMA President S. M. Barrett dropped by the new campus and spoke to the cadets, who were still housed in tents at the time. In town to speak on behalf of the League of Nations, the just-created association of countries founded with hopes of maintaining worldwide peace, former U.S. President William Howard Taft ended up spending most of the afternoon with Barrett, helping to draw up rules and regulations for the nascent academy.

A month later, the cadets were able to fold their tents and move into the newly built barracks. The building that housed the students was named for Oklahoma war hero Sgt. Maurice Meyer, who'd been mortally wounded in France late in 1918.

Maurice Meyer

According to Don R. Robards' excellent history of OMA, written as an unpublished master's thesis in 1947, "The organization of the Oklahoma Military Academy was not influenced to any great extent by other and better-known military schools. Events of the first year give insight into the matter and point to the fact that the school was the culmination of a life-long desire of Barrett and instead of being patterned after any other school it was based on his ideas."

Among those ideas was an emphasis on vocational education as part of the overall curriculum, as an article in OMA's first yearbook, the 1920 *Vedette*, explained:

> The need for vocational training was never fully realized by the people of this country until the recent war between the United States and Germany. The quick making and transportation of munitions is a vital factor in the winning of any war, and were it not for the fact that a large number of young men of this country were quickly, if not thoroughly, taught the use of machine tools, today's history would have been differently rewritten...The early training of boys along mechanical lines will do more towards placing our army and navy on a battle footing in a short time than any other kind of training. Mechanics requires precision, quick acting, self-reliance, and original ideas coupled with the ability to grasp and use the ideas of others. Any normal boy thoroughly schooled and practiced in these requisites will make an officer of the highest efficiency rating; the man who wins with the least sacrifices, the kind of a man who never wins on a foul or a streak of luck, the man whose work never permits a no decision verdict. This type of man is quiet, clear eyed, modest, and possessed of a magnetic personality that attracts and at the same time permits of no undue familiarity. This is the kind of man of whom everybody is proud to say, "He is a friend of mine." He is the kind of man the vocational department of the OMA, with the assistance of Uncle Sam, will train to handle the next national emergency with speed and decision...

Although most of the ideas that formed the bedrock of OMA's educational philosophy came from the veteran educator Barrett, a couple appear to have been established by OMA's predecessor on the Hill, Eastern University Preparatory School—something that seems natural, since Barrett also presided over that institution for a couple of years.

Like the preparatory school, OMA emphasized and saw considerable success with extracurricular activities. In the school years of 1920 and '21, for instance, the cadet football team lost only two games. Dubbed "the Miracle Team" by the *Claremore Progress*, and made up entirely of Oklahoma native sons, the 1921 outfit saw its sole defeat at the hands of Tahlequah's Northeastern—a team from a four-year teachers' college playing a group of high schoolers.

President Barrett also encouraged the formation of an OMA band, which began in 1920. Two years later, that group became the official band of the Oklahoma delegation to the Confederate Reunion at Richmond, Va. The trip included a swing by Washington, D.C., where the OMA boys played for the United States Congress and President Warren G. Harding.

Then there were the Barrett-planned excursions that were less spectacular but, in their own ways, noteworthy. One of these was chronicled in the 1920 *Vedette* under the title of "The Cadets Go on Hike to Claremore Mound."

Bright and early, May 1, the cadet corps of the Oklahoma Military Academy could be seen going over the endless chain of roads leading to Claremore Mound. They were going to camp on ground made famous by a big battle fought between the Osage and Cherokee Indians in 1828. When they arrived at the scene of action various details of men unloaded the big Pierce Arrow truck, which was driven by Captain Frost, put up tents and built camp fires in a comparatively short time. Mess was had about one o'clock, after which the cadets enjoyed themselves fishing, hunting, and swimming in and around the Verdigris River, which glided along the birches and willows growing along the side of the Mound. As evening drew near, the call for mess was sounded, cadets came from every direction and lined up for chow. Never did a bunch of boys do better justice to a meal.

About an hour after supper the boys could be seen gathered around the campfire listening to Colonel Barrett tell some Indian stories, as well as some of his own earlier experiences. As time went on, the boys themselves told stories and sang songs, then Captain Frost was called on to tell some deep sea stories. He told a weird ghost story and was soon hushed by the cadets. Taps was blown and all was silent. The camp was shortly lost in slumber, dreaming of bygone days.

The next morning many were in swimming before sunrise and some roamed over the surrounding country finding interesting Indian relics. Dinner was served at noon and camp was broken.

On the return trip the Pierce Arrow got stuck in the mud several times. It had to be pulled out by main strength by the cadets, by them it was pulled nearly to Sequoyah, where it was left. Two trucks were sent for and when they arrived the supplies were loaded on them. Some of the boys were left to take care of the trucks and the camping outfit and the others started for OMA by foot. It was not long before the school was in sight and a cheer rang out from the boys as they trudged up the road to the barracks. It was time for mess when the Academy was reached. All agreed that they had a good time and looked forward to the time that they would go on another such excursion.

(In a footnote to his thesis, Robards explains the "Colonel" appellation that all OMA presidents received, beginning with Barrett. "The military titles given to the member of the Oklahoma Military Academy faculty," he wrote, "were the result of being given an honorary commission in the Oklahoma National Guard and being placed on the Governor's staff. This rating did not carry any actual military duties except for those faculty members who were *bona fide* members of the reserve corps, guard, or regular army.")

Another notion Barrett retained from the prep school was its connection with the community of Claremore, a symbiotic relationship that found one of its greatest expressions in Barrett's allowing local boys to attend OMA without having to live in the barracks. This first happened in 1921, when a limited number of students—soon dubbed "day dogs" by the cadets—came to study by day and return to their own homes at night. Although the practice was halted later in the decade, it would return periodically throughout OMA's entire existence.

The same year that the day dogs first climbed the Hill to go to school, politics once again reared its head, as the Oklahoma legislature floated the idea of changing OMA into a hospital. The *Claremore Progress* registered immediate disdain for that proposal, maintaining that the abolishing of OMA in favor of a hospital would be a major loss for the city. One can only assume that the editorial reflected the thinking of a majority of the town's leaders and its other citizens.

Claremore's people had a right to be skittish, having lost their first state school only five years earlier. The hospital proposal, which really didn't go anywhere, seemed to spawn a kind of local paranoia about OMA's future at the hands of Oklahoma lawmakers. Of course, being teenage boys, some of the cadets figured a way to turn all the uncertainty to humorous advantage. Historian Robards writes:

> The rumors of the school being killed were so strong and persistent that when the legislature was in session mischievous cadets frequently would arise when reveille was sounded and shout that the school had just been killed by the legislature and go back to bed. The students would then remain in their quarters until Colonel Barrett came to see why the cadets were not in their classes.

OMA survived, and began steadily improving in both student population and resources, thanks in large part to the continued political clout and commitment of Claremore-based State Representative H. Tom Kight and the lobbying of Col. Barrett, who, according to Don Robards, "reportedly spent four days per week at the legislature and three days per week at the school" when the Oklahoma Congress was in session. Kight's continuing help during OMA's beginning years was reflected in the school's yearbooks, including the 1927 *Guidon*, which published a full-page picture of the representative over the slogan "A Stalwart Friend of OMA."

As mentioned earlier, the first OMA yearbook, which appeared in 1920, was called the *Vedette*—a term that, as OMA alumnus Glen Burke noted much later, meant "a small armed vessel used for scouting or escorting. That's the Navy definition. We refer to it as a mounted sentry in the advance of any army for observing enemy activities." It was the *Vedette* again in 1921, and then was called simply *OMA* for three years. In 1925 and '26, the *Vedette* title returned, and then it became the *Guidon*, retaining that name into the 1940s, when it finally changed back to its original title for good. (Meanwhile, the school newspaper, called the *Dragoon* upon its initial publication in the early '30s, became the *Guidon*.)

What did cadets find funny during OMA's first year? Here are a couple of vintage gags from the first yearbook:

> *She — "Can you see one good reason for the short skirt fad?"*
> *He — (enthusiastically) "I can see two of them."*

> *O.D. (To Guard) — "Has the furnace gone out?"*
> *Guard — "Not through here, Sir."*

* * * * *

In the fall of 1922, OMA's enrollment increased to 125 and a first year of junior college was added, making the academy a five-year school. In 1923, the second junior-college year was added, so that cadets could begin as high-school freshmen and graduate with two years of college credits. The Oklahoma legislature was responsible for expanding OMA's academics; at the same time, it set up a system of appointing cadets to the school. Beginning in 1923, each of Oklahoma's state senators was allowed to appoint two cadets and two alternates to OMA, with the appointed cadets getting a $100 break on tuition. These cadets would make up a major part of OMA's student population until 1941, when the practice was discontinued.

Colonel Barrett, on the other hand, discontinued his own relationship with the academy in 1924, resigning for what Robards calls "personal reasons." It's conjecture at this point, but perhaps Barrett's resignation had something to do with the downgrading of the ROTC program at OMA. He and OMA Board of Regents Secretary C.D. Davis had secured a Junior ROTC designation for the school with their trip to Washington, D.C. in 1919, and in 1920 the U.S. Secretary of War made it official.

From the 1920 *Vedette*:

> A unit of the Junior Divisions of the Reserve Officers Training Corps was authorized by a letter of February 1st, from the Secretary of War, to be established at the Oklahoma Military Academy, and was placed under the direction of Captain Clifford J. Matthews, USA, as Professor of Military Science and Tactics…
>
> The purpose of ROTC is not limited to qualifying students to become officers. In the application of its training it endeavors to give each student good health, a strong body and a correct physical bearing, all of which are assets in any walk of life. It strives to form the habit of precise and logical thinking that will enable one to arrive at correct decisions with ease and promptness. It endeavors to teach the student clean living and clean thinking, and to inculcate in him a high standard of honor, patriotism, fairness, firmness and aggressiveness; to teach respect for duly constituted authority; to teach him to go about his work with energy, earnestness, loyalty, and enthusiasm. If students of the ROTC are efficiently instructed in the above mentioned matters during their school days, many of them will be manifested in daily habits and conduct through life.

These qualities stand not only for success in military life, but in civil life also, and if any man has them constantly brought before him, it is highly probable that he will carry many of them into civil life, and derive from such training those qualities that will not only make him a good officer but a good citizen.

There was a problem, however, with establishing the first OMA unit, which was designated as infantry. The institution didn't yet have the number of students required to start an ROTC program. So, when it came time to get the go-ahead from an inspecting officer, a number of area World War I vets were asked by school officials to show up in uniform in order to plump up the numbers. The ploy worked, and the unit was given permission to exist. But in 1924, the same year Barrett resigned, the War Department downgraded OMA's ROTC program. Don Robards speculated that the artificially inflated numbers created by the borrowed veterans actually worked against the school later on, when OMA's enrollment didn't increase fast enough to compensate for the absence of the ringers who'd been brought in to help start things.

(A rating downgrade was bad for several reasons, but largely because it was tied to how much help—in the form of equipment, uniforms, military personnel and even financial aid—the federal government gave participating schools.)

The ROTC unit bounced back to its original designation in 1926, helped along by a favorable recommendation by Colonel Mayo, who had been inspecting the troops since 1923. After the 1925 inspection, he noted that the group had looked like a "mob" in 1923, but had since improved rapidly.

By the time OMA got its Junior ROTC rating back, Colonel Walter E. Downs was in charge. He'd taken over as OMA's president in June of 1925, with school dean Colonel W. S. Bryan filling in as acting president before that, following Barrett's resignation.

* * * * *

The Oklahoma Military Academy located at Claremore, Oklahoma, has the distinction of being the only military institution in the state of Oklahoma. It is rapidly forging to the front and it will soon occupy a position comparable with the best military schools of our country. There is no more serious responsibility than that of selecting the proper school for the growing boy who will be the citizen of tomorrow. Our school combines a system of general education with military training.

The PRIMARY LESSON for the FUTURE CITIZEN of DEMOCRACY is SELF CONTROL and that is achieved only through DISCIPLINE…

Military schools conserve the time and energies of the boy and direct his activities in proper channels. Regular hours for study, for military drill, for student activities, for sleep and regular well balanced meals result in broad shoulders, erect posture of body, deep chest, elastic step, alert mind, open, honest face, and fearless frank eye.

The Association of Military Colleges and Schools of the United States gave the following report relative to the merits of military schools: "Military training does not supplant or detract from the soundness of the academic work, but goes hand-in-hand with it. It serves:

—to develop initiative, self-control, self-reliance;

—to secure punctuality, orderliness, efficiency;

—to give erect carriage and manly bearing;

—to develop the ability to think clearly and act promptly;

—to promote a high personal standard of honor.

The military school puts efficiency into the work and character of the boy. It enables him to get a grip on his own faculties and realize his possibilities. In a military school manliness and fair play are taught, and the student is placed on his honor…

—Colonel Walter E. Downs, President (from the 1927 *Guidon*)

When creating the rules and regulations for the academy, Colonel Barrett had not included two characteristics that were *de rigeur* at virtually all other military schools: the merit system and the new-man system. As Robards put it in his history of OMA, "Under the 'Merit' system, merits and demerits are given on a predetermined basis for acts ranging from personal neatness to infractions of the code of honor. The 'New Man' system is a method of indoctrination and instilling in the new cadet the proper respect for authority, usually through menial tasks, but often through use of force. In most schools the cadet remains a new man until the end of his first year."

A few years after OMA began, the new-man system would be uniquely expressed on the Hill with the "rabbit" designation, which indeed began as a year-long ordeal. But the new-man practice unofficially began early in the '20s, originating with the OMA football team. One of its members brought in the idea from another military school he'd attended, and it apparently sounded good to the rest of the boys, who proceeded to make life a little harder for the new guys—dubbed "rats" by the upperclassmen.

Extracurricular activities of a different kind were documented in a May 7, 1925 article in the *Claremore Progress*. The newspaper told of the cadets' "favorite sport," which turned out to be a variation on the time-honored hotfoot. In this version, lumps of shoe polish were surreptitiously smeared on the shoes of a victim and then lit. OMA's administration frowned on such merriment, however; the story relates how a faculty member caught two boys in the act and "boxed their ears."

* * * * *

All cadets are required to refrain from:
Hazing in any form.
Leaving the campus without proper authority.
Gambling or betting, or possession of devices used for same.
Injury to property.
Taking, having, or using property of others without permission.
Use of profane or obscene language.
Contracting debts without permission.
Reading or possession of improper literature.
Possession of firearms other than those issued by the Military
    Department.
Joining any oath-bound or secret organization.
Selling, pawning, or exchanging personal effects.
    —from the Oklahoma Military Academy
        Book of Regulations, *circa* 1929

Colonel Downs would be the one to establish both the merit and new-man systems at OMA, but when he took the reins in 1925, the institution's long-term survival was still a far cry from being assured. Although the schools' relationship with Claremore and its citizens remained excellent, the jury was still out with many other observers in the state, including some political figures who were looking for schools to shut down or consolidate. A story in the periodical *Harlow's Weekly* reported that Governor M.E. Trapp and General Baird H. Markham —both members of OMA's Board of Regents—had given Downs a year to "make good."

If that's true, Downs turned out to be the right man for what had to be a pressure-packed job. It was under his presidency that the school entered what's considered its golden age; by the time he left in 1940, OMA was as solid an institution as it would ever be.

An Arkansas native, Downs was an Army veteran who'd served in World War I and an educator whose last job before OMA had been as superintendent of the Poteau, Okla., school system. Familiar with both the military and educational systems, Downs—who came from modest circumstances—also believed deeply that a military education shouldn't only be the province of the wealthy, and worked to make OMA an affordable alternative for middle-class parents. Although he didn't believe in hazing, he established an official new-man system at OMA soon after he took over—changing "rat" to the slightly less offensive "rabbit"—as well as a merit system. These two changes brought OMA more in line with other military institutions across the country.

Downs also continued the emphasis on extracurricular activities that stretched back to the school's beginnings—and even further, to its predecessor on the Hill, Eastern University Preparatory School. The 1925 football team, for instance, traveled to several other states for games, helping broaden publicity efforts for the school, and a year later joined a new Oklahoma junior-college conference.

Meanwhile, OMA's high-school department was accredited by the North Central Association of Colleges and Secondary Schools, an important step in establishing the educational legitimacy of the institution.

The rest of the '20s saw increasing enrollment and prestige for the school, with new buildings added and support increasing from all over— in spite of widespread pacifism following World War I—as reflected a couple of 1927 editorials in the state's two major newspapers. Both the *Tulsa Daily World* and Oklahoma City's *Daily Oklahoman* called for more state funding for the school, even as other institutions were in danger of being shutting down. The *World* put it this way:

> Nobody knows, of course, just what point of view a member of the legislature will take, but after reading some expressions pertaining to educational institutions we assume that an effort will be made to reduce the number. While there is much substantial and convincing argument in favor of cutting out some schools, we insist that the military school at Claremore is one which should receive just as much favorable consideration as the state university

or the A & M college in our educational affairs which cannot very well be included in the curriculum of either the university or the A & M, and, in most instances, accomplishes more for the boys of the state…

It would scarcely be a defendable act to perpetuate that institution merely to gratify local interests involved, or the sentiment of those closely connected with it. Unless the institution fills a larger place and can be made an instrument for substantial service to the state as a whole, it ought not to be maintained. It is the mature opinion of this paper that it has such a field and such a future, and that it is entitled to something more than mere maintenance; that the very best interests call for its enlargement physically and its improvement managerially. In short the World believes that Oklahoma should make its Military Academy one of the three major educational institutions. Which means, of course, that the legislature should now announce such a policy and begin without further delay the creation of an educational plant there where military training may be had, proportionately as important and as beautiful as the University at Norman or the A & M College at Stillwater.

The *Oklahoman* got even more specific about funding. After bemoaning the fact that many boys were having to leave Oklahoma in order to go to military school, simply because "the state has failed to provide adequate accommodations" at OMA, the editorial continued:

It ought to be easy for the legislature to pass judgment on the budget request of Oklahoma Military Academy for sufficient money to build an additional barracks. The present enrollment at the academy is large enough to exhaust the academy's barracks accommodations. No more students can be admitted unless the academy's facilities are enlarged. In the meantime, several hundred Oklahoma lads are enrolled in military training schools in other states. Many of these (possibly most of them) would take their training in Oklahoma if there were sufficient accommodations at the Claremore institution.

The objection of the pacifically-minded to military training will hardly hold in this case. Cherished opinion does not alter the fact that hundreds of lads who ought to be trained in Oklahoma are being trained in other states. Even if Oklahoma should withdraw entirely for the field of military instruction, hundreds of Oklahoma students would attend military schools just the same. Whether these boys should receive training in their home state or some other state is the question demanding legislative decision…

The newspaper support translated to legislative support, and construction soon was underway again on the OMA campus. President Downs summed the improvements up proudly in the 1928 *Guidon:*

> The total value of the buildings, furniture and fixtures is approximately one half of a million dollars. All the buildings are of brick, fire-proof construction, lighted by electricity and provided with hot and cold water. The Baird H. Markham Barracks and the Central Heating plant have been completed this year providing not only for an increased enrollment of one hundred and fifty cadets but also ample heating facilities for all the buildings.

General Baird H. Markham, the new barracks' namesake, had been a member of the OMA Board of Regents for some time. A year or so earlier, he and Representative H. Tom Kight had gotten into a disagreement over the hiring of a new adjutant at OMA, and Markham had actually resigned from the board over it. That situation proved to be temporary, however, and by the time the barracks bearing his name were completed, Markham was not only back on board but also, apparently, in a giving mood. In what may seem in retrospect a case of gilding the lily, the regent gifted the campus with a working cannon to go along with the new barracks. The idea was that the cadets were to fire the weapon every day at 7 a.m. and 5:30 p.m. This attempt at a new tradition on the Hill proved short-lived, however; the cannon's substantial morning thunder not only awoke the students, for whom it was intended, but much of Claremore's population as well, and it was silenced after a number of civilian protests reached the ears of the academy's administration—and the pages of the *Claremore Progress.*

Sometime during Downs' early years as president, Oklahoma Military Academy became known as "the West Point of the Southwest." Although it's unknown where, or by whose hand, that appellation first appeared; by 1926 those traveling through Claremore could see the slogan printed across a big sign outside Claremore's railroad depot.

Downs and his staff also presided over a steady increase in attendance during the latter part of the 1920s, helped along by a program in which the parents of prospective cadets were sent letters touting the benefits of an OMA education, followed by faculty members touring Oklahoma to follow up any expressions of interest with in-person visits. But it was another idea that would prove to have even more of an effect on OMA and its attendance as well as its reputation, leading not only to upgrades in the institution's ROTC program but also to the establishment of a team of cadets whose prowess in a then-popular sport would eventually reach to Southern California—under the sponsorship of Hollywood's top box-office draw of 1934.

The Hill Roars
Through The 1920's

Company Formation in Camp ~ 1920

Gallery Practice ~ 1923

Rifle Team ~ 1925

Cadet Corps on Parade ~ 1925

Federal Inspection Collage from 1927

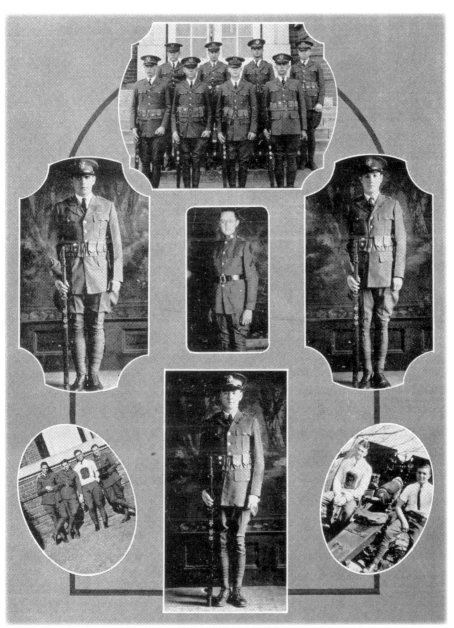

Scenes from 1928

Pistol Attack! ~ 1936 Guidon

The 1930s

I absorbed into my brain and blood and bones the spirit of the cavalry. The cavalry was elite, the crown of the service. Its history was the schema of the nation. The cavalry had been born in the Revolution, opened the Frontier, fused the Union, and conquered the West. America was made on horseback, carved by mounted soldiers; our identity as a people was dictated from the saddle... There were no equals, only followers, for the cavalry was always first, the cutting edge of steel and spirit. Youngbloods sought the same spirit in airplanes; the more sluggish in armor. But all of them envied the horsemen, and we were they.
— Edwin D. Ramsey with Stephen J. Rivele
Lieutenant Ramsey's War (Kingsbridge Publishing Co., 1990)

In 1929, OMA President Downs had applied to the U.S. Army's Adjutant General in hopes of getting an ROTC cavalry unit for OMA. He filed the application after seeing a report showing that other military schools had doubled or tripled their enrollment after obtaining a cavalry unit, and that fact probably had a great deal of influence on the decision to try to acquire one for the institution.

The Adjutant General, however, turned down the request, and the '20s ended without any horses on College Hill.

Undaunted, Downs and his staff tried again the next year, and this time, they were successful. Among those helping to get it done were OMA's longtime champion, Representative H. Tom Kight, as well as U.S. Senator Elmer Thomas, who tacked a request for a cavalry unit at OMA onto a war-appropriations bill that was headed through the legislature in Washington.

Another Oklahoman, Patrick J. Hurley, was Secretary of War at the time, and the story goes that he sent an army colonel to OMA to

Col. Patrick J. Hurley ~ 1931

check the feasibility of establishing a cavalry unit on the campus. The colonel returned with, according to historian Don Robards, "about a dozen reasons why such a unit should not be established at the academy," and Hurley countered by asking him to instead find a way it could be done. As it turned out, the colonel knew of a cavalry unit in Oregon that was being disbanded, and although several other institutions had requested the unit, Hurley made sure that it made its way to the Hill instead.

Whether that tale is completely true or not, the fact is that OMA's new cavalry unit did come from Oregon, and that the 1931 yearbook, the *Guidon*, was dedicated to Hurley for "his espousal of our interests in matters so vitally concerning the institution."

A new building waited in Claremore for the sixty horses allocated for OMA's cavalry program. Eleven Army enlisted men accompanied the horses, staying on the Hill to help run the new program. The War Department designated the newly formed unit a Senior ROTC Cavalry Unit, which was another big step for the institution. The infantry unit, which had been around from the beginning and included the cadets in the OMA band, got its own senior designation a year later. Because of the rising popularity of the cavalry unit, however, infantry was dropped from the school's ROTC program in 1936.

The upgrade from "junior" to "senior" was good for OMA for a couple of reasons. Essentially, the presence of a senior unit on campus meant that a cadet could take four years of ROTC at OMA, beginning with his junior year of high school (rather than as a freshman in college, which was the norm), and get a certificate of completion that would enable him to be commissioned a second lieutenant—after he went to a four-year college and completed the requirements for a bachelor's degree. Also, a school with a senior unit got more aid from the federal government, both financial and otherwise, and that helped lessen the pressure on the state and its lawmakers, who didn't have to appropriate quite as much money to keep OMA up and running.

Soon after the horses arrived and the senior unit got underway, OMA put together its first polo team, coached by Lieutenant Sam Houston III, a great-grandson of the legendary Texas soldier and politician. By 1931, Houston's outfit, which consisted of four players along with alternates, was not only taking long road trips to play teams at schools like the University of Missouri, Iowa State University and New Mexico Military Institute—it was winning as well. The team, dubbed the Flying Cadets, quickly attracted the attention of native son Will Rogers, who was then living on his ranch in Santa Monica, California, enjoying his status as one of America's top movie stars. Rogers was, in fact, the top-drawing movie star of 1934, as well as a nationally syndicated columnist. In the fall of 1931, he visited the school as part of his gala homecoming, climbing into the saddle himself to join the polo players in a match—and scoring six of the team's nine goals.

Lt. Houston

Rogers' attention to and pride in his hometown boys led to the Flying Cadets' most famous contests, played three years later at the Uplifters Club near Rogers' West Coast ranch with the middle of three matches moving to Rogers' own field.

"The Uplifters Club was primarily a polo club, and the first match [with the OMA team] was played there on December 23, 1934, against a team from Stanford University," said Steve Gragert, the editor of Will Rogers' papers. "Rogers didn't literally take the team out to California, because he lived there. Dr. Jesse Bushyhead, a physician in Claremore and a cousin of Will, accompanied them on the trip. Will Rogers financed it, however."

"The year I came to OMA was the year they sent the polo team to play Stanford and the University of Arizona," recalled Colonel John Horne, who began at OMA in the fall of '34. "In fact, what I remember most about the polo team is that they decided to have a little workout with the polo mallets, and they'd get up on chairs and have us post up—bend over and grab our ankles—and back up to the chairs where they were standing, and then they'd hit us in the butts with those polo mallets and see if they could knock us down." He laughed.

It was quite exciting in those days. I remember we knew they

Will Rogers with the 1934 Polo Team

were going [to California], and we knew they were going by train, and taking their own horses with 'em. They had to leave at some horrible early hour in the morning, maybe 4 o'clock, to get to Tulsa and the railroad station. When first call sounded, we all usually got up out of bed and went to the bathroom immediately and got our clothes on, because when they blew reveille we had to go out and form up. And that morning, there was a cascade of water running down the north steps of Markham Barracks, and we all got wet, going to the bathroom. Of course, most of us had on slippers, but we got our feet wet, and we couldn't figure out where the water was coming from. Well, there was a fire extinguisher [water hose] in the middle of the upper hall of Markham Barracks, and they'd turned it on before they left.

By that time, the team itself was long gone, en route to points west. And the boys acquitted themselves very well, as Rogers noted in an unpublished piece that was apparently intended as one of his daily columns.

Just come from the polo game, Claremore Oklahoma played

Stanford University, score 10-8, when you think there ain't anything but rope throwers and comedians come from Claremore you are sure wrong, its a military school, its only a preparatory school, but they sure do know how to play polo. . .

Seven cadets took the train trip, along with Lt. Houston, Dr. Bushyhead, and the team's horses. At Rogers' suggestion, the group stopped off in Phoenix, Arizona, to play a practice game with the University of Arizona's team, which the Flying Cadets won 7-5. Then it was on to Southern California, where they won the first two of three matches played over a week's time against a Stanford team that included Will Rogers, Jr. The Flying Cadets received—from the wife of famed director Frank Borzage—a 14" tall loving cup dubbed "The Will Rogers Trophy."

An article in the *Claremore Progress* was understandably ecstatic about the cadets' showing:

> The Claremore team turned in a brand of polo that drew column after column of publicity from sports writers in Los Angeles and other Pacific Coast newspapers. This valuable publicity, along with news-reel releases and radio broadcasts, in which Will Rogers "told the world" about the Oklahoma Military Academy Polo Team from Claremore, is worth untold dollars to the school on the Hill, and the city of Claremore.

As guests of America's biggest movie star, the OMA teammates watched Stanford and Alabama play in the Rose Bowl and also got a first-hand peek at the Hollywood dream factory, which was arguably at its peak of production at the time. They toured the 20th Century-Fox lot (which the *Progress* noted was "about three times as large as the city of Claremore"), watched Rogers shoot a scene for *Life Begins at 40*, and even crashed another film-in-progress. As the *Progress* noted:

> Another set visited was one on which Evelyn Venable is doing a Southern picture, in which she and another member of the cast were engaged in heavy love making in an old fashioned garden. Will led his party up to the rear of the artificial garden and thrust his head through the bushes and said, "Hey, everybody! I want you all to meet my polo team from Claremore."
>
> "Cut," said the director, then, "Bring 'em on in, Mr. Rogers."

Such was the power of a box-office champion like Rogers. And the matches with Stanford for the Will Rogers Trophy would likely have been an annual event, with fresh-faced polo-playing cadets from Oklahoma getting glimpses of Hollywood glamour and Claremore-style hospitality, if not for the death of the beloved actor, comedian, and writer in the plane crash with his pilot friend Wiley Post the very next year. Still, the polo team remained a first-class outfit, winning a national championship in 1938 and maintaining a winning record until the early 1940s, when World War II halted intercollegiate play.

* * * * *

...Today we have more reason for pride in the Oklahoma Military Academy than ever before. Great things have been accomplished in a very short time. For those of us who have toiled daily, either officially or cadet, these things are, in many respects, imperceptible and intangible, things that have come gradually only through hard work, loyalty, esprit, co-operation and co-ordination. These things are the accomplishment of the entire school, Faculty and Cadet Corps, working harmoniously toward a definite end. With this spirit and team work nothing can keep the Oklahoma Military Academy from assuming its rightful position as one of the States three greatest schools and the peer of any essentially Military School in the country...

Today, there is greater loyalty and esprit in the Cadet Corps than ever before. The discipline is commendable, the uniform is decidedly improved, and the Academic standard is acknowledged to be superior to what it has been in the past. Greater facilities, created by the utilization of all space and materials, have added much to efficiency. Morale, that intangible quality so essential for success, has been steadily improving. The formation of a Cotillion Club, class spirit, intra-mural athletics, organization of the Dragoon, the issue of a splendid annual; the inception of a natural, friendly athletic rivalry with the New Mexico Military Institute; the performances of a great football team and a magnificent polo team, the inauguration of OMA - Civilian Horseshows, the splendid work of an un-excelled band and the formation of Crack Cavalry and Infantry Units, second to none, have all played their part in this irresistible Movement...

Much remains to be done. Always will there be chafing at

restraint and discontent at regulations. But an essentially Military School could not exist and prosper without the imposition of restraint and impartial enforcement of regulations. Our goal this year is to make the Oklahoma Military Academy an Honor Military School. We must not falter in our determination and forward progress. . .
— from *The Dragoon*, Vol. 1, No. 1 (December 17, 1931)

It took a little longer than the *Dragoon* editorial writer hoped, but OMA did indeed receive an honor rating from the War Department, beginning in 1933. It was the first try at the honor rating for the institution, and it became the youngest military school ever to receive the designation. OMA held onto that rating, which had to be renewed annually, for the rest of its existence.

An honor rating was given, or withheld, following each yearly inspection by members of the Washington, D.C. - based War Board. As a June 17, 1937, Tulsa World article pointed out, however, "The War Board visits only a limited number of schools recommended by the officers of the various corps area and it is an honor to be selected for this inspection regardless of whether the honor rating is accorded."

In addition to the prestige afforded a school that earned the honor, there were some practical advantages as well. The faculty of an honor school, for instance, could designate one cadet and two alternates each year for entrance to West Point, with the usual requirements of entrance exams and a congressional appointment waived.

In 1934, the inspectors for the War Board included an unusually distinguished officer, General Johnson Hagood, who was the Commanding General of the Third Army of the United States and the Eighth Corps Area, which included Texas, New Mexico, Arizona, Colorado, and Oklahoma. As befitting his stature, Hagood and the rest of his party were met in Claremore by a mounted escort and accompanied to College Hill, where they witnessed, according to Don Robards, "a parade and review...followed by a sham battle, silent drill, and equestrian maneuvers consisting of jumping and a saber course." Hagood was impressed. A *Claremore Progress* piece from January 15, 1934, quoted a part of the general's speech to the staff and cadets:

I've visited many military schools in my capacity as an Army commander. I have visited the expensive schools where there is no lack of equipment; I have seen academies where there were more cadets; more money to spend, and finer buildings; but I have never visited one where as much is being done on as little as the Oklahoma Military Academy. You have many reasons for being proud of it, and supporting it right down the line.

A few months later, Colonel Downs received word that OMA had been given the honor rating for the second year in a row. Out of more than 300 schools across the country inspected by the War Board, only 20, including OMA, had been chosen. In a story about the honor rating publishing in the June 3, 1934 *Tulsa World*, the OMA president used the opportunity to do a little promotion for the school. "Please remember also," he told the paper, "that the cost of attending OMA is less than half the lowest cost of attending any other school given honor rating."

Cost, of course, was a major factor then, with America in the relentless grip of the Great Depression. In December of 1931, the very first issue of the school paper, *The Dragoon*, had published a small but ominous filler item noting, "The depression has affected military schools materially in the matter of enrollment this year, almost all being considerably smaller and a few having closed their doors." And while OMA's enrollment had been going up through 1931, it hit a snag the next year, with the number of cadets dropping from 330 to 270.

Undoubtedly, that was a major reason that President Downs decided to reinstate the "day dogs" program, which had been dropped back in 1925. These day students came from around the area and lived at home, thus negating the need to pay for room and board, laundry services, and hospital fees—although they had to have uniforms and attend all classes, formations, and inspections. (The school's numbers ultimately rose again, and by the end of the decade enrollment would be nearly 400.)

Donald Ruggles, a cadet in the '30s and former professional musician, said that many of the day dogs of that time were musicians, recruited by OMA's crackerjack music director, P. H. Kelley. Ruggles remembered it this way:

In 1936, I was in the band down at Claremore High School. The OMA band was going to the Texas State Fair, and Captain Kelley needed another trombone player. So he came down to the high school and I auditioned and got to go with the band. I was only 14 years old or so—I was in the Army at 13 or 14 years old. They put me in uniform and taught me how to turn a corner and I had a big time. When we got back to OMA and I started to turn my uniform in, Kelley said, "No, I think we'll need you from now on. So if you'd like to, you just go to school at OMA." Well, I thought that was pretty nice.

Ruggles lived at home in Claremore for the next two years, participating in all the drills and classroom work, but leaving the Hill every evening. As day students, he noted, they were exempt from the rigors of the rabbit semester. "We kind of hid out," he said with a laugh. "The day students were a different breed of cat. There was a piano player who was really good, and a baritone player, Frank Peters, out of the boys' home in Sand Springs. Basically the day students were strictly musicians, and they didn't care too much about marching around the field. They just wanted to sit down and play."

After his first two years, however, Ruggles became a cadet, as well as band captain and Capt. Kelley's assistant director. It was in this capacity that he devised a new way of leading the marching band, based on what he'd experienced in the OMA cavalry program.

We developed an open-type marching system, same as the cavalry had, and we developed it where we could do it with hand and arm signals. That's the way the cavalry did it, because, you know, you couldn't give a verbal command, because everyone couldn't hear it. Some people would be too far away to hear it. But if you wanted half your group to go one way and half to go the other, your hand and arm signals could do that real easily. It would confuse the heck out of things if you tried it by just shouting commands. The first time anybody saw us do that, any outsider, we were at Skelly Stadium in Tulsa. And anybody in the band business just flipped on that type of thinking, because it gave them so much more leeway, and latitude as to formations they could put in. One guy could stand out there and do hand and arm signals for the whole troop. It was an exciting thing.

* * * * *

Nineteen-thirty-four was a big year for the academy and its programs. A few months after General Hagood gave his glowing speech to the faculty and cadets, and not long after the school was notified of its second straight honor rating, Tulsa's Spartan School of Aeronautics joined with OMA in establishing an aviation flight and ground school

Will Rogers Airport

at Will Rogers Airport, which was then being constructed just north of Claremore. According to a 1992 thesis by historian Larry Dean Wright, Spartan and OMA had joined forces to create an aviation department at the school several years earlier, making it "the first junior college in the nation to have flight instruction included in the curriculum."

In an article written for the Fall 1985 issue of *College Hill*, published by the Rogers College Foundation, former Spartan employee Julian Q. Myers remembered the beginnings of the airport project:

> ...I was placed in charge of all aviation activities under the direct supervision of OMA officials. This responsibility included completion of the airport, airplane hangar, airport office, lecture room, practical school work shop, and ground and flight instruction. The labor for all phases of construction was paid under an authorization by the Federal Emergency Relief Administration. During some periods, 75 or more workers were active at any one time on the field and in the hangar. The pay scale ranged from 25 cents to 50 cents per hour. Any one laborer was permitted to work a maximum of three days per month. A painter was allotted one day per month. Other craftsmen had similar schedules.

Myers and his group hustled to get everything ready for the fall 1935 semester at OMA, but they ran into a roadblock when the Department of Commerce—whose Bureau of Aeronautics was the forerunner of today's Federal Aviation Administration—refused to authorize lighting for the airfield. The reason, noted Myers, was that "it was not designated an 'emergency field' because of its proximity to the Tulsa airport."

OMA, Spartan, and Claremore officials insisted that adequate field lighting was necessary for safety reasons, and even enlisted Will Rogers' help in trying to persuade the Commerce Department to reconsider. But that didn't happen until after an American Airlines passenger plane made a forced landing—during a ground-school lecture—at the field. Myers and the cadets found a broken fuel line, repaired it, and sent the flight on its way to St. Louis. A grateful American Airlines president sent a letter to OMA, offering to help the new airport any way he could. Recalled Myers:

> We wrote to him outlining our problem regarding our lighting. We thought that since American had used the field in an emergency, the company could put in a good word or two at the proper time and place.
>
> Apparently, the company did, for, in a few weeks, the airport was designated as an emergency field with complete lighting.

Throughout the '30s and into the '40s, the OMA aviation department produced many pilots and technicians who would later serve in World War II. Among those was A. Blaine Imel, Jr., who, as a Marine lieutenant, would be one of the first fighter pilots to attack Tokyo, participating in 65 other combat missions during World War II. For him, he said, it started at OMA. "They had a hangar out there at Will Rogers, and they offered CPT, civilian pilot training," he said with a chuckle. "The hardest part was getting the $35 from my dad to take the course."

A. Blaine Imel, Jr.~ 1941

In the late '30s, a bill was introduced in the U.S. House of Representatives to award OMA an ROTC aviation unit—which would've taken the place of the then-disbanded infantry unit—but it failed to pass. Eventually, with the blessings of the Department of Commerce, OMA itself took over the management and administration of the flight school, ending its affiliation with Spartan School of Aeronautics.

* * * * *

NEXT TO WEST POINT
The Most Beautifully Situated
American Military School
—headlines from a 1935 promotional brochure for OMA

By 1935, Oklahoma Military Academy had a lot of things to be proud of, including its honor rating (given to only 20 out of 300 military schools); its senior ROTC units for both infantry and cavalry (OMA

Coach Cline

was one of only three junior colleges in the nation to have a cavalry unit); a complete aviation-training program, and a nationally known polo team along with competitive teams in football, baseball and boxing. The veteran coach Murl "Tuffy" Cline had already helmed the academy's football squad for several years, creating a first-rate outfit and running it with an iron fist. Coach Cline, who'd starred at halfback in the '20s for both OMA and the University of Tulsa, helmed some outstanding football teams during the '30s, with his 1938 squad rated as the No. 2 junior college team in the nation by one pollster. One of the legends about Cline was related in a memoir by '50s cadet Sam M. Matthews:

Coach Cline maintained iron-clad discipline with his teams. One day, during a grueling practice on Soldier's Field, a disgruntled player back talked Tuffy after a chewing-out. This was a no-no. Tuffy told the offending player to start running laps around the cinder track and not to stop until he was told to. The practice resumed, and when completed the team left for the showers and Coach Cline headed for his home in Claremore. Sitting down at the supper table, Tuffy jumped up, grabbed his hat, and raced back to Soldier's Field on the Hill. Sure enough, there was the mouther, still running laps around the cinder track. Coach Cline had forgotten to tell him to stop running at the end of practice.

The OMA band and orchestra, as well, were top outfits. Helmed by the working musician Kelley, the groups played a number of events throughout the year and appeared every Thursday evening on Tulsa radio station KVOO, a 25,000 watt flamethrower (its wattage later doubled to 50,000) that reached halfway across the country and was best-known at the time as the home of western-swing stars Bob Wills and the Texas Playboys.

"We had audiences everywhere that would write in to KVOO about us," said Lt. Gen. William E. Potts, a cadet in the '30s who played baritone in the orchestra and went on to distinguish himself as OMA's highest ranking military alumnus. "It was a terrific band and a wonderful experience for me. They put us in a bus, took us to Tulsa, and we went right in and did our thing. As soon as it was over, they put us back on the bus and brought us back to the Hill.

"We played the '1812 Overture,' some marches, things like that," he added, remembering the group's radio repertoire. "We played all kinds of music. Captain Kelley was a professional in every way, but he was also a very good instructor and disciplinarian— and human being, too. I just thought the world of him."

Besides touting academics, military

Lt. General William E. Potts

honors, and sports and music programs in their recruitment publications, the faculty and staff of OMA could play the esthetics card as well. As the beginning of the 1935 brochure stated:

> Oklahoma Military Academy crowns a gently sloping hill, rising 200 feet above the attractive city of Claremore, famed as the Oklahoma home of Will Rogers, humorist, and as a radium-water health resort. The beautifully landscaped academy site commands enchanting views of the romantic Osage Hills. The unusual charm of the landscape adds greatly to the cadet's contentment and enjoyment. No other American Military School except West Point, in the Hudson river highlands, is so beautifully situated...

As for as the cadets themselves:

> Boys of a high type—and none other—attend OMA. Approximately 40 percent of the entire student body makes the Dean's Honor Roll each year—a record impossible except to a splendid class of youth. Applicants with records of incorrigibility are not received, as the Academy is in no sense a reform school. Its discipline is strict, but not tyrannical, and it does not attempt the redemption of boys whose conduct calls for severe measures. "Strict discipline" does not mean converting boys into automatons.

Academy life is made enjoyable for the cadets by every means possible, and the boys invariably regret the closing of the school year and their departure from "The Hill."

Although it was reduced in length as the years went by, the "rabbit" period—which was OMA's version of the time-honored "new man" program—began as a year-long ordeal for all incoming cadets. Here, the "strict discipline" referred to in the brochure found its most extreme manifestations, as upperclassmen, often gleefully, took on the task of converting newly admitted students to a military way of life.

"Well, it was pretty tough back in those days," reflected Colonel Robert B. Lewis, who came to OMA in 1937. "They would actually sometimes beat you with a saber. One guy would put a glove on one hand and a saber in the other and kind of pop it. I remember one time when a guy was popping it and I got a couple of slices cut out of my pants. Then, they'd take a clothes brush and pull out all the bristles and beat you with that.

"But it wasn't too bad. I had a couple of friends from Oklahoma City there, and I could go to their room and kind of relax, hide out a little. I was a fairly good rabbit, I think."

"There was an adjustment in the first year, because of the plebes thing, the rabbit year," agreed Colonel Edwin D. Ramsey, who would go on to lead a band of Filipino freedom fighters against the Japanese during World War II, a remarkable story related in his 1990 book, *Lieutenant Ramsey's War.* Ramsey came to OMA in 1934 for his senior year of high school.

"There was another student, an upperclassman, a full-blooded Osage Indian, and for some reason I had irritated him," Ramsey remembered. "He beat me so badly that I had a blood blister on my bottom about an eighth of an inch thick. To get even with him, I was out in the field and found a dead rattlesnake, and I put in his bed. He almost died of a heart attack." Ramsey laughed. "He couldn't prove it, but he had to know where it came from. So he never bothered me again."

Colonel John Horne recalled the day his mother drove him to OMA for the first time, and he got out of the car with his footlocker in front of Markham Barracks. "These friendly guys came out and took me up [to the barracks] and helped me get unpacked, and I said, 'What a friendly place.'" He laughed. "Then school started, and things began to happen, and I wasn't so welcome then.

"It was quite an experience for me," he added. "But it didn't hurt anybody, really. We all got used to it. I think you were less likely to bully the new kids from then on. It gave you some self-discipline, and you knew what they were going through. I never used a paddle on anybody. I had one used on me one time, that's all. And that was a couple of upper-class cadets."

In addition to the self-discipline that Horne noted, the rabbit period was designed to teach new cadets how to receive, accept, and give orders, along with such traits as responsibility, self-reliance, and reliance on others to help achieve goals. Rabbits were kept so busy and physically challenged that there was little time for reflection, which kept down the amount of homesickness they might have otherwise felt. The discipline was more benign, but nonetheless strict, when it came to study habits. As Col. Lewis noted, "They *made* us study, basically. You sat down from seven to nine every night, and you hardly moved your chair. They forced us to study, and we learned to study that way. I started making good grades, and when I graduated I was number two in my class, academically."

As both a member of the honor roll and a part of the cavalry unit, Lewis got to join like-minded cadets in the school's honor troop. Apparently, Col. Downs and the rest of the OMA faculty decided that the mounted-escort reception given General Hagood's inspection party on its 1934 visit should be repeated each year for each inspection team. As Lewis recalled:

> I was in the honor troop, I think, the whole time I was there, and one of the things I really enjoyed was when the War Board came to make an inspection. They would come to give us our accreditation as a military school, and if you were on the honor troop, you would line up and put your uniform on and all that, and go down to the railroad station in columns of fours to meet the War Board inspectors. To be on the honor troop, you had to have a certain grade average and be able to stay on a horse, too. You'd be riding and the guy next to you would kick your horse, just for the heck of it. I was thrown a few times.
>
> Our horses were what were called remounts. They came from El Reno, Fort Reno, and they weren't really wild, they were broken, but they hadn't been ridden for a long time. And early in the season they were really tough. The stables had a very low clearance, and boy, if that horse took off for the stables and you got there, you'd just grab him around the neck and get down. But I had a lot of

good experiences with the horses.

"Fort Reno was a remount station for the United States Cavalry," added Col. Horne, "and a lot of those horses were thoroughbreds. The cavalry had found out a long time ago that a horse will do more on its heart than on anything else."

* * * * *

Early in his tenure as OMA president, Colonel Downs had not only put the institution in line with the military-school tradition of the "new man"; he'd also instituted the merit system, another characteristic of military academies. Most former cadets, including Colonel Lewis, seem to remember getting demerits more than merits. "You got *de*merits if your shoes weren't shined, or your bed wasn't made—if you goofed up and did something like that," he noted. "To work off demerits, you had to walk the bullpen with your uniform and rifle. The bullpen was an area where you walked in a circle, like on a track, for a long time."

Even with the threat of demerits and other strict disciplinary measures, however, some cadets just couldn't resist misbehaving. As Lewis remembered:

> We had a guy, unidentified at the time, who would go into the latrines at night and shoot off firecrackers and then run back to his room. Finally, they all got fed up with it and said, "We're going to find out who did it." So in the middle of the night they marched us down toward the Verdigris River; we were out practically all night, marching. And he finally admitted it. But he was so stupid that nobody really took offense at it, you know.

Nighttime marches to the Verdigris River were not only one of the favored ways of flushing out wrongdoers on the Hill; they were also examples of the principle of mass punishment, in which cadets were made to realize that their individual actions affected everyone around them. Mass punishments, like the forced marches, were training and learning experiences for the cadets—even if the lessons learned were occasionally about beating the system. Blaine Imel recalled a late '30s incident involving a cadet named George. "I never can say George's last name, but he came from Pawnee," Imel said. "One night he dumped the trash cans downstairs, those metal cans, and, boy, they called us down in front, and we went clear to the Verdigris River before we finally got to turn around and go back." He laughed. "I think the smart cheaters kind of hid a little ways out and waited and caught everybody coming back."

* * * * *

One of the most ambitious building programs of any school its size in the nation is now underway at the Oklahoma Military Academy, which stands high on a hill west of Claremore. Right now the academy is having its particular hill remodeled at a cost of hundreds of thousands of dollars, for the purpose of further strengthening its position as one of the outstanding military institutions in the country. Those Oklahomans who have not visited the academy in recent weeks may have difficulty grasping the full extent of the many changes now underway on the hill, changes made possible through PWA and WPA projects. They are, it is apparent even to the layman, much needed changes, fulfilling not only the hopes of those connected with the institution but making possible a broader field of service for the school and providing manifold benefits to cadets for generations to come.
—Lavere Anderson, the *Tulsa Daily World*, March 29, 1936

Bushyhead Field House

As anyone who lived through the Great Depression knows, the PWA was the Public Works Administration, and the WPA was the Works Progress Administration, two agencies in the alphabet soup of New Deal government programs begun under President Franklin D. Roosevelt. For OMA, the participation of these two entities meant a massive change to the campus, including a new drill hall and field house— to be constructed at a cost of $110,000, according to the *World* article, and to "contain...one of the largest swimming pools to be found in any school west of the Mississippi River"—along with an 800-

seat auditorium ($95,000), five faculty officers' residences ($5,000 each), and upgrades to the school's power plant, sewage system and area around its hangar at the Claremore airport.

Will Rogers and his Oklahoma aviator pal Wiley Post had lost their lives in a crash near Point Barrow, Alaska, shocking not only the home folks but all the world, a few months before the OMA construction project began. And while there was serious talk for a time about renaming OMA the Will Rogers Military Academy, Rogers' name instead graced the new auditorium, with the name of his cousin, Jesse Bushyhead—the Claremore physician who'd accompanied the polo team on its California adventure fewer than two years before—appended to the field house. On October 29, 1936, formal dedication ceremonies for the two new buildings were held on the Hill, with more than 1200 onlookers hearing Oklahoma Senator James Nance declare OMA "a favorite with members of the state legislature because of the high type of students it turns out."

Just about a year later, the OMA and Will Rogers connection was again demonstrated, when cadets participated in a ceremony—held on November 4, 1937, the 58th anniversary of the great humorist's birth—marked the beginning of the Will Rogers Memorial. Col. Robert B. Lewis, then in his rabbit year, remembered what it was like on that chilly autumn day: "We stood at parade rest, and the governor and everybody in the world talked. It was bitter cold, and they wouldn't let us wear overcoats. So we stood for a long time—it probably wasn't that long, but it seemed like it—with our rifles out, cold as the dickens, and when we got ready to march off a bunch of the guys fell down."

* * * * *

The OMA school year is properly balanced by social activities. Notable events are the Christmas and Commencement Farewell hops. The calendar includes an average of three formal dances each semester. Cadet's parents have standing invitations to all events of this nature.
—from the 1935 OMA promotional brochure

A cadet in the '30s didn't have a lot of time to pursue amusements, especially during his rabbit year. With enforced study periods from 7 p.m. until 9 p.m., most of the students only had the part of the weekend between Saturday morning inspection and Sunday afternoon dress parades (during spring semesters) to devote to fun. As the brochure indicates, however, the Hill threw some pretty good dances.

"The cadet band was extremely good, so we had a lot of dances up there," said Col. Lewis. "Some of the girls I knew in Oklahoma City would come up for the dances. We had a very, very good band."

"It was a very formal affair," added Gen. Potts. "We would have a grand march, with every couple in columns, and we would walk around in front of all the people, down and around and back and forth. It was all inside the [Bushyhead Field House] hall there, with that swimming pool at the end. We went around that and back again."

Potts remembered the "planned intricate patterns" of the grand march, which was always led by the ranking cadet. "That was the cadet colonel," he explained. "Then, the battalion commanders were cadet lieutenant colonels, and then the company commanders were cadet captains. Then, in the battalions, you had executive officers, which were cadet majors."

The cadet officers and their dates would fall in for the march according to rank, although, Potts added, "It wasn't always disciplined that way. That was the way it went when people got in there and got organized."

Those dances were held on Saturday night, once a month, and drew girls from all over the area, "whose mothers, aunts and, sometimes, fathers drove them to the Hill, joining faculty members and their wives to sit around the circumference of the gymnasium throughout the evening," said Potts. "There were nearly as many chaperones as there were young ladies. A lot of the ladies came from Tulsa and surrounding areas like Bartlesville, all those towns, and they would like coming up for the dances because the cadets had known most of them as they were going through high school, before they became cadets at the military academy. The cadet invited whomever he wanted to and they all came really turned out."

In the movies of the time, Fred Astaire and Ginger Rogers were famously and elegantly dancing cheek-to-cheek. However, there would be none of that at the OMA dances.

"Mrs. Esther Taulbee Roberts and her husband gave dance instructions and some basic etiquette lessons to cadets, and there was to be no cheek-to-cheek dancing," Potts remembered. "It was a very formal and disciplined thing all the way. The dances started at a certain time and as soon as the dance was over the parents would take the ladies back home and the boys had to be taken back to their barracks, where they would stand inspections."

Off the Hill, there were also attractions in Claremore, including a couple of movie theaters. "There weren't too many," recalled Lewis. "Of course, nobody had cars back in those days. We always made a decision whether to walk downtown or take one of the two taxis. I think it cost about 10 cents to take a taxi downtown.

"On Thanksgiving and Christmas, Captain Huffman, one of the instructors, would load a bunch of us up and drive us to Oklahoma City," he added. "I think we paid him $2.50 or something to drive us there, and we'd stop in Bristow at a place called the Hamburger King."

Those like tennis player Lewis, who participated in sports, also had several opportunities to travel off campus. The boxing and basketball teams reached high points in the mid-to-late '30s as well, and polo continued as a high-profile OMA sport throughout the decade, with the 1938 national-champion team winning 23 straight matches before being defeated by its main rival, New Mexico Military Institute—which it had previously beaten three times.

The 1934 Boxing Team

In 1939, however, the bottom fell out of OMA's athletic program, thanks in no small part to an edict from Governor Leon C. Phillips, who decreed that the school could not give financial aid to athletes. Before this pronouncement, the school's Board of Regents and President Downs had been able to assign janitorial and other service jobs to athletes, who would get their costs of attending the academy reduced in return for their work. Not all varsity athletes got these jobs, of course, and some other students were employed by the school as well.

Apparently, Governor Phillips forbade this practice for political reasons. As historian Don Robards wrote in his thesis, *A History of the Oklahoma Military Academy:*

The cause of this and the many other changes brought about by the Phillips administration go back to an old political fight between H. Tom Kight, Sr., and Phillips. In 1935, Phillips aspired to become Speaker of the Oklahoma House of Representatives. Governor E. W. Marland favored another candidate. While all the facts were not clear, it is evident Kight's vote and influence contributed to Phillips' defeat. A feeling of bitterness began with this incident.

Indeed, Phillips' rancor appears to have found a convenient target in OMA, as he zeroed in on the institution that Kight was instrumental in founding. As the '30s closed, the clouds swirling ominously around the college on the Hill weren't just the harbingers of the upcoming World War, but hints that the school's very existence would once again be threatened by forces much closer to home.

*　*　*　*　*

A state institution will always, to some degree, be at the mercy of political trends, ambitions, and power struggles. Oklahoma Military Academy, however, seemed throughout its history to be more affected than most by the prevailing winds in the state capitol. Its predecessor, Eastern University Preparatory School, had died when Oklahoma's governor pulled the plug on its funding back in 1917. Then, only a couple of years after OMA's birth in 1919, there were those in the legislature who thought the infrastructure on the Hill would make a better hospital than military school.

The academy survived that threat, and came through the '30s in good shape. However, in early 1939, OMA became a battleground when the long-simmering conflict between new Governor Leon C. Phillips and longtime Rogers County Representative H. Tom Kight erupted, with Col. Downs becoming the major casualty. The battle also involved Kight's son, H. Tom Kight, Jr., who had been appointed to the OMA Board of Regents in 1936, as well as others close to the veteran state representative.

It began with a private audit of the school's financial records, ordered by the governor, and expanded to the state senate, which passed a resolution in February calling for an investigation of the academy's finances. Lines were drawn, giving Kight's political opponents an opportunity to go from the political to the personal. Senator Jesse Taylor of Woodward, for instance, let loose a volley claiming that only problem boys were sent to OMA, the tuition was too high, and the school itself had been created, as the February 19 *Daily Oklahoman* reported, to reward Kight "for his work in the impeaching of two governors."

For his part, Kight claimed that Phillips was using a number of people, as well as the *Tulsa Daily World*, to smear the school and his family.

A state senate investigation committee finally suggested that finance officer Ted Adams be released from his duties, with Col. Downs assuming those responsibilities until a replacement could be hired. Meanwhile, Governor Phillips struck again, appointing a new Board of Regents for the school, which included Tulsa attorney Joe Chambers, a former member of the legislature who was apparently a friend of the governor. The Oklahoma House of Representatives fired back with a resolution calling for an investigation of Chambers' wife, who was an employee of the Oklahoma Tax Commission. Things got both angry and personal in a hurry, with Kight, at one point, threatening to shoot a *Daily World* reporter who was covering the story.

Things quieted down for a few months, only to erupt again in late summer, when Governor Phillips fired another blast at OMA, calling its financial management "shocking" and dubbing the senate investigation earlier in the year "white washing." He even charged that animal feed bought for the school was instead being fed to Kight's livestock.

An audit a couple of months later showed a deficit of more than $16,000, with auditors laying much of the blame on the football program and the inability of some team members to pay what they owed the school. And in a few more months, the man who had led Oklahoma Military Academy for a decade and a half was gone, the victim of forces that, unlike the cadets on the Hill, were simply beyond his control.

The Administration Building

The Stables ~ Built in 1930

The Auditorium ~ Built in 1936

Thrills on the Hill in the 1930's

The Aviation Department ~ 1938

Baseball Team ~ 1938

The Undefeated Varsity Polo Team ~ 1938

The Varsity "Jitterbugsters" ~ 1939

Collages from 1938

Troop F ~ 1939

Training Squads ~ 1939

Eighteen Wins in a Row! ~ 1939

Aviation School ~ 1939

Lt. Col. Richard E. Anderson
President, 1940–1941

Capt. John C. Hamilton
President, 1941–1944

Col. W.S. Bryan
Interim President
Multiple Terms
1924–1948

Col. Kenneth S. Perkins
President, 1944–1948

The 1940s

...(T)he year 1940 brought to a close the term of Colonel Downs who had for fifteen years so ably guided the destinies of the academy. His term which had brought the greatest growth known to Oklahoma Military Academy ended with the bitter political fight in which he was an innocent bystander. The Colonel, like any other human, made his mistakes but he was at all times working for a better school and was sincere in his dealings with the students and faculty. He was kind and generous to a fault and believed in giving any student who broke the rules another chance if at all possible...

To meet the requirements of the presidency of Oklahoma Military Academy and its unique standards and strong political backers who demanded a share in its operation, the Colonel more than lived up to expectations. True there may have been better schools in some respects but it is doubtful that more could have been accomplished under the conditions that existed...

—Don R. Robards, *A History of the Oklahoma Military Academy*

One of the reasons the new OMA Board of Regents gave for Col. Downs' dismissal was that they wanted a president who had graduated from West Point. They got their man in Colonel R. E. Anderson, who'd not only graduated from that famed academy in 1912 but had also served two stints there as an instructor. His resumé also included service as an ROTC officer at Cornell University and Pennsylvania Military College and, just before assuming the OMA presidency, executive officer and member of the commandant's department at the Citadel, South Carolina's noted military school.

While waiting for the 1940-41 school year to begin under its new president, Governor Phillips announced that all student jobs at the school had been dropped, except for cadets who were already working there. They would be allowed to continue their jobs until graduation. (As it turned out, this ban didn't last very long. Although the no-working-students policy was never formally renounced, some students soon began taking jobs at the school again, since it didn't take long for the administration—and the governor—to realize that adults willing to do that kind of work for those kinds of wages were hard to find, especially since America was recovering from the Great Depression.)

Football players, who had been some of the major beneficiaries of the student jobs, were hard hit by the new edict. Several of the OMA lettermen, along with many other students unhappy about the resignation of Colonel Downs and the new rules and policy changes on the Hill, went somewhere else after the '38-'39 school year ended. The result was that the once-vaunted football team won only one game per year until 1943, when varsity athletics disappeared from the Hill, a casualty of gas rationing and other wartime factors. (While intramural sports were still played within the student body after the spring of 1943, the varsity program wouldn't resume until after World War II ended.)

Another change implemented in 1940 was the discontinuation of the day-student program. Governor Phillips insisted that the inspecting officers from the War Board, according to Don Robards, "had expressed their disapproval of the crowded conditions and the allowing of day students to attend the school," with a subsequent letter arriving from the War Department in Washington indicating "that unless these conditions were changed the federal support would be withdrawn." Others, however, saw it as just another attempt by the governor and his board to further disassociate the school from the City of Claremore—and, not coincidentally, its resident lawmaker H. Tom Kight. This notion is bolstered, as Robards pointed out, by the fact that no such letter has ever been found in the OMA files.

Colonel Anderson ended up being one of the shortest-lived of OMA's presidents, taking a leave of absence after the 1940 fall semester and never returning. The ostensible reason for his departure was his desire to return to active duty; in fact, as Robards wrote, "the real reason for this action was his inability to get W. C. Steger, the [OMA] business manager, to work with him. Steger was an appointee of the Phillips board and the governor upheld him by announcing that 'all Steger knows is to be honest and make other people stay in line.'"

At the same time, rumors were once again flying about OMA's demise. Those in the Claremore area who knew of Governor Phillips' conflicts with Representative Kight, and who further believed that Phillips was taking his anger out on the school, were ready to assume the worst. And it looked like the worst was on the way when the governor's plans to talk to Washington about changing OMA into an Army training school, financed and run by the feds, came to light. While Phillips' announced intentions didn't help his standing with Claremore's city leaders or the staff and cadets on the Hill—and may also have had something to do with Col. Anderson's departure from the president's post—this period of tension for the school lasted less than a month. By the first week of February, the *Claremore Daily Progress* had reported that the Army wasn't interested and Phillips was now talking about improving OMA instead of changing it into something else.

In the summer of 1941, after a shakeup in the school's board of directors, Captain John C. Hamilton was appointed OMA president. A former commandant of cadets, he'd been acting president since Anderson's departure. Like Anderson, he was a West Point graduate. He also had cavalry experience, a definite plus for a school with an ROTC cavalry unit.

"The story was that he had received a much-unwanted medical discharge from the U.S. Calvary as a result of a horrific accident when the Horse Cavalry was being mechanized," said Kenneth D. Kirkland, a wartime cadet at OMA. "He had been thrown from his tank in a collision and been struck by the next tank. Some said that he had been run over by the tank. When asked how that could be without killing him, the answer was, 'It was Captain Jake and it was just a light tank.'"

A few months after 'Captain Jake' assumed the helm at OMA, the *Daily Oklahoman* published a long, photo-illustrated article on the new president. Written by Gilbert Hill, it ran under the title "No Place for Sissies," and said, in part:

> A school is judged by the men it produces. Upon this simple philosophy, a new, and perhaps brighter, chapter is opening in the troubled history of the Oklahoma Military Academy at Claremore. The philosophy is that of Capt. John C. Hamilton, USA, retired, a West Pointer with a love of thoroughness, appreciation of leadership, and respect for "bull-headed boys like you find in Oklahoma whom you'd want beside you on the Bataan Peninsula if you were there." Hamilton, 44 years old, was retired in 1935 for

physical disability after a series of accidents in line of duty first with the cavalry, then in the first cavalry unit to be motorized. But with three-fourths of his army pay guaranteed him for life, he found that "retirement" was growing extremely boring in 1940 after he had fixed up his home in Virginia, the state where he was born. Friends in the war department prevailed upon him to come to Oklahoma Military Academy as its commandant. He stayed, to become acting president, then president...

During Hamilton's presidency, upperclassmen were organized into supervisory "rabbit details" and the first *Rabbit Manual* was published. That small but indispensable pocket-sized book contained everything from a brief history of Oklahoma to a guide to buildings on campus to a glossary of military, and OMA, terminology—along with several pages under the heading of "New Cadet Regulations." The *Rabbit Manual* also introduced many young men to the concept of an honor code, telling them:

A code of honor cannot be rigidly defined other than it consists of each man living up to his inherent sense of right and wrong. A code of honor deals solely with the ethical and moral attitude of the individual in relation to himself, his companions, and to society. A code of honor cannot be written in a book but a man's conscience tells him when he has violated it. An individual should not profit in any way by a violation of this code nor should he escape the results that must necessarily follow any transgression of this code. No act, thought, or word should be tolerated which might discredit those with whom he is associated or the community in which he lives.

Honor has no shades of meaning. To fail to tell the whole truth is a cowardly way of stating a falsehood. Evasion is more contemptible than deliberate lying. A cadet always has the privilege of resting upon his constitutional rights to refuse to make a statement, on the grounds that it may incriminate him, but a statement, written or oral, once made is binding...

For cadets, the most significant statement under the honor system consisted of only two words: all right. A verbal report of "all right" meant that the student, on his honor, had done what he was supposed to have done. The *Rabbit Manual* gave four examples of what could be conveyed by an "all right" response:

1. *In Checking Out:* That a cadet is going to the place specified and none other, and that no undue advantage of the privilege will be taken.

2. *In Checking In:* That a cadet has been to the place specified and none other, and that no undue advantage of the privilege has been taken.

3. *Inspection for a Lost Article:* That the cadet has conscientiously searched for the article and that it is neither in his possession nor does he have any knowledge of its whereabouts.

4. *Confinement:* That the cadet was at the authorized place at the time of inspection and that the confinement was not violated in any way.

The *Rabbit Manual* concluded its "Code of Honor" section with a declaration designed to drive the deep importance of honor, ethics and integrity into every rabbit's soul:

A man's greatest asset is his integrity of character and when he loses it, he loses everything. It is also true that an institution is rich only when the integrity of its graduates is unquestionable. Without this primary virtue, no amount of buildings, students, or publicity can justify its existence. This code of ethics is the highest possession of the Oklahoma Military Academy and all members of the Corps of Cadets shall see that it is kept intact.

If an ethical lapse was severe, a cadet could be brought before a committee of his peers, with the very real chance that he could be drummed out of the corps. As DeAtley Hampton remembered:

An offense that involved honor—stealing, lying, cheating—was a serious offense, and you didn't want to be brought before the honor committee. About the only penalty that the committee could come up with was to kick the person out of school, and to my knowledge, the president always took the recommendation of the honor committee. During the time I was here [1944-48] there were maybe 10 people kicked out.

* * * * *

From the 1946 Vedette ~ A rabbit "thinning out"

While the power of cadet officers over rabbits expanded during Capt. Hamilton's tenure, the old Army officer didn't particularly care for some of the forms of hazing that had arisen in the '20s and '30s. That's according to the *Daily Oklahoman's* "No Place for Sissies" story, in which reporter Hill wrote:

> ...Hazing had become standard practice at OMA, as had been the habit of sending "rabbits," new boys, on errands, or blacking boots. Hamilton talked it over with the corps. It was agreed that the only reason for hazing was for the "satisfaction and egotism of the older boys," and it was ordered stopped. As always, someone tried to get away with it. A "rabbit" was sent on an errand. When it was discovered, the older boy did one mile of punishment tour [marching on the gravel-covered lot of the "bull ring"] for every yard the rabbit was sent and the hazing stopped.

That, of course, didn't mean that the rabbit period suddenly became a cakewalk. In fact, certain forms of hazing continued, as Anthony Massad, a cadet in the 1940s and later an Oklahoma Senator, explained, recalling his rabbit days:

> Every night at nine o'clock we had to stand to. That's what they called it. You stood outside your door, and, normally, they'd ask

you to thin out. That's when you get up against the wall, kneel down halfway, hold your hands out, and just sit there. Well, that wasn't bad. That was easy. The hard part was when they took your footlocker while you were in that position and put it on your arms. And you would sit there and sit there. Finally, you just couldn't take it any more, and you'd drop it. Then you'd get your butt eaten out good and proper, and they'd get you back in the position. This lasted for about 45 minutes every night.

"Shortly before I came, there were big paddles," added DeAtley Hampton, who came to the Hill as a new cadet in 1944. "That was a big deal with the paddles, and it was definitely forbidden when I got there. At about that same time, in the Army, there was a change where the military could not have personal physical contact. It may have been that the War Department made those changes for ROTC at the same time they made them for the Army, but Captain Hamilton was the guy who enforced it [at OMA] and it was very strict. I never had anybody lay into me with a paddle."

Capt. Hamilton would get a reputation as a no-nonsense disciplinarian during his few years as head of the academy, something anyone reading the *Oklahoman* piece could've foreseen. "Perhaps," Hamilton told the *Oklahoman* reporter, "appeasement of the young, letting them have their own way all the time, doesn't work with children any better than it does in diplomacy."

Kenneth D. Kirkland remembered a first-hand example of Hamilton's toughness, and, as well, his almost preternatural powers of observation. As a cadet in the early '40s, Kirkland had paid 50 cents to a former cadet for a used pair of boots; he planned to wear those to Saturday drills, keeping his newly issued boots ready and gleaming for inspections. The old boots he'd bought, however, rubbed blisters on his heels, and by the time he'd limped back to his barracks, he simply threw the old boots in his laundry bag, rather than getting them in shape for Sunday inspection. As he recalled:

The Sunday room inspections were usually conducted by one of the faculty officers. It was rare for Captain Hamilton to conduct them, but I had learned to recognize that distinctive cough that always preceded him and knew for sure that the toughest inspector of all was about to arrive. I took a quick nervous look at the laundry bag for any telltale bulges. I had buried the boots well in the center of the dirty laundry and I thought I was safe.

Captain Hamilton greeted me with his usual, "Good morning, Kirkland," and I responded, "Good morning, sir," with unusually mixed emotions. With hardly a look at anything else in my room he went directly to my laundry bag and started feeling it. I couldn't believe it. No one could have told. No one else knew.

"What is this I feel?" he asked.

"My boots, sir."

"And why are they in your laundry bag?"

I hesitated. "They are in my laundry bag because they are dirty, sir."

He paused for a bit. "Kirkland," he started, and I knew this wasn't going to be good, "is this where your boots are supposed to be?"

"No, sir."

"Kirkland, where are your boots supposed to be?"

"In my closet, sir."

He started looking around the rest of the room and running his white gloves where dust might be. Now, he stood directly in front of me. "Kirkland, why didn't you shine your boots and put them where they belong?" he asked.

My mind was of no use. "I didn't have time," I stammered.

Captain Hamilton turned away, then back again. "Kirkland," he said, "there is no such thing as not having enough time. Either you are inefficient or you need help." And with that, he left.

I threw the boots away and watched for the gig list that was posted each week, listing the infractions that had been reported and the demerits that had been awarded. Not shining your boots was a two-demerit offense, but when I found my name, the offense listed was "making an irrelevant remark—five demerits."

I am in my late seventies and I still have bothersome bone spurs on my heels that developed from that one march. I have never ever again used "I didn't have enough time" as an excuse. My children and any of my working subordinates can tell you that there is no such thing as not having enough time. You either are inefficient, or you need help.

Many other cadets over the years found themselves working off demerits earned because of infractions during inspections. A cadet's room had to be immaculate enough for the inspecting officer to run a white glove across any surface and not pick up any dust or other foreign material. This white-glove treatment extended to rifle inspections, and students soon found out how to scrub inside the barrels of their weapons with soap and water to eliminate any trace of rust or powder residue.

In addition, every item in a cadet's room, from underwear to insignia, had a specific way to be placed, hung, or folded. The slightest deviation usually meant demerits, and the effort to get things exactly right stayed with many cadets long after their days on the Hill. "My clothes in my closet, they've got to be lined up and a certain length," noted Anthony Massad with a grin. "My shoes have to be shined, and they have to be put in order. I can't stand an unmade bed. My wife's aware of this, and we still roll my socks the same way I was taught."

Demerits, of course, could also be extremely capricious. "One of my jobs in the wintertime was to go and heat up the stool in the latrine," recalled Hampton with a laugh. "I had to go sit on it and warm it up. One of my memorable demerits came when it was still cold, and the guy I was doing it for gave me a demerit."

* * * * *

When Pearl Harbor happened, I was in my room in the corner, upstairs in Markham barracks overlooking the tennis courts. We were listening to the radio and looking out the window at guys playing tennis, and it came over the radio. The enormity of it didn't strike me at the time, but everything was going to change.
— former cadet Louis Miller

We had breaks at various times, and so there were several of us in the post exchange, a little place up on the Hill where they served soft drinks and things like that. We heard this on the radio and we got very serious about it, you see.
—Gen. William Potts

That day, the OMA polo team was playing the team from Oklahoma University in Claremore. The enlisted cadre told us Pearl Harbor had been attacked. Being great history buffs, we had little notion of where or why Pearl Harbor!

Our team went on to serve with the 1st Cavalry Division in the Pacific, and all survived and came back to dear old Oklahoma. I can't remember who won that game, but I do remember the OU

guys had their trunk full of beer. We didn't get any.
—former cadet John E. Martin

December 7, 1941, changed everything in America, and OMA was no exception. In mid-1942, a bill was introduced in the U.S. Congress to turn the school into the second United States Military Academy (after West Point). That effort failed, but a few months later, OMA went to a 12 month school year, consisting of three 17 week semesters. Via this accelerated program, students could graduate more quickly, thereby supplying the military with much-needed officers.

A. Frank Cochran, a rabbit in '43, recalled that a cadet's day began at six a.m. with reveille and a school bell, giving the cadets 30 minutes to "dress, make our beds, straighten the room, and wash and brush teeth." Then, reveille and the bell sounded again, with cadets allowed five minutes to get in platoon formation for assembly, where reports and any announcements were made.

After marching to breakfast in the mess hall, cadets returned to prepare for morning classes. "Each cadet went to his classroom and his allotted desk, placed his books on the desk, and stood at attention until the instructor arrived," recalled Cochran. "The senior cadet present then reported the class to the instructor and upon receiving permission gave the command, 'Seats!' Classes lasted 50 minutes, at the end of which we were called to attention, dismissed, and allowed to move to the next classroom."

After morning classes came the noon meal, with the Doogie Band— the school's drum & bugle corps—"playing us into the mess hall," said Cochran. Two hours of classes followed, then athletics or military training, which included, during this period of ROTC cavalry at OMA, lessons in horsemanship. There was also the mandatory study period from 7 until 9 p.m., following the evening meal.

Although weekends provided a respite from this schedule, they were still full of required activities, as Kenneth Kirkland remembered:

> On Saturdays we had extended-order drill in the morning, then immediately after lunch, field inspection. On Sunday morning before chapel came room inspection. Saturday and Sunday afternoons were the two-per-weekend pass-privilege times, when you could go into town and take in a movie, grab some non-mess hall food or perhaps mingle with the Claremore girls at the drug store or in the hotel coffee shop.

The Sunday morning worship services were obligatory, but students had the option of attending chapel on campus or going downtown to a place of worship in Claremore. During this time, Claremore's Catholic church was a particular favorite of the cadets; those who stayed on the Hill on Sunday mornings attended services led by Academic Dean Col. W. C. Bryan, who exhibited a particular fondness for the old hymn "Church in the Wildwood," with its two-part, march-time chorus.

Sometimes, the church service was all a cadet had to look forward to on a weekend. Instead of hanging out at the Will Rogers Hotel sipping coffee and flirting with the town girls, he found himself confined to the campus, working off demerits. Said Kirkland:

> For infractions of the many rules, you were allowed 10 demerits per semester. Any over that required confinement to your room and "punishment tours" —which, if you were a corporal or less, were one hour of marching back and forth between Markham Barracks and the mess hall, shouldering your rifle. Each hour reduced any over ten demerits by one, and if you marched them all off you were released from confinement and could take your pass privilege. You could march off as many as six demerits in a weekend.
>
> If you were a sergeant or higher, confinement meant that you were confined to your room. There were no tours, and for each pass privilege your total was only reduced by one demerit.

The intensified training of the cadets was, of course, because of the war that raged across the world. But at least once, the war brought them something well out of that routine. Lt. Col. Harlan G. Koch, who became a rabbit in September of '41, (and who would much later become a novelist with *Homer's Place*, his tale of life in the '30s and '40s) recalled an incident that brought the war very close to the Hill, if only for a few minutes:

> One of my classmates was cadet first captain Ben Boyd...Ben's big brother was already a pilot in the U.S. Army Air Corps, was a native of Claremore, and he wanted to revisit his hometown, give sleepy Claremore and Ben a thrill of what was to come. I'll never forget that afternoon in 1942 when I casually looked down off the Hill toward Claremore. I couldn't have been more electrified had it been a screaming tornado. Coming straight up the road at a level *lower* than the Hill was a genuine B-17 Flying Fortress.

A proud OMA aviator ~ 1941   I

couldn't believe my eyes! I'd never seen a real B-17 except in Movietone News and the newspapers. There was little sound as it sped nearer and nearer. Then, it suddenly pulled up between our two barracks—so close that I could see the facial expression of a gunner, see him rotating his machine gun in the bubbled enclosure. All the gun bubbles were manned. Every window on the Hill shook and clattered. Cadets and faculty streamed from the buildings. Windows went up. The B-17 quietly disappeared into the sun and everyone was momentarily stunned to silence. Finally, someone said, "Wow. Didja see that? Didja see that? Where'd he go?"

The pilot, of course, was Ben Boyd's big brother, who circled the huge bomber around on the outskirts of Claremore and flew over the town and campus a couple more times before leaving.

It was magnificent. It was mesmerizing. Four large thundering engines—I'd never seen such a huge airplane—spellbinding because we could actually see eyes and noses in the cockpit. Again, he pulled this behemoth of an aircraft just above the barracks buildings, its growling engines causing everything to shake and shudder. That morning I'd read of Stuka bombers, and now I was imagining the terror on soldiers and civilians, especially if the guns were actually shooting, if bombs were destroying buildings.

Just the sound was petrification enough...

That sound, he added, "caused someone's chicken farm to go wild," with some of the flock "impaling themselves on chicken wire." The flyover, he also noted, "brought a smidgen of the war to OMA, and I remembered we cadets began listening more closely to what the old cavalry sergeants had to say."

Lt. Col. Koch also remembered the Army coming to the school shortly after Pearl Harbor and collecting "every cadet's ancient Springfield rifle" for military use. And if the students needed any more evidence that the war had hit College Hill, they could have found it on the dedication page of the 1943-44 *Rabbit Manual,* the second volume of the handbook. A full-page photo pictured Marine Second Lieutenant Roy L. Booth, who not long ago had walked among them. He was one of the first OMA cadets killed in action in World War II. The tribute opposite his picture summed up both the sadness and pride of his fellow cadets:

Booth ~ 1941

> Over half of us had the privilege of being in the Corps with you. Many of us were helped through difficult times by your example and understanding. You were at once the most rugged and yet the gentlest of us, and you will live with us forever. You stand for what is best in our state and in the Academy, for you overcame every difficulty that was thrown in your path without complaint or defeat. You were, and always will be, a very gallant gentleman.

In the same volume of the *Rabbit Manual,* cadet captain Ben F. Boyd—whose aviator brother had buzzed the campus a year or so earlier—told the new men in no uncertain terms about the purpose of their time on the Hill, not to mention their time as rabbits:

> As a cadet of the Oklahoma Military Academy, you must realize the importance of the education and training you will receive here. We are at war, and every part of the course and daily life is carefully planned to make you of the greatest value to your country when the Academy and War Department certify that you are ready. Avail yourselves of this opportunity, as here you qualify two years earlier than in any but one other state school. We are in the greatest war of our national history, and you are being trained

as leaders of troops in that war. This calls for willing obedience to customs and regulations; prompt and cheerful execution of orders. The man who cannot pass through his Rabbit year shows himself to be unfit officer material. There is no place for the playboy among a corps preparing itself for the field of battle. There is no place for a man who evades or temporizes with courage, honor or truth…

"What they did—and I can see it now—was when you came to Oklahoma Military Academy, you probably had no discipline, and they wanted to tear everything down and rebuild you the way they wanted you to be rebuilt," explained Anthony Massad. "It was probably six months before I realized I hadn't made the biggest mistake of my life." He laughed. "You were a rabbit for the first semester, six months, and then you became what we called a half-ass. You weren't exactly a full cadet, but you weren't a rabbit anymore." DeAtley Hampton summed it up this way:

> You told your folks goodbye, took off your civilian clothes, put on a pair of coveralls that didn't fit, and went around a bunch of people you didn't know. If you had any hair, you got it cut off. But they did not leave you any time to think about your poor state of affairs. They kept you busy all the time. You felt like a really little bitty cog in a great big wheel.

"If my folks hadn't already left," said Joe McBride, another wartime rabbit, "I might've gone home with 'em."

During those wartime years, rabbits like Hampton and McBride were not allowed to leave the campus for any reason during their first month. After those long first weeks, they finally got to leave for a few hours, going across the road for a tour of the Will Rogers Memorial. It might've been a short trip, but the temporary break in the grueling routine was deeply appreciated by most of the youngsters.

Even before the rabbit semester (which had been reduced from the original year-long ordeal) started, the new men had already been deeply immersed in the ways of the military life in general, and the academy in particular, as wartime cadet A. Frank Cochran recalled:

> I entered OMA about the first of September, 1943. That was about two weeks before schools started and the period was used for

"indoctrination." One of the first things in the leveling process and introduction to the lowest form of humanity—rabbit status—was the removal of all our hair. Believe me, it was a cultural shock that removed the vinegar from all of us.

We were also fitted for our dress and semi-dress uniforms and issued some one-piece fatigues and ROTC uniforms that were furnished by the Army. The pants were actually riding britches and a pair of full-lace riding boots and a shirt completed that uniform.

We were then marched to the barracks, assigned a room with a roommate, and taught how to properly "display" all of our clothing in the closet and in the drawers; how to make the bed tight enough that a quarter, when dropped from a height of three feet, would bounce a foot; how to dress rapidly and assemble in platoon formation in front of the barracks in the least possible time; and how to march in formation, perform the manual of arms, and do the other intricate movements demanded during close-order drill. By the end of that first two weeks, we were thoroughly indoctrinated and integrated into the corps…Some of our class that had problems adjusting to this rather dramatic, drastic, change in lifestyle…for the most part, had returned home and were no longer enrolled in the academy…

Cochran observed that, for the first few years during WW II, OMA's cadets trained with wooden rifles, since America and its allies "needed nearly everything that was available"—including, as Lt. Col. Koch noted, most of the rifles that had been used by the cadets. Cochran recalled the academy having a few World War I-vintage Springfield rifles during the period—obviously, those unfit for use by the Army—but, he added, he and the other cadets "learned about these weapons in class, but we were not armed with them until early 1944."

Of course, OMA was still a cavalry school, and the students also learned how to ride horses, first bareback and then using the government-issue McClellen saddle. Hampton noted:

By the time you finished your rabbit semester, you were able to go out and ride. You started out riding without any saddle. You rode around, around and around, it seems to me like five days a week. Bridle, no saddle. Then you got the saddle, but you didn't have any stirrups. The last thing you got was the stirrups. If you

Riding Practice ~ 1941

fell off or were thrown from a horse, you got up and rode that same horse immediately if you weren't hurt. If you were injured you rode that same horse as soon as you recovered. If the horse ran away, you walked back to the stable.

After a cadet mastered riding with stirrups, next came instruction in mounted drill, which, noted Cochran, "was completely different. Dismounted drill was performed by responding to voice commands," he explained. "Mounted drill was performed by responding to hand and arm signals, voice command, and sometimes bugle calls, and the system of movement was completely different." Remembered Hampton:

> You kept going to riding classes. You would progress from riding around this little corral until you got to the point where you could go out and go on what they called the Russian rides— which was 'follow the leader' on horseback. Jumping was also a big deal. There was a Lieutenant Trost, a great rider, who taught jumping classes. You started without reins, just using your legs to guide the horse. Then you jumped with a glass of water, about half-full, and you couldn't spill it.
>
> And then there were the real pros. A tall drink of water from

Springfield named Ghers, a polo player and a real horseman, jumped blindfolded with the water. He was the only guy I ever saw do it.

"Every Saturday morning, we had what we called 'the problem,' a maneuver with the two companies," said Alex Adwan. "One had the horses and the other would walk. We would have a march, a battle, a problem—a military drill of some kind. The problem might be that the red army was invading from Chelsea, and we were going to meet them at Oologah. They had cavalry, but we only had infantry.

"So, if any horse cavalry column had marched into Oklahoma from Germany at the time, we would've certainly been ready," he added with a laugh.

* * * * *

I was fifteen, in uniform, and the nation was at war. It was exciting and fun.

—A. Frank Cochran

The year 1943 was noteworthy on the Hill for at least two things. First, the Oklahoma Military Academy Coat of Arms, which remains one of the school's best-known symbols, was adopted and approved by both the OMA Board of Regents and the Oklahoma Historical Society. Designed by Capt. Hamilton, it incorporated a crest depicting the helmet of Passas, Greek goddess of warfare and wisdom, over a Greek sword, that had been used by the schools since the early '30's. To that was added the Indian war shield emblem found on the Oklahoma flag, and a scroll bearing the school's motto: Courage, Loyalty, and Honor.

The 1943 class was the first official class to graduate during wartime on the Hill. It consisted of 22 men, whom Hamilton officially addressed. "To you young Oklahomans, I speak with the most sincere pride and respect," said Captain Hamilton to his charges. "In my two years here, I have never seen you fail, nor have I seen a fence too high for you to take. Although a graduate of our oldest military school, I have never experienced nostalgia, for the best in it is what I find in you." It was an inspiring speech, and all the more so when one considers that, even then, Hamilton knew that forces were massing against him and his presidency. Some of the same players who had forced Col. Downs out of the top office at OMA were once again making the academy a football, kicked and thrown back and forth in a deadly serious political game between longtime rivals.

* * * * *

Control of the Oklahoma Military Academy, fifth ranking school of its kind in the nation, was assured for Gov. Robert S. Kerr today when the state senate passed, without amendment, a house bill calling for a new Board of Regents for the school. While Governor Kerr will be chairman of the board, and will name the two members, the new regime is expected to see the return of Representative H. Tom Kight of Claremore as the power behind the throne. Representative Kight was the principal author of the bill which passed today...

—Lorren Williams, "Governor Voted Control of OMA"
Tulsa Daily World, Jan. 30, 1943

The term of Governor Leon C. Phillips was over, and as 1943 dawned the see-saw battle between him and the father of OMA, Representative H. Tom Kight, found the latter in control. Although the conflict between Phillips and Kight stretched back to Phillips' failed 1935 bid to become Speaker of the House, OMA hadn't been drawn into it until 1939. That was when Phillips, who by then had moved to the governor's mansion, began investigating the school's financial records, which ultimately led to the dismissal of then-President Col. Downs, who'd been backed by Kight. It was the Phillips-appointed board that named Capt. Hamilton—and his brief predecessor, Col. Anderson—to the post, and now that Phillips was gone it was Hamilton who came under scrutiny.

According to a 1947 interview with longtime OMA coach Murl "Tuffy" Cline, conducted by historian Don R. Robards, many people in Kight's hometown of Claremore didn't like the changes that Gov. Phillips—and, by extension, Capt. Hamilton—had implemented at the school. During Hamilton's tenure, the relationship between the town and the academy had become more distant, especially after he dropped the day-student program at the beginning of the 1940-41 school year. There were even rumors that Hamilton had told a staff member not to associate with the townspeople. Add to that the highly publicized attempt Phillips had made to sell the academy to the feds for use as an Army training school, and it's not hard to see how there could've been lots of local support for a regime change on the Hill.

On the other hand, Hamilton and his no-nonsense disciplinary approach were popular with many cadet parents, whose tuition and fee payments now financed more than half of OMA's operating budget.

Some, in fact, who enrolled their boys for the 1943-44 school year, said they would withdraw their students from OMA if Hamilton was replaced. The cadets themselves defended him as well, ultimately resorting to a series of broadcasts over Tulsa radio station KTUL in defense of their beleaguered president.

At first, it looked as though the students and parents would get their wish. The *Tulsa Daily World*—which had frequently been accused of partisanship by Kight—announced in an April 24, 1943 story that Gov. Kerr and the new OMA board was convening for its first meeting "with strong indications that Capt. John C. Hamilton will be retained as president of the school." In a statement that may give some credence to Kight's accusations, the article went on to note, "Attempts have been made by old-line politicians to oust Capt. Hamilton, a thoroughly military man who has re-organized the school and established it on a high plane of scholarship and discipline." It continued:

> Governor Kerr recently announced that he would not change heads of educational institutions for political reasons, and as far as is known all are being retained. When this announcement was made parents of cadets at OMA breathed easier and are entering their sons there again in the only strictly boys educational institution in the state.

Only a couple of weeks later, however, Hamilton was in Oklahoma City for a contentious two-day hearing to determine his fitness for the office. A *Tulsa Daily World* story of the time gave a laundry list of accusations voiced by H. Tom Kight against the OMA president. They included charges that Hamilton was "a habitual drunkard, a user of narcotics, unscrupulous, untruthful, [and] unfitted temperamentally for the position," with "his conduct before the cadets at times unbecoming a man in his position." Most of the witnesses against Hamilton were people who'd worked at OMA, or other Claremore citizens, while Hamilton's defenders came mostly from the ranks of cadets and their parents.

The results were inconclusive, with both sides claiming victory, but when all the parties left the capitol building's Blue Room, where the hearing had been held, the handwriting was on the wall.

While all of this was going on, Kight had fired another OMA-related volley, charging that former governor Phillips, now a rancher in Weeletka, along with a former member of the OMA Board of Regents, had rented out OMA property to Bill Flippin, "the king bee bootlegger of Oklahoma...for $50 or $100 a year," according to a Lorren Williams article in the Feb. 27, 1943, *Tulsa Daily World*. The claim was made before a special house committee. An Associated Press story reported the ex-governor's response:

Gov. Phillips

Former Gov. Leon C. Phillips made quick and hot denial tonight to a charge by H. Tom Kight, Rogers County legislator, that he entered a land rental deal with eastern Oklahoma's "king bee bootlegger."

"Of course, there is no truth in it," Phillips retorted. "It was through my agents that the man was sent to the penitentiary. It was Milo Beck, one of my staff, who put him there.

"The committee will find there is no truth in it pretty soon when it investigates it." ...

The property in question was approximately 420 acres around Canyon Lake, where OMA cadets would regularly bivouac for war games and other training. And, despite what Phillips told the Associated Press, there indeed was some truth to Kight's charges.

Ray Bingham, the country-music booking agent and manager, lived several of his childhood years on the Canyon Lake property. His father, Walter Bingham, was a well-known moonshiner and bootlegger with connections to then-dry Oklahoma's "king bee bootlegger."

"Flippin took their stuff and sold it, and he also sold bonded whiskey that he'd get from out of state," said Bingham, who still lives near the area. "My dad and Ollie Davis made the whiskey on that property. I can walk right to where the still was. About three creeks run into that lake, so there was ample water. They'd do it at night, because if they'd done it during the day the revenuers could see the smoke."

Bingham believes that he and the rest of his family lived in the hunting lodge on the property from '39 or '40 "until they closed it in the late '40s. We were living there in '43, I know, because I wasn't quite old enough to go to school, but I'd walk there to visit."

Employed by OMA, Bingham's father "even spent a little time up on the Hill, mowing and stuff." But his main job was as caretaker for Canyon Lake and the grounds, which included a couple of barracks and a large mess hall. Recalled Bingham:

> I remember that there'd be bunches of cadets down there, shooting their weapons. They'd train there, just like the 45th [National Guard Unit] trained at Claremore Mound. As little boys, my brothers and cousins and me would watch 'em marching and all of that, and then we'd try to play what they were playing. It was a big thing for us. There was a war going on, and we'd listen to news about the war on the radio at night and then watch 'em train during the day.
>
> In decent weather, they'd always be out there swimming. There were canoes all over the place. And after they'd gone back to the Hill, we'd all go down by the lake and gather up all the white t-shirts they'd left. My mama'd wash 'em, and my older brothers and cousins would wear 'em. We never had store-bought stuff like that.

* * * * *

Capt. Hamilton managed to hang on at OMA until the summer of 1944, bolstered by a group of parents determined to see him stay, and by their sons, his cadets, who apparently thought quite highly of him. In early August, several members of OMA's student population put some cash together and bought time on Tulsa station KTUL, where Cadet Gerald Johnson went on the air to tell listeners that the OMA cadet corps "wishes the state of Oklahoma to know they are solidly behind Captain Hamilton and admire and respect him as their president."

By that time, however, it was too late. The OMA Board of Regents, including Governor Kerr, had sent Hamilton an August 2 letter giving the president an ultimatum: resign by August 15 and get a 15-day paid vacation, or don't resign and get dismissed on that date. In a terse statement published in the Aug. 9 *Tulsa World*, Hamilton said he wouldn't resign. "If they want to discharge me," he added, "it's their business."

By August 12, however, he'd changed his mind. "In order to terminate all unrest and any movements in my behalf which might disrupt the academy, at this time I hereby tender my resignation effective at your discretion," he wired OMA Regent A.E. Montgomery. "I assure you I will continue to assist the state of Oklahoma and the Oklahoma Military Academy. I have urged all cadets and personnel to remain at their work to maintain the academy's splendid record."

The day before had seen some of the hottest debate between the Board of Regents and the parents' association, whose president at the time was Tulsan J. L. Burke. In an August 11 article, *Tulsa Tribune* capital correspondent Joseph E. Howell related one particularly impressive exchange between the two factions:

> Burke charged that due to the long standing fight between Hamilton and Kight, many patrons of the academy felt Hamilton was being removed to satisfy "local politicians" in Claremore. Burke also charged that Kight had "called" a meeting of the board to consider Hamilton's ouster a year ago. The governor said Burke was "highly entertaining" but George Ade Davis, president of Oklahoma Gas and Electric Co., who with Kerr and A.E. Montgomery, Tulsa, is a member of the board, spoke up. "If the governor does not rise to his own defense, I will! The governor can't say 'I am honorable. I am virtuous,'" said Davis, "but I can."
>
> His finger pointing sharply at Burke and his chin thrust forward, Kerr declared, "When you said any outsider called a meeting of this board, that statement is false. I had either to laugh at you or close the meeting." ...

After accepting Hamilton's resignation, the board asked him to disregard the August 15 resignation deadline and instead to stay on until the end of the summer session. This came after an assembly on the academy campus, during which Hamilton told the students:

> If you want to do something for me, I am asking you now to carry this corps onward so that it will be bigger and stronger and finer than it ever has been. There comes a time when continued fighting merely causes useless loss—when you are actually destroying what you are trying to help.
>
> I know how you cadets feel about me, and God knows this corps means more to me than anything else in life. Constituted law and order decreed that I am to go. It is up to me to respect that authority. I want every cadet to return to the academy next semester for re-enrollment. You must come back with a determination to make this school ever better and better. No matter what my personal feelings are, this academy is greater than any individual. No one person is indispensable. I have never asked you to be loyal to me. I have demanded loyalty to the school.

Hamilton's speech "produced a settling effect upon the corps of cadets," noted an August 13th *World* article. A student petition to Gov. Kerr asking for "a good and sufficient reason" for removing Hamilton never made it to Oklahoma City, and the final of three KTUL radio broadcasts was canceled by the cadet corps. Cadet Johnson, who'd been behind the mike for the first two, instead told Tulsa newspapers, "The corps of cadets has been deeply impressed by Captain Hamilton himself but the principles of good soldiers that he has instilled in us impresses us far more. Because we are proud of OMA and the State of Oklahoma we shall continue to make OMA greater than ever before and we shall give our new leader our complete support and loyalty."

At the end of Hamilton's tenure in September, 1944, OMA Dean Col. W. C. Bryan, became acting president, turning the reins over to Col. Kenneth S. Perkins on November 1st of the same year.

* * * * *

An Army officer for more than 36 years, Col. K.S. Perkins took retirement leave from his post commander position at Fort Sill in order to assume the OMA presidency. He was a Virginia native and a graduate of the Virginia Military Institute, where he returned after World War I to help establish its first ROTC unit.

"The new head of the academy moved cautiously and made an effort to become acquainted with the situation before making any sweeping changes," wrote historian Don R. Robards.

Indeed, in a *Tulsa Tribune* piece published a little over a month after Perkins assumed the reins, the new president played it close to the vest:

> Colonel Perkins disclosed today hopes for an expansion program in the future which will provide for an enrollment of 500 students, practically doubling the present enrollment of 270 cadets. The present enrollment taxes the building and facilities now available on the OMA campus. Asked for additional information on future plans for the academy the colonel said he was not in a position at this time to furnish detailed information…

In the same article, headlined "No Drastic Changes Are Planned for OMA," Perkins announced that the academy now was able to appoint one graduate a year to both West Point and the U.S. Naval Academy at Annapolis, Maryland. The new president also made athletics a priority, although wartime travel restrictions still didn't allow for any varsity sports—even the fabled OMA polo team could only train and play inter-squad games. The story noted, however, that 89 boys had come out for the basketball team, "and from this group the academy expects to mould a top-ranking quintet to compete with other schools over the state when travel and other war time restrictions are lifted."

* * * * *

Even though Will Rogers was gone, the relationship between OMA and the memorial for the famed Claremore humorist, columnist and movie star remained as close as their respective grounds, which both shared on the same hill. Rogers had been buried in Los Angeles following his fatal 1935 plane crash, but, nine years later, his widow asked that his body and the body of a son, Fred, be moved to the Will Rogers Memorial, where an elaborate final resting place for Rogers and his other family members had just been built. The next year, 1945, saw a squad of movie stars and newsreel photographers descend on OMA for Will Rogers Days, an annual event still observed in Claremore. Bob Hope and his sidekick, Jerry Colonna, broadcast a radio show from the Bushyhead Field House before joining other dignitaries and OMA cadets in the Rogers burial ceremonies. Cadets Alex Adwan and DeAtley Hampton were both involved in the event. Recalled Hampton:

> Governor Turner and Bob Hope were both carrying a wreath, and myself and another member of the color guard were on either side. The procession was from the south side of the museum, down the series of steps to where the tomb is. Everybody was trying to be solemn—and Bob Hope was telling jokes. By the time you'd get to the bottom of the steps, everybody would be laughing except Bob Hope. And the Movietone [newsreel] man would say, "Take it again." We must've done that at least four times before Bob Hope finally shut up.

Will Rogers Days attracted other Hollywood celebrities over the next few years, although none made quite as big an impression as superstar Hope. As Adwan remembered, "I was a host for one of the actors who came here, the number two guy in the Cisco Kid series, Leo Carillo. I talked to him a lot. He was a lot of fun. Of course, we all listened to Bob Hope, because he was a big star. And man, he was Bob Hope all

Distinguished Guest ~ Bob Hope

the time. He was having a great time around these kids."

Even without Hollywood stars on the campus, however, the cadets sometimes felt as though they were in a movie. As Adwan explained, "The horses—that's what set us apart from everyone else. Everybody had seen John Wayne movies, but, hell, we *did* John Wayne movies. We'd do all of those maneuvers and everything they did in [the Wayne film] *Fort Apache.*"

The benefits of having an ROTC cavalry unit were far-reaching, leading to such unusual applications as band captain Donald Ruggles' earlier-mentioned adaptation of cavalry hand signals to lead marching bands. Blaine Imel also found that the horsemanship lessons he learned on the Hill served him well as a World War II fighter pilot. "What a wonderful thing it was," he said, "because the discipline we had to do with the horses was almost identical to the protection of the forces in aircraft. We learned to go in sections and divisions of four, just like it was set up for our aircraft. And we got more discipline there than you got in the pre-flight schools or the secondary schools. Any of the kids who had gone through a military academy were way ahead of anyone else. If orders were given, they knew we'd respond."

The cavalry unit also provided the cadets with competitive activities, especially during the wartime restrictions on travel that put a temporary end to intercollegiate sports. Young riders participated in horsemanship contests called gymkanas, and sometimes rode their mounts to Tulsa for horse shows, which Hampton recalls as being "Quite a deal—we'd ride into Tulsa, bivouac at Mohawk Park, and sleep on our saddles."

The end of the war, however, brought about the demise of the cavalry as well. While the federal government, in 1946, selected OMA as one of only four junior colleges in the country to receive a full senior ROTC program, it also abolished the ROTC cavalry units across the country, including the one on the Hill. "Well, this is four years into a war with atomic weapons and people are still riding horses around, so they decided it was time to make a change," explained Adwan. "They closed the units at Texas A&M and New Mexico Military Institute, too.

"Why they kept it all during the war was just because, well, the war was going on and nobody seemed to be making any changes," Adwan added. "A guy—I can't tell you his name—made a great speech [at OMA] several years ago. I wish I had a copy. He said this was a remarkable place, where well up into the 20th century they were trying to train young men and prepare them for the modern world by teaching them horse cavalry. He said, 'You can't believe it, but it really worked.'"

A 1946 *Tulsa World* article suggested that, although the cavalry unit was being dismantled, "it is expected that the War Department will continue to furnish the horses and equipment necessary for the conduct of mounted instruction as an extra-curricular activity, in order that there may be available a group of young reserve officers trained in horse cavalry should the necessity for them arise."

It was not to be, however. By January 1949, when Colonel James Morrison arrived at OMA for his rabbit semester, there wasn't a horse to be found anywhere on campus.

"They had them at a lady's ranch, by some little town south of Claremore," he recalled. "We used to go down and ride 'em. But we did not have horses on the Hill."

And so passed the horse cavalry era of OMA. The ROTC unit was now mechanized cavalry, with tanks and other vehicles replacing the flesh-and-blood animals that had helped bring national attention to the school on the Hill. In addition, ROTC students now had to attend a summer camp between their third and fourth year of training, spending six weeks at a regular Army post like Camp Hood, Fort Sill, or Camp Gruber as a mandatory step on their way to a commission.

* * * * *

Slightly under a thousand former OMA cadets served in the armed forces during World War II in all grades from private to colonel. Sixty-two of these young men gave their lives in their country's service…

—*Tulsa World*, Aug. 18, 1946

The war was over, and it was a new day across America. Things had changed, and Oklahoma Military Academy reflected many of those changes. With the need to turn out officers for the war no longer a factor, for instance, OMA returned to the regular two-semester school year. The cadet population also decreased, tumbling from 304 in 1943 to 202 in 1947. Lots of reasons were given for this slide, including the lack of interest in a military academy by veterans returning to school on the G.I. Bill of Rights. They'd already had military training, and the idea of repeating it—even combat veterans had to go through the rabbit period—wasn't very enticing to many. (Some vets, however, did choose to go to school on the Hill, along with at least one POW.) Those who returned from combat may have initially resisted, but ultimately made the most of their time at OMA.

Meanwhile, Murl "Tuffy" Cline, who'd been OMA's athletic director since 1927 resigned in 1945, succeeded by Lt. Col. Lee Gilstrap, a returning Army vet who'd been Cline's assistant before the war. Gilstrap also became public-relations director for the academy, but he wouldn't last long in either position, becoming the center of another political firestorm at the end of the 1946-47 school year. (When varsity athletics started back up at the academy in 1946, the level of competition was lower, with what historian Robards describes as "Class 'B' high schools" providing much of the competition.)

Also in 1946, H. Tom Kight, the father of OMA, died. A powerful Oklahoma politician and longtime Claremore resident, he had continually championed the school, taking on anyone he perceived as working against its best interests. His combative attitude and strong will had sometimes led to political scuffling, but he'd also done more to keep the school going and growing than any other figure in history.

Unfortunately for OMA, the political wrangling didn't end with Kight's death. In 1947, an attempt by Oklahoma Senator W.A. Waller of Nowata to get funding for a metal and woodworking building and a shop to handle the new mechanized equipment on the Hill brought a stinging response from fellow Senator Phil Lowery of Loco. According to a March 27 *World* article, "Lowery charged the tuition has 'almost doubled in the last two or three years at OMA,' and demanded to know 'why?' 'A few years ago a boy could go to the school for $600 a year. Now it costs more that $1,000.'

"I am against appropriating money to make a rich man's school out of OMA and fixing it so that the ordinary man can't send his boy there," Lowery said.

Waller defended the charges "due to higher costs and the fact that all other state institutions also had almost doubled living expenses," according to the story, but the bill—its amount already reduced from Waller's original figure—was sent back into committee.

Waller was more successful that year with his introduction of a senate bill calling for a new OMA Board of Regents. It passed, and the subsequent group was different from earlier boards in a number of ways. For one thing, there were three members instead of five, with staggered terms of office. The governor would not serve on the board; in fact, none of the members could hold any state office. No two members could

Gilstrap

be from the same county or even from the same profession. In this way, Waller and the other backers of the bill—including Col. Perkins—hoped to eliminate, or at least keep to a minimum, the partisan wrangling that had marked OMA's history from the beginning.

It was a noble idea, but it didn't work. A few months later, Col. Perkins relieved Col. Gilstrap and two instructors of their duties in what he later called an effort to reduce expenses, touching off another conflict. As the *Tulsa World* reported in a May 29 article:

Col. Lee Gilstrap, a faculty member at Oklahoma Military Academy at Claremore for the past 20 years and one of the most popular school executives in state educational circles, has been dismissed from his position as public relations director and director of athletics, it was learned Wednesday...Contacted at his home in Claremore, Col. Gilstrap confirmed the report of his ouster but said he had declined to make any previous comment for publication as he did not "wish to place the school, with which I have been connected so long, in an embarrassing position." Col. Perkins would not discuss the dismissal. The OMA commandant merely stated: "I have no comment. You will have to get the facts from Col. Gilstrap."...

The dismissal of Col. Gilstrap has stirred up a storm of protest among residents of Claremore and from hundreds of OMA graduates. Telephone calls to members of the Board of Regents asking that Col. Gilstrap be retained have been made and it was understood that an appeal has also been made to Gov. Roy J. Turner.

A state senator, who asked that his name not be used, said he had been "deluged with letters, telegrams and telephone calls from Claremore citizens and a large number of OMA graduates," all asking that Gilstrap be returned to duty with the school...

Some sources attributed the dismissal of Col. Gilstrap to activities among the colonel's friends to have him named as president of the school in an effort to build up a larger student enrollment...

Col. Gilstrap said that he was planning "no individual action in regard to the dismissal—what follows is up to the Board of Regents and my friends." ...

The regents, however, were divided. In another newspaper story, Oklahoma City-based Board Chairman T. Murray Robinson was quoted as saying the OMA president "was following his instructions from our board" when he made the dismissals. But Roy Wilkinson, a board member from Nowata, said, "it looks like Col. Perkins is tearing down the school instead of building it up," indicating that the action originated with Perkins, not the board. In fact, as a May 30 *World* story reported, "Members of the board revealed they had not been notified of Col. Gilstrap's dismissal, nor of the ouster of two other OMA faculty members. Capt. E.E. Claunch and Capt. Milton Phillips."

Col. Gilstrap was not reinstated. But within another year, Col. Perkins would also be gone. By the second semester of the 1947-48 school year, attendance on the Hill had dropped to 141, even as enrollment in most other state-supported schools was growing. Homer M. Ledbetter, who would become the next OMA president, wrote a doctoral dissertation a few years later that offered several theories for the decline:

Among these reasons were the lack of interest in the military academy by the returning young men who had been in the armed services; the natural tendency to turn away from the military school at the end of a great war; the lack of proper advertising; and the poor public relations that had developed through the past decade as a result of political embroilment of the school with several colorful figures in the political arena of the state. There were those who said the age of the president prevented his possessing the dynamic leadership so necessary at this particular time to the promotion of the schools' welfare.

It is the writer's opinion from his own observation that a combination of the reasons given above with others to be mentioned were the contributions to the poor interest in the academy at this time. Factional strife among members of the faculty; a complacent lethargy on the part of the faculty and the administration; a spirit of defeat within the student body; and a determined desire to react to the stern military routine developed during the war years—all of these provided the background for the decline of enrollment. The lack of a staunch political friend was also felt at this time.

In a meeting during March of 1948, the board decided to ask Col. Perkins to resign. They also began a search to replace him, contacting Oklahoma educational leaders for recommendations. According to Ledbetter, the board came up with three specific qualifications. He wrote, "This man was to be young; he was to have an educational background; and he was to have had military experience."

A native Oklahoman who'd served in Gen. Patton's Third Army during World War II, Ledbetter was recommended to the board by the principal of Tulsa's Central High School, where he'd started teaching in 1938. When he was appointed to the presidency of Oklahoma Military Academy on June 1, 1948, he was 34 years old. Then a captain, he would later become a colonel (like the other OMA presidents, the title reflected an honorary appointment to the Oklahoma National Guard). He would also remain as the academy's president for the next 16 years, tying the longevity record of Col. Walter E. Downs.

* * * * *

The recent football trip to Wentworth Military Academy gave me the first chance I'd ever had to compare another military school with my own. Both schools are Senior ROTC, Junior College institutions and therefore approximately equal. Maybe you'd like to see my comparison.

WMA is located six blocks from the business district of Lexington, Missouri. The campus covers about three city blocks and is surrounded on all sides by Lexington homes. Most of the space is occupied by picturesque but old and slightly beaten buildings. The campus is crowded to the extent that formations are held right in a normal city street. Compared to OMA's spacious campus and new buildings, Wentworth didn't stand a chance.

OMA won by a landslide in the uniform category, too. Wentworth's "wool C" uniform consists of regular army O.D. wool pants with a black stripe down the side and an O.D. jacket. Black shoes, black tie and a khaki shirt are worn with this, plus an overseas cap. Their dress uniform is black or dark blue pants and blouse with a large red stripe down the side of the pants. This is worn with a white shirt, black tie, black shoes, black and red Garrison cap and a black leather belt similar to our guard belts. Their overcoats are like ours, only black. All our uniforms are worn by WMA's faculty and tactical officers. That should be argument enough for us.

Military? We win again. Wentworth is an Infantry School while we are Armored Cavalry. That means a lot if you don't like to walk all the time. They still carry the old Springfield rifle M1903A3 instead of the newer, thumb grabbing, M1 Garrand. Wentworth does beat us in manpower, having close to 350 cadets and is therefore formed in a battalion instead of a squadron.

One thing the Red Dragons got my vote on is the Mess Hall and the food there. Cadets are served family style by colored mess boys or K.P.'s at tables with tablecloths. Although the football team got a better meal than Wentworth's Corps, such things as biscuits for breakfast, ice water, glasses and all the milk you can drink, for all, gave WMA the edge over us there.

Last, but not least, at least to parents, is the cost. WMA costs about $1500 per year. Much of the uniforms are rented, not purchased, so the cost is approximately the same each year. Compare this to OMA's $1000 per year for New Cadets and $800 per year for Old Cadets. Another best, for us.

Although Wentworth was the very best of hosts and the friendliness of their cadets did much toward making it a swell trip...Yep, I'm still going to OMA and mighty glad about it, too.
—Robert M. Gomez, "Editorial: OMA Wins My Vote"
OMA *Guidon*, Dec. 1948

When Capt. Ledbetter took over, the total enrollment at OMA was 72 men. Speaking of himself in the third person for his doctoral thesis, Ledbetter wrote, "He believed that it would take good public relations, plenty of hard work, and a great deal of improvement of the educational program, before he could hope for any lasting results."

Ledbetter set to the task. Before the fall semester began, he had made 58 speeches across the state, which fell in line with policy statements he gave to a Claremore Rotary Club meeting in early January, 1949. "Ledbetter outlined two major policies adopted since he became president of the school last summer," reported a January 6, 1949, *World* article. "One calls for increased enrollment to the academy's maximum efficient capacity of 300. The other deals with good public relations throughout the state."

Although other staff members also contacted potential students throughout Oklahoma, Ledbetter certainly did his part. As Tulsan Bud Inhofe, who came to OMA in 1949, recalled, "One evening this guy came out to the house. His name was Colonel Homer Ledbetter. He had a real clean-looking, happy—almost cherubic, if that's a good word—face, and he told us all about the wonders of coming to OMA. I will never forget him telling us, oh, how wonderful it would be up there.

"So I came up, my folks went home, and they took me and shaved my head and gave me clothes. I was about 105 or 110 pounds then, and they shoved me in a room. The guy who alphabetically became my roommate, George Hudman, was a little over 200 pounds, a great athlete. He could press *me*, literally.

"It was a real lonesome day," he concluded, "but it wasn't as lonesome for me, because I was going to make sure I stayed alive with George Hudman."

It also helped that Inhofe had Tulsa friends like Harry Poarch going through the rabbit semester with him. "I think there were 125 in our class, and about 50 of those dropped out," noted Poarch, who went on to become a colonel in the Army. "My parents had told me that the first semester was pretty tough, and if I ever got to where I couldn't deal with it, then I could leave. But one way or another, I made it through. I just had the perseverance, I think, to see if I could do it."

Col. James Morrison, who began as a rabbit in January of 1949—during Ledbetter's first full year as OMA president—had been attending high school and living with his transplanted Oklahoma family in California. His trepidation about returning to his home state for an OMA education wasn't helped by the weather on his arrival. "We got into New Mexico on a train, and the train couldn't go any farther for awhile, so they offered to put us on a bus," he said. "Our bus came to Claremore, I got off the bus, and if I had seen a bus going the other way, I would've gone the other way. Oh, it was terrible. Ice was on the road. Terrible weather. I slipped and fell down and I couldn't believe I'd done something that foolish."

Once the rabbit semester started, "We weren't supposed to go out of town for five weeks," Morrison added. "I went to Tulsa the second week. Yeah, I was about half smart-aleck. I walked off the damn Hill, went down and got on the train and went to Tulsa.

"When I got back, I was wet, and the corps commander saw me and he said, 'Well, if you're going to go to Tulsa, take a raincoat.'" He laughed. "It hadn't rained in Claremore."

* * * * *

With the recent graduation of Oklahoma Military Academy's 28th class, Capt. Homer M. Ledbetter marked the first anniversary of his taking over the reins of Oklahoma's only state military school. During that year the enrollment of cadets at OMA has almost doubled and present enrollment of new cadets gives every indication that with the school year 1949-50 the academy will be operating at full capacity for the first time since the conclusion of World War II...

Always one of the leading military schools of the country in the eyes of the United States Army which provides the staff for the ROTC training of the cadets, the school year just completed was no exception. Army War Board inspectors once again awarded OMA its highest rating...

OMA cadets receive more military training in their four years of ROTC at the academy than do selectees in their 21 months of service, Captain Ledbetter points out, and do not suffer the ill effects of interrupted education, for according to the latest selective service regulations, regularly enrolled cadets are not subject to the draft. Military training at the academy is effected through armored cavalry platoons making use of light tanks, assault guns, armored cars, half tracks, personnel carriers, jeeps, and planes. Training in radio supplements this work.

—"Captain Ledbetter Finishes First Year at Helm of OMA,"
Tulsa Tribune, June 24, 1949

As the 1940s ended, the efforts of Ledbetter and his staff were bearing fruit, with enrollment at the institution on the rise. During the first school year of the Ledbetter era, 1948-49, the number of students increased to 215, which press reports claimed was double the total of the previous year.

Among those finishing their tenure on the Hill at that same time was Robert L. Dean Jr., an accomplished piano player who entertained at many OMA dances and functions. After moving to Italy, he became a well-known jazzman, but ultimately achieved lasting fame with his bronze monuments of General Dwight D. Eisenhower.

OMA's president seemed to have an instinctive knack for coming up with ideas that would get him and the academy ink in Oklahoma's newspapers, thereby spreading the word and reaching potential new cadets. In August of 1949, for instance, a few weeks before the start of the new school year, Ledbetter announced the beginning of a drive to find "the lost army," a dramatic but effective term for, as a *Tulsa World* article explained, "the 1,200 youths who attended out-of-state military schools last year."

"Despite an enrollment boom," the story continued, "OMA officials are opening a full-scale offensive to halt the siphoning of the state's military recruits."

At the same time, things were going well enough on the Hill that Capt. Ledbetter was able to also announce that just anyone couldn't waltz onto campus and expect to be accepted. As an August 21 *World* story noted: "Pre-school talks with parents have brought requests from nearly 700 students for 1949-50. However, a new method of screening applicants will cut into this figure. All applicants will be interviewed by an examining board and only the 'cream' of the prospects will be admitted, Capt. Ledbetter said."

Col. Glen Burke was one of the cadets who first arrived on campus during that last school year of the '40s. After being named a Distinguished Alumni at the 2002 reunion, he said, "Whatever I am today, I give the credit to God and OMA," adding:

> I had a lot of *first* experiences here on the Hill. First time away from home, first time I ever wore garters, first time for a tie—and I didn't know how to tie it. Wore it with the same knot for the first year. First bathrobe. Only problem was, my folks forgot to buy me a bathrobe. My squad leader told me to wear my raincoat to the latrine. The first sergeant met me in the hall and said, 'What's the matter, Burke? You think it's going to rain in here?' Finally, the bathrobe came in the mail. It was white with red stripes. Met that same sergeant in the hall and he said, 'Burke, you look like a damn peppermint stick.'
>
> About those garters. Do you have any idea how hard it is to keep your garters up when you are a skinny-legged little kid? I was always dragging garters behind me when double-timing across campus.
>
> Oh, yes. That was another first...running everywhere I went. Ran past a couple of officers one day and gave them a sharp salute as I whizzed by. They stopped me. 'Mister, you should come to a quick-time when saluting an officer.' They made me go back and try again. Thinking I wasn't quick enough, I ran by faster the second time...

On the other end of the 1949-50 school year were seasoned cadets now facing life in the outside world, including the unnamed writer who reflected on his time at the academy in the "Bull Session" section of the May 1950 *OMA Guidon*:

> Well, gentlemen, we have come through another year at OMA. I know that is what is said at the end of each year. However, that is something that you never get tired of hearing.
>
> Sure, there has been a lot of dissension about this year, but the hearts always get a little softer at the end of the year. Things are never as bad as they seem, so let's all just bid a fond adieu to our friends until such time as we might see them again.
>
> There have been a lot of good times, though some of them were slightly illegal. We have made a lot of friends. Never forget them. And never forget what you have learned at OMA. The training you have received is going to come in handy, and I don't necessarily mean military.

The graduating boys leave this school in your hands. We hope that you keep up the traditions and spirits that have been bequeathed on this school by the past. You have a good school, please don't ruin it. Never let anyone take the good things away from you without a fight.

It has been nice living with you—BE GOOD.

The world would be besieged by changes in the 1950s, from the beginning and end of the Korean Conflict to the start of the Cold War. On the Hill, the tanks would leave during the '50s, and the ROTC would reorganize into a branch general unit. Still, through it all, the good things would continue. And so would the fight.

OMA Excels
in the '40s

1941's Aviators ~ Contact!

1942 Rifle Inspection

*Heavy Machine
Gun Practice ~ 1942*

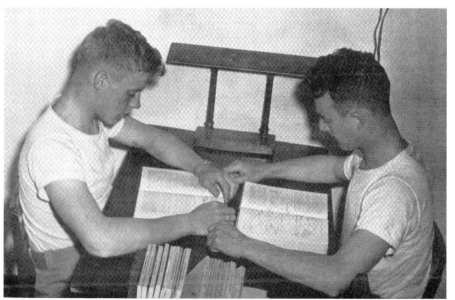

Call to Quarters ~ 1944

Summer Uniforms with Pith Helmets, Pegs & Boots ~ 1944

Aerial View of campus ~ August, 1944

Horsemanship Training
~ 1944

Col. & Mrs. K.S. Perkins ~ 1944

OMA's 1945 Polo Team

Mounted Honor Guard ~ 1945

Chow! 1948 Vedette

President Truman honors OMA ~ 1949

Doubling on the Triple Bar ~ 1946

The 1946 Jumping Team

Color Guard ~ 1946

Mounted Drill Team ~ 1946

Cpt. Ralph Baird Teaching Math ~ 1948

The Guidon Staff ~ 1947

Honor Guard ~ 1947

*Supply Sergeant
with Machine Guns
~ 1947*

Sgt. Davis' Retirement Parade ~ 1947

*Class of 1942 Former Cadet
Dale Robertson revisits
the Hill*

R.L. Dean
1947 National Rifle Champion

The 1947 Rifle Team

Maj. Paine Teaching ~ 1948 Vedette

Cadet Capers ~ 1948 Vedette

*Rabbits after a few hard weeks of
training ~ 1948 Vedette*

Douglas Lake

*Preparatory Hall (Administration Building) with
Bushyhead Field House in the background*

The 1950s

Col. Homer M. Ledbetter, President
1948-1964

As the 1950s began, OMA president Ledbetter and his staff continued their recruiting efforts, and enrollment on the Hill inched upward. For the 1951 and '52 school years, attendance was near the 300 mark, even with somewhere around a third of the new boys dropping out before completion of their rabbit semester—a figure that had stood at roughly the same percentage for several years, according to cadets of the time. And while Ledbetter had earlier vowed in print to admit only the "cream" of the prospects under his regime, there were still many young men arriving each semester whose academics and attitudes were less than stellar. Many of these couldn't take the rigors of being a rabbit and left; others stayed to find themselves transformed.

Among the latter was a young man from Muskogee named Jim Barker, who would go on to serve as Oklahoma Speaker of the House. As he recalls:

> I attended Muskogee High School my sophomore year, and I was not doing well. Frankly, I was running with a pretty rough crowd. My mom and dad had divorced when I was five, so she was fully responsible for me, and she heard about the military academy. We lived in an apartment at the time, and [Dean of Academics] Col. Baird came and we talked and we decided I would come to OMA as a junior. I was probably one of the meaner kids who went there. I thought I could beat the system.

Of course, he couldn't, but like many other successful OMA cadets, he learned to work within it.

> The first year was really tough and I really did not like it. I wanted to leave and my mom said no, so I stayed. And when the second year started, I thought, 'Well, I'm really going to start trying.' You had to sit and study for two hours each night, and you had to be making pretty good grades or you would have one of the professors in here with you—they'd come in and help you. If you were deficient, it went even further than that. You'd have to meet with them more often. It was a really good atmosphere for someone who was on the wrong track to begin with, like I was. So it worked out really fine.
>
> I attended OMA for four years, and by the time I got to junior college I was making the honor roll. I was on the junior-college football team. I really started liking it and, consequently, I graduated second-highest cadet. My mom and this school really turned my life around.

Barker even came to realize that valuable lessons came out of the extreme circumstances of the early '50s rabbit semester.

> We stood outside many, many nights and had what they called a Chinese fire drill. They had those real often. What they would do was have us in a formation outside and then announce a uniform. They'd name maybe 15 items that you would wear out or carry out—like maybe carrying a mattress cover, which was on the

bottom of the bed.

You didn't have a paper or pencil to write anything down, and if one person had it wrong, then you had another fire drill. So when you got out there, if you disappointed your fellow cadets, you had all kinds of problems. It got to a point—and it didn't take long to get there—that you wanted to please them. It was a team effort, and I think that no matter what we do in life, it's always a team effort.

When I became Speaker of the House, I ran against a good friend of mine, David Riggs of Tulsa, and I didn't beat him by very much. So we immediately started off with a pretty divided house because we had a very close race. And then you had to start trying to make a team out of 101 politicians. It all went back to how you built a team back then: You give other people credit, you share the credit, and everyone looks good.

New cadets trudge across the drill field

During the rabbit semester, however, it was hard for the new kids to see the future benefits of this sort of training. Most of them were like Sam M. Matthews, an early '50s cadet, who felt at first as though they were entering a strange new world—and, in fact, they were. "The campus was absolutely immaculate," Matthews recalled in his memoir, *My Memories of OMA*. "There was not a blade of grass out of place, no signs of peeling paint, no rust on iron work or dirty streets. There were no paths across the grassy areas and no discarded cigarette butts."

As Matthews lined up with his fellow rookies and their parents outside the registrar's office to enroll, "a big kid a few heads in front named Gene Barrett" entertained the group with wisecracks and humorous observations. But, he added, "I cannot say a person did not feel a little nervous and queasy preparing to sign up for a lifestyle into the unknown. Everyone seemed a little edgy. Even Barrett's quips seemed a release of

Rabbits await their fate

nervous anticipation."

Barrett and the others, of course, had every right to be nervous. Their lives were changing forever, and they knew it. And while each cadet had the choice of staying or leaving, it was a rare young man who didn't at least entertain some notions of ditching the Hill during the rabbit semester, especially during the intense period known as Hell Week.

Hell Week was the last week of the rabbit semester, that, as an article by Bob Milam in the Dec. 16, 1954 *OMA Guidon* explained, "gives the members of the NCD [New Cadet Detail] a chance to see if their teaching has been any good…[and] gives the Rabbits a chance to see if they really deserve to belong to the OMA Corps of Cadets."

Milam's story went on to detail many of the special challenges faced during a rabbit's final week:

> Hell Week began with a bang at "First Call" Monday, December 5th. Five minutes later, there was a "Room Inspection" with NCO's gleefully pointing out "corrections."
>
> Hardly had the Rabbits had a chance to get their breath when, lo, five minutes later—a "Personal Inspection!"
>
> You who are reading this may think five minutes is not long enough to straighten a room after NCO has inspected it and, on top of that, prepare for a personal inspection. But ask any Rabbit—if you can't make a bed after it's been torn up, clean up a

room, shine a pair of shoes, polish several pieces of brass, sew on buttons, do several laps around the barracks, and then fall out into a formation—all in five minutes...then you don't belong here.

Six hours of relative relaxation comes with classes until the noon mess hour. This gives the Company commander time enough to organize a few inspections and to send his Rabbits on several tours around the lake. It also means another square meal drill—or an extra hour of time for the NCO's to dream up special work for the long suffering rabbits.

Things return to normal after school call for everyone except for a few who are so unfortunate as to have the afternoon off. They spend the time either in hiding out under their bunks or in the "Opportunity Hours" [the time that was allotted for extra studying] which suddenly become popular.

Thus time rocks along until CQ [call to quarters] is over, when the rabbits are introduced to 15 minutes of the fastest and toughest "physical training" the company CO can think of.

Best of all, there was the Saturday 14-mile hike to look forward to...

"There was a lot of hazing that went on during Hell Week," says Gene Crose, who arrived on campus in the fall of 1950 as a high school freshman. "They'd have you in a half-squat holding up a chair or footlocker and you would have to do that until you almost passed out. I did it for about 28 minutes one day and I couldn't even walk. They called a formation and I started to run out to the formation and I fell over the banister in the barracks. My legs just weren't there."

Even before the final indignities of Hell Week, however, early '50s rabbits, like their predecessors, faced constant reminders of their low-rung status. "They cut all your hair off and you had to sew your side pockets shut," recalled Rob Roy Routh. "You had to eat what they called square meals in the mess hall, sitting on the front few inches of your seat. And if an upperclassman was in the hall, you had to brace up against the wall with your neck pulled in."

"It was tough," added Crose. "I really never thought about giving up and going home, though, because I wanted to make my parents proud of me. I think I would've gone to hell for that," he added with a laugh. "Well, I felt like I was in hell some of the time down at OMA."

Crose ended up staying throughout high school and getting his junior college degree from the institution, becoming OMA's—and, a bit later,

Tulsa's—first rock 'n' roller along the way. But initially, staying with the program took some serious adjustment on his part.

> When you're a rabbit, you have to square every corner and run everywhere you go on the campus. At the corners, you have to do a right face, a left face, and then take off running again. And in the mess hall, you have to sit on the first three inches of your chair. You have to keep your back straight and look straight ahead. And you can *not* talk. When I first went down there, I'd never heard of such a thing. They told me to look straight ahead and I said, "*You* look straight ahead."
>
> These guys were big guys, and they grabbed me and threw me up against the wall, and, boy, I fought 'em. But that just made it worse. That went on about a week, until I realized that I wasn't going to beat it. So I figured I might as well join 'em and do what I was supposed to do. So I tried to do that. But I still had a lot of trouble. Even when I got to be an old man, I still ended up on con a lot.

A cadet became an "old man" after the first year. By that time, he had not only survived the rabbit semester, but also the next semester of being a "half-can" or "half-ass," a transitory kind of place where a student wasn't suffering the harassment given rabbits, but wasn't exactly a regular cadet, either. And even after a cadet had reached his second year and old-man status, as Crose noted, he

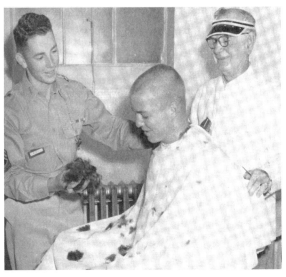

A rabbit gets a haircut

still could be punished by going on con. Wrote Sam Matthews:

> After accumulating a given amount of demerits, a cadet was placed on "con." I believe the definition of "con" was "confined." His town pass privileges were taken away and in most cases the

cadet was required to work off "con" or walk "con." Walking "con" consisted of walking back and forth across the drill field carrying his M-1 rifle all afternoon on Saturdays.

The daily guard detail was responsible for the people on "con." In some cases, these condemned cadets were assigned to polish the brass doors found on the campus and the two Naval twelve-pounder cannons, used during the War Between the States, in front of the Pershing Rifle Range…

These unfortunates, he added, were the young men who'd been "stuck" by a staff member or cadet officer. "Getting 'stuck' meant receiving a demerit or demerits as applied to the offense," wrote Matthews. "To be stuck, a cadet would be guilty of unshined shoes, unpolished insignia, needing a haircut, or a dirty M-1 rifle. Messy barrack rooms would certainly be a stick. Nonregulation parts of the uniform would get you

a sticking, and Captain Bill Bess was death on these regulations."

Bess was a legendary tactical officer in those days, the assistant to the Commandant of Cadets. "I believe to this day," noted Matthews, "that Captain Bess had psychic powers and eyes in the back of his head."

Bess wasn't amused when he caught an early '50s cadet, Ted Wright, flaunting the rules. As Wright

Lt. Col. Bess   remembered it:

I kept a car down at the bottom of the Hill. I used to come up through Owasso and in around the back way, park my car at the bottom of the Hill in a bunch of trees, and run up the side of the Hill.

One night I was AWOL. I had just dropped my date off in Tulsa, and I was headed back to the Hill. I pulled up at a red light at Fourth and Main in downtown Tulsa—and Bill Bess pulled up next to me in his car. He looked over and saw me, and when the light changed I turned right and took off, running through every light there was until I got back to Claremore.

I parked my car, ran up the side of the Hill, got to my room—I was in a four-man room—and shut the door. I hung my combat boots on the top sill by the heels, so when you opened the door the boots would fall down. Then, I jumped on the top sack, where I was sleeping. I'm lying there thinking, 'What am I going to say? What am I going to do?' And it wasn't five minutes before the door opened and those boots fell and hit him—and boy, was he mad.

He yelled "Wright!" and I said 'yes, sir,' and jumped out of that sack. I'm standing at attention in my skivvies and he gets right in my face, his nose about an inch from mine, and he says, "Were you in Tulsa tonight?"

I didn't answer him for what seemed like an eternity, but it was probably only a second or two, and I said "yes, sir."

He said, "I *thought* so," and walked out. Left me. I thought, "Oh, my God." I went back to bed and I don't think I slept all night long.

About a week or 10 days later I missed a class or something and I had to report to him. You had to report at a certain time of the week to answer your demerits. He gave me an hour of time for whatever my infraction was, and I stepped back to salute and do an about-face and leave, and he said, "One more thing. That trip to Tulsa? That'll be *five* hours." So he hadn't forgotten.

Wright was hardly the only cadet taking unauthorized trips off the Hill in the early 1950s. And while many were caught and punished, some were not, even when their offense was so blatant that it's hard to see how anyone could get away with it. A perfect example was related by Col. Harry Poarch, who recalled an audacious escape from the OMA campus during the 1951-52 school year.

Being one of several who were pretty much wallflowers at the cadet dances, I rarely attended these events. On one Saturday evening, John Long and I decided a visit to one of the local bootleggers was in order, since we were not participating in the dance festivities. As cadets will remember, Oklahoma was a dry state at the time.

A major problem, however, was that we had no mode of transportation to visit such a place of degradation. Not to be defeated in this effort, we proceeded to a maintenance shed where a farm-type tractor belonging to the school was stored. With John driving and me standing on the rear axle, off we went, right down the Hill, out the main entrance, and on down Will Rogers Boulevard to our destination, a location I do not specifically remember.

How we made it there and back without being seen—at least by anyone who cared—is beyond me, but we were successful in our mission.

Other missions, however, were deadly serious. While it was not mandatory, some cadets also belonged to the Claremore-based National Guard unit, which not only gave them a legitimate reason to get off the Hill on the weekends, it supplied them with pocket money as well.

Eighteen members of the 45th Reconnaissance Division, including both cadets and faculty, were called to active duty when the conflict in Korea began to escalate. Young cadet guardsmen were abruptly swept away from their studies and dropped on foreign shores. There, they joined several OMA graduates who were serving in the Far East, including First Lieutenant Frank L. Brown, a standout at the school in both academics and sports. A highly respected squadron commander during his years at OMA, he was killed in Korea on Sept. 2, 1951.

* * * * *

OMA's school president was Colonel Homer M. Ledbetter. The Colonel was a professional public educator with a thorough understanding of the science of politics. With this political savvy, President Ledbetter accomplished many positive contributions in improving the school. It was Col. Ledbetter's dream to create a four-year college of OMA. He stated his ambitions to us one evening during an informal assembly of the Corps in front of the auditorium.

OMA was bucking strong competition in constructing the Colonel's dream. It was felt that the state's two major universities, OU and Oklahoma A & M, fought this possibility vigorously. Another principal obstacle in Col. Ledbetter's way was the struggle to increase the school's enrollment. This would help place it in a position to be considered by the State Legislature as qualified for its new status and insure their vote of approval…

—Sam M. Matthews, "My Memories of OMA"

Col. Ledbetter may indeed have had a dream of converting OMA to a four-year college—but it was a dream born of necessity. In early 1953, with the war in Korea still raging, the Department of the Army directed that senior ROTC programs could no longer be offered at junior colleges, a move that affected 42 military schools across the country, including OMA. Under this new edict, the academy would not only lose its senior ROTC designation, but also the accompanying federal funds and other government help that went with the program. Apparently, the Pentagon felt that this reduction in the number of senior ROTC units across America would save the government money.

The announcement, understandably, put Ledbetter in a quandary. At a June 1953 meeting with the state Board of Regents, the OMA president heard at least three proposals for the future of the institution: convert it to a four-year college, drop the junior college program and become a high school with a junior ROTC unit, or continue as a four-year high school and two-year junior college, without a senior ROTC unit. If the latter plan were followed, there was even talk about making the junior college co-educational. "This," explained *Tulsa World* reporter Joe Reilly in a June 16 article, "would put the school on a par with other state junior colleges serving primarily a local area."

Ledbetter traveled to Washington in search of guidance, finding out that all military junior colleges, including OMA, would be given a three-to-five year transition period to convert to a four-year college, provided that the conversion started by the first of September, 1954. He met again with the state regents for higher education just after the beginning of the fall 1953 semester—and the end of the Korean War—telling them that OMA's enrollment had dropped from 300 to 228 because of the "adverse publicity" concerning the Department of the Army's action. "I feel very definitely that if I am to make the conversion, or if I am not to make the conversion, I need to know," he told the state regents. "I need to know how to stop this adverse publicity."

According to a Sept. 29, 1953, *World* piece, "The commandant [Ledbetter] said Army officials had waived requirements that a senior ROTC school must have an enrollment of at least 100 college freshmen. The only enrollment requirement now, he said, is that the school turn out 25 graduates each year." At the time, OMA had 144 high school students and 84 college students.

Ledbetter came to the board with a plan, noted the *World* story:

> He asked that the board authorize a gradual conversion into a 4-year college by adding one year of college training and dropping one year of high school work each year until the transition is complete. That way, he pointed out, all students currently enrolled would be able to complete their training.

In order to make the change, he estimated an additional $25,000 in state funds would be needed to meet salaries of new instructors. He estimated an extra $25,000 would be desirable, but not absolutely necessary, for new equipment and other facilities the first year.

Ledbetter buttressed his position by telling the regents that closing the academy—which was apparently also an option at the time—would mean that a six-million-dollar physical plant would be shut down. He described it as the best one at any military school in the nation, with the exception of West Point. And he put a dollar figure on the help OMA was getting from the federal government: $865,000 for equipment, $75,000 for payroll, and $5,000 for supplies.

Johnston Murray, the governor, came down on Ledbetter's side, recommending that the regents do what they could to help convert the academy to a four-year military college, especially because "apparently it would involve such a little bit of additional money." The Board of Regents, however, did not vote to finance the expansion.

Luckily for Ledbetter and OMA, the Army changed its mind after a few months, allowing the academy's ROTC program—and those of other military junior colleges across the country—to continue for at least another three years. "Under this program," explained Joseph E. Howell in a *Tulsa Tribune* article from April 10, 1954, "OMA offers two ROTC programs, a junior program which runs through the four years of high school work the school offers, and a senior program which encompasses the last two years of high school and the first two years of college."

Howell wrote that military schools across the country, including OMA, had been having a dialogue with the Department of the Army on the issue of junior colleges offering senior ROTC programs:

> At first blush, according to Ledbetter, the army idea that ROTC commissions should go to men with college degrees seemed to have merit. However, as the military schools studied the proposition they came to the conclusion the round-the-clock military life in a military school was an educational factor not to be ignored.
>
> Spokesmen for the military schools pointed out to the army that by comparison, ROTC is a part time matter in the average four-year college and regular army men agreed with them, Ledbetter added…

That same argument had been put forth before. In that September 1953 meeting with the state regents for higher education, Ledbetter's commandant of cadets, Col. George E. Butler, told the group that the Pentagon had issued an order that no second lieutenant should be sent to combat in Korea without first undergoing specialized training, the kind ROTC students got only at military schools. He said that college grads with only ROTC training "were losing not only their own lives, but the lives of many others along with them."

The *Tribune* article also mentioned that the military schools had been able to show that eliminating their senior ROTC programs would actually cost the government more in increased training costs for graduates from regular four-year colleges.

Eventually, the military schools that didn't offer four-year degrees, like OMA, managed to convince the Department of the Army to continue allowing them to offer senior ROTC programs by combining training in the last two years of high school and the two junior-college years. The Army even abandoned the requirement that a school graduate 25 students with commissions each year—another good thing for the school on the Hill, which had a total enrollment of only 208 at the end of the 1954 school year, the lowest since the late '40s. Ledbetter felt that all the speculation and uncertainty about the school's future had been a major factor in its population decline, and admitted to the Tribune's Howell that he had "misgivings" about trying to convert OMA to a four-year college. "Our problem now," he said, "is making people see that the school is stable."

* * * * *

A snapshot of cadets' lives during this time can be found in the March 31, 1954, issue of the *Guidon*. In an article titled "You Wouldn't Believe It, But We'll Tell You Anyway," student writer Bill Combs claimed to have spent "two weeks and the soles to a pair of good combat boots" running down info for the piece, which chronicled the yearly consumption of various things by the academy's cadets and included figures from the school canteen—2,160 sweet rolls, 40,500 soft drinks and 12,000 cups of coffee—and the mess hall: 18,000 "big Irish potatoes," 102,600 half-pint cartons of milk, and 21,600,000,000 English peas!

"Then here's a figure to make your feet ache," Combs wrote. "The corps of cadets drills a total of 192 hours each year on Monday, Wednesday, and Friday. Then, to keep the rifles in shape, they use over 25,000 rifle patches and 25 quarts of oil in cleaning rifles during a school year."

According to the Maintenance Department figures, cadets use plenty of what it takes to clean the barracks. Ask a "Con" man about the job of painting the barracks…they used something like 225 gallons last year.

And you privates…ever see any of that "GI" soap? They use 2,475 gallons of it here each year to make sure your hands are soft and sweet.

And then there are those "Police" formations…ever stop to figure out how many match sticks you pick up during a year? Our figures say something like 360,000 are thrown away each year. Let's hope most of them get into those GI Cans.

By the way, there are some cadets here who do study or at least make a show of it…the PX sells over 2,500 nickel pencils during the nine months you are "studying." Besides that, they sell 700 pairs of shoe strings.

Each week, we go to the Business Office for our allowance…we get between $1 and $3.50 each week, to the tune of $24,000 each year…and we're still broke…

* * * * *

During the mechanized-cavalry era of OMA, which lingered through the first part of the 1950s, the boys on the Hill trained with a variety of both weapons and vehicles. Bill B. Harris, in a memoir titled "OMA Thoughts, 1951-54," remembered them well:

The weapons we learned about were mostly weapons of the WW II era. They were the 30 and 50 caliber machine guns, the 45 pistol, the machine gun known as the "grease gun," the M1 Garand and the M1 carbine. We marched with the M1 Garand and learned how to take them all apart, clean and maintain them, and use them as a firearm.

The military vehicles we had at the time were two M4A3 Sherman tanks, a half-track, an armored car and several Jeeps. These were the tanks we had my last two years at the school, but the first year the tanks were reconnaissance tanks and I don't remember why they were changed to the M4 Sherman. We used these vehicles in our war games and also for military parades and such.

Of course, for many young men, just the sight of a tank conjured up the romance of the big war, and the possibility of getting to drive or ride in one surely fueled many boys' decisions to attend OMA. Harris was a young man who enjoyed getting in the driver's seat of one of those old war wagons, and he remembered how the experience could be addictive enough to make even a good cadet do something he knew he shouldn't.

One Saturday afternoon, Phil Doerner and I went to the military department and got permission to drive one of the M4A3 Sherman tanks over to the area where we usually had our war games. After Phil and I had taken turns driving the vehicle around the area, we decided we would drive the tank around the drill field before we took it back to the military department. When we got back to the department, Sgt. Wilson ate us out severely, but he obviously didn't report to the powers that be, because nothing ever came of it. We were very lucky.

Mechanized maneuvers

They—and their fellow cadets of the time who loved to drive and ride around in real-life Army tanks—were lucky in another way. They were on the Hill at a time when the tanks still rolled. OMA had dodged a bullet when the Army changed its mind about two-year colleges and senior ROTC, but the Pentagon brass weren't quite finished. In 1955, the whole ROTC program was reorganized, and the armored cavalry unit on the Hill was abolished. The tanks on the campus rolled one more time, but this time it was off the Hill, never to return. The armored unit, there since 1947, was replaced by a branch general unit—which was, essentially, very similar to the infantry program that OMA had started with decades ago.

Unlike the threat to take away the senior-unit designation, however, this change had little effect on the institution's enrollment. By the 1956-

57 school year, the student population was beginning a climb that would last well into the 1960s.

The mid-'50s rebound extended to the academy's athletic programs. Sam Matthews, OMA class of '55, remembered active golf, tennis, fencing, rifle and drill teams, and a football program with two competitive varsity squads, one for high school and the other for junior college. "I think there were 90 out for high school ball my junior year," he noted in his memoir about OMA, suggesting also that the junior college team's George Hudman was "an athlete on the same level with OU's Steve Owens."

Hudman & Teammates ~ 1952-53

OMA alumnus B. G. Jones, who went on to a successful career as a high school football coach, remembered a particular example of *esprit* involving the team and its fans in the late 1950s.

I was a cheerleader my junior and senior year in high school and my freshman year in college. I had some money because I'd worked all summer, and I wanted to get some kind of car because of this junior college team—as cheerleaders, we could drive to see them. So I went down to Claremore, to the junkyard. They had an old '47 Pontiac hearse that had been used to shoe horses—red felt in the back, with a stack of coal and a tin piece under it so it wouldn't burn down, and a guy had been driving around the rural areas and shoeing horses out of it. It needed a new clutch, so it was just junk.

I asked the man how much he wanted for it, and he said 25 dollars. I had 25 dollars, so I gave it to him and we brought the hearse up to OMA. To get my 25 dollars back, we sold 50-cent tickets for a chance on 25 dollars, and guess what? We drew the name of a faculty member and he gave us the money back.

So we took the hearse over to the maintenance department and put a new clutch and a new pressure plate in it. George Thompson, the maintenance director, hooked up a valve-cleaner bottle where the passenger sits that went all the way to the carburetor, so you could turn this valve and it would suck in this valve cleaner and just smoke the whole stadium up. Then he put a siren in the front. We had our won-lost record—which was all wins—on the side.

We would go over and get the opposing cheerleaders. They'd be thinking we were bringing them back around the track to our side to cheer, and we were. But first, we'd drive around and speed up past our stands. We had women's panties we'd bought down in Claremore, and we'd throw them out, and then we'd throw an old mannequin out the back.

He laughed, noting that it was all designed to make the crowds wonder what was going on in the hearse with the opposing cheerleaders —who were, of course, a different gender than OMA's. "After that," Jones said, "we'd go back around again and stop, and they'd do a cheer, and then we'd go over to their side and do a cheer."

Virtually all of the schools the academy teams played were regular high schools and colleges in the area, and as Jones' story points out, the cadets were a breed apart. While they all lived, technically, in Claremore, the students on the Hill were not immune from the usual conflicts found between citizens and students in any college community. In fact, the relationship between the OMA boys and their counterparts in Claremore may have been more challenging than most, thanks in no small part to that old saw about how women love a man in uniform. "Every once in a while there would be a car load of town kids making the circle up here, honking their horns, throwing beer bottles, and generally raising hell," remembered Col. Harry Poarch. "We had some pretty nice dances up here, you know, and I'm sure the competition for girls was part of it."

Added Poarch's fellow '50s cadet Sam Matthews:

There were always hard feelings by the Claremore Dapper Dans toward the cadet corps. The cadets were always drawing the attention of the eligible Claremore girlies and leaving the Claremore Don Juans empty-handed and frustrated. It was an age-old dilemma for the Claremore cavaliers.

One night, a group of brave Claremore buckos agreed it was time to wreak vengeance on those despised "rabbits" occupying the Hill. About seven of these raiders decided to storm the OMA bastille and teach those tin soldiers a lesson in becoming more respectful and keeping their attentions away from Claremore territorial assets. Each raider, no doubt, thought himself equal to any 10 of the military boys. I'm not sure which one of the barracks these raiders assaulted, but I have always believed it was Markham. The Claremore commandos entered the building sometime after taps to wreak their havoc. Some cadets, still awake, were able to block all avenues of escape. The corps was almost instantly on defense in superior numbers.

It is said that before first call the next morning, there were seven pairs of civilian pants flying at full mast on the post's main flagpole.

* * * * *

One of the main periods in a cadet's life is his rabbit or initiation period. This is a 15-week period in which the new cadet learns, in short, to fetch for himself. He must learn to keep a tidy room always but most certainly during the time that he is a rabbit. At first the rabbit is enrolled and he is yet still bewildered by his new surroundings with only a vague notion of what is going on around him. (Up to this time, a rabbit has usually depended on others to pick up after him, run errands and take up for him.) All he can see or is supposed to see are good examples around him. Sharp uniforms, shined shoes that he can see his face in. He sees the "old men" standing tall, with their shoulders back naturally, which is something you acquire after you've been at the school a while, and he already had a feeling of *ESPRIT DE CORPS...*
—Don Gish, *OMA Guidon*, December 18, 1958

The school on the Hill was nothing if not a respecter of tradition, and as the 1950s rolled toward the '60s, many of the traditions first

The Brace ~ 1956

begun in the '30s—or even the '20s—were still parts of every cadet's life. There were, for instance, the mandatory two-hour study periods on weeknights, the Sunday parades, the annual anxiety-wracked War Board inspections, the formal dances, the demerits and their punishments, and, of course, the new-man "rabbit" system. Originally a school-year-long ordeal, the rabbit period had been reduced to one semester in the 1940s. But even at half the length, it still drove away those who couldn't accept the sudden, intense, change in their lives. It was the rare rookie cadet who didn't experience bouts of homesickness and regret at the beginning. Many were very young, like B.G. Jones, whose first-day impressions echo those of many mid-'50s newcomers to the Hill.

I was 13 years old, my first time away from home. My folks dropped me off, and I remember looking out the window at Markham Barracks at that black-and-white Plymouth, '57, with the big fins, and then seeing my parents and my sister at a distance, our eyes meeting as they drove away.

And then it hit me. I realized I was alone for the first time in my life. That's when I crawled in the closet and closed the door and started crying my eyes out.

"Once the parents left," he added, "the new-cadet detail, which was in charge of all the rabbits took over, and so they came in and then all hell broke loose."

Jones was one of the ones who managed to stay with the program and graduate. As mentioned earlier in this chapter, however, some did not. In an article published in the *Tulsa Tribune* a couple of weeks after the beginning of the 1955 school year, Col. Ledbetter admitted to writer Joseph E. Howell that reaction to the rabbit system had cost the school as many as 15 students in other years, although only five had left so far that semester. He also told Howell that during his early days as OMA president, he'd been inclined to favor abolition of the rabbit system, but he was now for it—not only because it helped teach the new boys to respect authority, but also because it helped the older boys to exercise it. "Sometimes we have to bust a little old boy who has been made a corporal and given a squad of rabbits," Ledbetter noted, "but it helps him learn a valuable lesson."

Fifties student Donald K. Routh learned a different kind of lesson as a cadet corporal at OMA, one that helped put him on a path toward a career as one of the nation's top psychologists.

I guess it must've been my second year, and I was a corporal and put in charge of a squad. I had what I still think of as a golden bunch of kids. Just wonderful. They seemed to be winning awards all the time—room inspections, whatever. My memory is that they were the best drill squad that year, which was kind of a big thing for us. I was also, I think, priding myself on my leadership—that it was my doing that got these wonderful results out of this squad. And I think that if my life had continued to go that way, you know, I might've been a veteran like a lot of these other [OMA] fellows. But the school's response, oddly enough, was that the next squad I got was known colloquially as the f--k-up squad. They were the sorriest group of kids that you ever saw, the most dysfunctional or whatever term you want to use. There was one fat guy who couldn't run, another guy who couldn't wash properly...and I just dealt with them as best I could. I learned that they weren't going to be the squad I had last time, so for them to survive, just to get through all the discipline and crap they had to put up with would be a major accomplishment.

It was my first experience with people who were not behaving well. They were catching the consequences of that, and I was trying to help them.

"Every young man, 14 to 24, needs some disciplinary training of the kind we give," said Ledbetter in the *Tribune* story. "There is nothing a boy needs any more than discipline, and certainly he is not getting it in the average school or home today."

The colonel, of course, was promoting the kind of military training that cadets got at OMA, even as he noted that some of the old ways had been slightly amended in order to, as he put it, "compete with fraternities."

"We used to have plain concrete walls and Army cots," he told the reporter. "Now, we've painted the walls in the boys' rooms in three different colors. We've put in Venetian blinds, comfortable beds, and steel desks. We've equipped the lounges with good furniture and TV sets."

He added that students now got to keep a car on campus after their rabbit semester, as long as it was kept in the designated parking lot, the boy had a driver's license and car insurance, and school authorities had a duplicate key.

Ledbetter seemed to harbor some ill feelings about college fraternities. They came out in the *Tribune* piece, when he admitted that he wasn't crazy about the notion of a student having a vehicle on the Hill and then made an odd statement to rationalize the action. "It's a popular thing," he said, "for the son of a rich family to be given a convertible when he is graduated from high school, and for him to take it to school the next fall and join a fraternity."

* * * * *

As many cadets of the era recalled for this book, the formal balls in the '50s—held in conjunction with special occasions like Christmas, parents' day, and graduation—brought some of America's top musical talent to the Bushyhead Field House. Big names that played for the cadet dances included Billy May, Ted Weems, the Glenn Miller Orchestra—carrying on after the death of its leader during World War II—and Louis Armstrong. (Sam Matthews recalls that the immortal Satchmo "would remove his coat and shirt, put on a pair of green shades and read a novel" during the breaks of his OMA show.) The school, also, had a dance band during those years called the Cadets, a separate entity from the marching band.

"They used to have a reunion for the Army reservists over in Tulsa, and our dance band would go over and play," recalled former cadet Jon Hines, who played saxophone in both the dance and marching bands. "My roommate, Phillip Barrett, and I also did Homer & Jethro-type stuff, pantomiming records. I'd dress up in a cowboy suit and my roommate wore big overalls and put big black freckles on his face. The band director, Capt. Thomas, would take us all over the place."

Hines said that the Glenn Miller Orchestra played the Graduation Ball in '58, but the year before it was a band out of Hollywood called the Cell Block Seven. "They were all dressed like convicts," he noted, "like Elvis Presley in that *Jailhouse Rock*."

In fact, OMA had gotten its own version of Elvis a year before that,

Backstage with Louis Armstrong ~ 1960

during a performance of the academy's annual talent show, Cadet Capers.
Explained Gene Crose, who'd been a cadet since 1950:

> I was going to do some country music on Cadet Capers, but
> then I saw Elvis on TV on Tommy Dorsey's show. It was his first
> show, and I just happened to be sitting in front of the TV in the
> barracks when it came on.
>
> So, when I heard Elvis, I thought, 'Oh, my goodness. There is
> no way I want to sing country music now.' So I took a Carl Perkins
> tune, 'Blue Suede Shoes,' and I liked it so well I thought I would
> sing that. And I did 'Forgot to Remember to Forget,' which was
> Elvis' second Sun Records recording, and some other song I can't
> remember now. We did two songs, and then I came back out and
> we did 'Blue Suede Shoes,' and gosh—they just went wild. I wasn't
> really trying to copy Elvis. I just loved the music and the feel and
> that kind of thing.

Even with only a couple of actual musicians in his four-man band,
Crose was an immediate sensation. The rock 'n' roll train was just leaving
the station, and OMA had its own star on board.

> After that, they asked me to travel with the Cadet Orchestra,
> so I did. They would do their thing, and then they'd take a break
> and we'd do two or three numbers. We got so popular that they
> started leaving us—the bus would pull out and leave us. The man

in charge of the orchestra, Capt. Thomas, would pull the cord out of the wall so the microphone wouldn't work. It took me a while to figure out what was going on.

Although the band director obviously preferred pantomimes of the countrified comedy of Homer & Jethro to this new raucous rock 'n' roll music, he was hopelessly bucking a trend. The kind of rock 'n' roll Crose performed was roaring across the country and the world, indisputably the new music of America's youth—including those who happened to be in military school. Crose and his band of players from the Hill made a successful appearance on a brand-new local TV show, *Party Lane with Chris*, and soon Crose was working with a group of Tulsa musicians and playing jobs around town as Gene Crose and the Rockets. By the time he graduated from OMA in May of '56, he was already on his way to becoming Tulsa's first homegrown rock 'n' roll act.

But he—and Elvis—had started something on the OMA campus. Rock 'n' roll music became a regular feature of Cadet Capers, as can be seen from a report on the 32nd annual staging of the talent show in the April 21, 1959, *OMA Guidon*. The event began with a performance by the cadet dance band, some comedy dancing by students in drag, a piano solo, an accordian solo, and a minstrel routine done by a couple of cadets in blackface. "James R. Long," noted the article, "was then introduced to match his crooning against the rock 'n' roll singing of Gary Rastelli, who offered his renditions of 'Endless Sleep' and 'Swingin' Baby Doll.' Rastelli was accompanied by the Rock N' Roll Band, which is composed of Barry Baker, Tom Clark, Rick Conger, Thomas Orndorff and William Scudder."

Historians tell us that rock 'n' roll was about rebellion, and authority figures like the plug-pulling Capt. Thomas may have sensed that. A military school was no place for rebels, though, and OMA's early rockers—and the administration—learned to adapt. "I'm not sure how rebellious it was," said late '50s-early '60s cadet Bill Ramsay, who played guitar in an all-cadet band. "I guess it was a little bit. I mean, we had Presley at that time. But I don't remember being discouraged by the faculty. I don't remember being particularly *en*couraged, either.

"They let us have our time, and our forms of expression, but I think they were as mystified as most of the older generation," he added with a laugh.

* * * * *

In the early 1950s, the school's administration began presenting a series of stage shows for the cadets designed to be both educational and entertaining. Modeled after the old Chautauqua programs popular around the turn of the century, they were named after the auditorium near Athens where Aristotle had taught. Chances are, however, that the famous philosopher of ancient times didn't have to put up with the criticism that the modern-day equivalent got in an April 30, 1954, *Guidon* editorial by Dean Bradley.

> Each Friday night at exactly 7:30 p.m., if you happen to be in the vicinity of the "Hill," you can hear the weary feet of the Corps tramping toward the auditorium where they are "requested" to listen to some person lecture on "How to Come Out of Your Shell," or some other absurd topic in a program commonly called a "Lyceum."
>
> It seems that many of the supposedly educational "Lyceums" are not suited or selected to interest the cadets.
>
> In most schools these "Lyceums," which prove so "interesting and beneficial" are held on the school's time and not on the students'. Personally, I don't mind using up my very limited spare time on a good program, of which there have been a very few this year, but if they want to present a program to the Corps like some that I have seen on MY time it "tees" me off no end! A lyceum of that type should be left to the option of the cadets, not to the policy of "you all come or get fifteen [demerits, presumably]."
>
> I have heard it said that one should not criticize if he cannot suggest a possible remedy. Well, some of the cadets have suggested that instead of having so many lectures on such uninteresting topics—that they should have movies as we had last year...
>
> Furthermore, it would undoubtedly be cheaper to show a good movie, and if they can't have a good lyceum, let's just not have one at all.

The lyceum presentations, however, continued through the '50s, although they diminished in frequency to about once a month. In the '58-'59 school year, the program included TV, movie and radio actress Virginia Sale, doing a presentation called "American Character Sketches"; hypnotist Howard Klein; record-setting runner Wes Santee, who brought along a film of his career highlights; retired Air Force general Orvil A. Anderson speaking on "Our Conquest of Space"; and the return of a Russian-born entertainer named George Jason, dubbed "the one-man entertainment company," who seemed to be a particular hit. As a December 18, 1958 *Guidon* article noted, "The program, according to Mr. Jason, was divided into three parts—the first 'in which I talk,' the second 'in which I play the piano,' and the third 'in which I perform with this magical stuff.' Each part was enthusiastically received by the corps, as were the 'volunteers' he selected to help him in the final part of his act."

* * * * *

OMA's cadets—particularly those in the drill team and band—were also a source of entertainment to others, participating in parades and other events not only in Oklahoma, but also in other areas of the country. Bill B. Harris, an early '50s member of the drill team, remembered performing everywhere from a downtown Claremore parade to the Holiday in Dixie event in Shreveport, Louisiana, while band member Jon Hines recalled traveling to Oklahoma City for the opening of the sesquicentennial Oklahoma legislature. "The drill team performed outside and the band played on the south steps," Hines said. "There was an honor guard, we all lined the inside of the chamber, and they opened the '57 session of the legislature."

While the drill team and band often performed together, a real rivalry existed between the two, according to B.G. Jones.

> I played with the band for five years, freshman in high school through freshman in college. Then I left the band my sophomore year in college and went to the drill team as the guidon.
>
> The unique part about that was, you see, that the band and the drill team were always at each other. They weren't friends at all, and a lot of vulgar things were said between the two. But if anybody said anything against us—the camaraderie would come to the front.
>
> Still, if you were in the band and wanted to come over, they didn't want to let you. And if they let you in, and you did the initiation, you might not live through it.
>
> They were pretty easy on me, though.

* * * * *

For most of the '50s, life went on atop the Hill in time-honored fashion. An April 18, 1957, story by *Tulsa Tribune* reporter David Corbett could've come straight from a newspaper two decades earlier, as he wrote how OMA had once again prepared for its annual honor-rating inspection, which it had passed every year since 1933, focusing on a couple of young cadets to start the piece.

> Seventeen-year-old Cadet David Gordon of Tulsa slept on his floor Tuesday night. And his roommate, Cadet Jim Lasseter, slept in the closet. They didn't have to, for inviting and impeccably clean bunk beds awaited them if they cared to move just a few feet away. But Wednesday was the day of the annual federal inspection of the Oklahoma Military Academy here, and the eagerness which led Gordon and Lasseter to such lengths to avoid disarranging their carefully made beds was the same throughout the campus...

The piece pointed out that OMA had a staff of three regular Army officers and eight NCOs to "supervise military training," and that all 19 members of the faculty were members of the Oklahoma National Guard. And, of course, there was a quote from Col. Ledbetter, who solemnly noted that "Our aim is to develop in young men the integrity and manhood of which they are capable."

Legendary officer Bill Bess was also still around in the late '50s, although his rank had been promoted to Lt. Colonel and his title to commandant of cadets. As might be imagined, his charges knew better than to question anything he did. Jon Hines recalled an incident from 1957:

> I was on my way to my room one morning and I heard my name called over what we called the bitch box: "Report to the commandant's office." I didn't think I'd done anything wrong, but I hotfooted it over there.
>
> Col. Bess asked me, "Cadet Hines, have you got a clean Class B uniform?" That was the one with the Eisenhower, the Ike, jacket.
>
> I said, "Yes, sir."
>
> He said, "Go put it on and come back."
>
> I was in fatigues, so I went over and changed, and when I got back, he said, "Report to the guard house."
>
> See, out where the flagpole is now, there was a visitors' center

and a guard at the gate from, I'd say, six in the morning to probably midnight. They had a sergeant of the guard, a corporal of the guard, and three privates who were rotated on that gate.

Well, I thought I was in trouble. So I got out there, and they took my picture for the 1957 annual. I'm the man at the gate in the first picture in the annual. And to this day, I don't know why he called me.

Jon Hines mans the Guard House ~ 1957

A few years earlier, the guard house and its gate had been a place where cadets going off campus had to check in and out, under the watchful eye of the officer of the day and a couple of orderlies. With the OMA mail room adjacent to it, the guard house was also the place where students assembled for mail call, the high point of the day for many a cadet.

Now, the guard house had transmogrified into a visitor's center, one of the small changes that crept onto the Hill before the end of the decade. And there were other, bigger, changes as well. In 1956, the day-student program was reinstated, and this time it would stick. Then, in 1957, the academy opened its doors to night students as well, starting an evening-college division.

It's not likely that many saw these moves as foreshadowing the end of Oklahoma Military Academy. But with the benefit of hindsight, it's easy to see that these were a couple of small things that helped open the campus on the Hill to groups other than cadets, and a first tiny step toward becoming a regular junior college.

Life on the Hill in the '50s

A Mechanized Military ~ 1950

*A cadet's work is never done.
Studying ~ 1950*

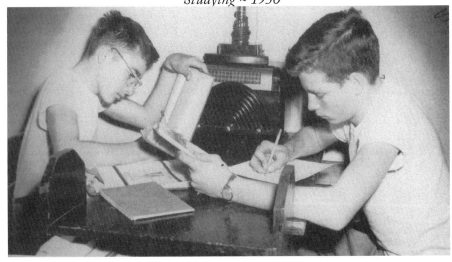

Combat Vehicles ~ 1950

Light Tank ~ 1950

1951 Parade

Holiday Ball ~ 1951

Major Paul Kelly ~ 1952

Guard Duty ~ 1952

The 1952 Track Team

A rabbit's first haircut ~ 1953

The 1954 OMA Marching Band

The 1956 Fencing Team

Color Guard ~ 1957

The 1955 "Big Team"

The 1958 Swim Team

1959 Cadet Capers

YOU KNOW YOU ARE ALWAYS A CADET FROM OMA WHEN...

- Someone yells "rabbit" and you don't look for the Energizer bunny.
- You hear the word "brace" and don't think of orthopedics.
- "The Hill" does not mean Iwo Jima or San Juan.
- Someone mentions the word "townies" and all you can think of is girls.
- You clean the house on Friday nights thinking there will be a Saturday morning inspection.
- You tell the kids "lights out" to get them to go to bed and "make reveille" to get them awake.
- You "form up" the kids to get them organized.
- You call information seminars "lyceums."
- You still make the bed using the "forty-five degree corner" technique.
- You call a restaurant a mess hall.
- You can fondly remember sending someone to the Commandant's office for the key to the flagpole, to the nurse for his masturbation papers, and to the PX for rubber chevrons for his raincoat...

—B.G. Jones and Phil Goldfarb

The 1960s

Maj. Gen. John F. Smoller
President ~ 1964-1968

Written by two '60s graduates long after their days on the Hill, that humorously nostalgic list would indicate that things didn't change much for the institution as the '50s became the '60s, that Oklahoma Military Academy stood as a bastion of immutability in a sea of change. In many ways, that was true. Although the rabbit period would shorten to six weeks, during the latter '60s it was still a full semester throughout much of the decade. And the testimony of those who were there indicated that it had changed little from the '40s. Recalled Gen. Timothy Malishenko, a rabbit in 1960:

Being a rabbit was difficult for everybody. There's no preparation for being a rabbit. I mean, I was probably four-foot-eleven and weighed 90-95 pounds. They shaved your head and put combat boots on you, and you ran everywhere and drilled with M1's. If I put a bayonet on an M1 and stood at attention, it came up to my ear.

At dining hall during rabbit period, you had to sit on the front six inches of your chair, looking straight ahead. You could look straight ahead, and you could look down, and you had to square to eat—bringing the fork up straight until it was level with your mouth, and then straight into your mouth.

But the real routine was with the water pitcher. You had to sit there on the front edge of your chair, looking straight ahead, and ask for permission for water. Well, when they gave you the water, your right hand went out vertically away from you and you held the pitcher rigid, asking for permission to pour the water. If they wanted to be difficult, they'd wait a while. They'd say things like, "Well, just hold it. I'm not ready yet," or "Don't move until I tell you you can move," until your shoulder and arm could start trembling. When a 95-lb. kid is holding a water pitcher out in front of him, it builds deltoids and strength real quick.

Malishenko came to OMA midway through the school year, so his rabbit class was comprised of only a couple dozen rookies. As he said with a chuckle, "I don't know if that was a good thing or not, because when the group's that small and everybody else has already been through it, there are a lot more people to focus on the 20 in your class.

"But there were some great folks in that group, and a lot of friends came out of it," he added. "I'm sure that's probably true of all rabbits. It's that Marine Corps or boot-camp analogy of a few good men. You grow up and survive and you become a lot stronger because of all of it."

David Raper, a cadet at the time, said that many families sacrificed heavily to send their boys to OMA, which gave some rabbits added impetus to make the grade—even one who stood 4'5" tall and weighed 70 lbs., as Raper did when he first reported to the Hill.

James Elder arrived at the Hill from Tulsa in the early 1960s. He became a noted attorney, and in a speech following his 2004 induction into the Oklahoma Military Academy Hall of Fame, he recalled his rabbit days. "I suspect there was not a day in my life that I felt so alone," he said, "and at the same time filled with the anticipation of what I could achieve with the opportunities open to me."

Before I came to OMA, I had probably never made my bed. I'd probably polished my shoes once. I was practically an only child because my sister had married when I was six, and I was spoiled rotten.

My father was a very shrewd man. On the day of enrollment, he called me into the business office as he was about to pay my tuition, and he made me stand there as he counted out 25 one-hundred-dollar bills and laid them on the counter. And he looked at me and said, "Now, anytime you think about leaving I want you to think about me paying this money, because I'm not going to get any of it back."

Two weeks later, after I was firmly entrenched in the so-called rabbit period, I felt like I had perhaps been double-crossed. So I sat down and wrote a letter that said, "Dear Dad: If I hadn't seen you count out all that money for tuition, they would see my dust from Claremore to Tulsa. Your son, Jim."

He carried that letter with him until he died.

One of Elder's particular bugaboos as a rabbit was the "poop sheet," which all newcomers were required to learn.

The poop sheet was a 13-15 page typewritten document that they mimeographed, and it smelled like alcohol. That tells you how old it was. It had the cadet prayer, a couple of speeches, general orders, some of the history of the school, various and sundry things that you were expected to memorize and recite on command to upperclassmen. It was the same thing they have at West Point; I'm sure all military academies have them.

Memory work, though, was very difficult for me, and when I was given that document to learn, I thought, well, I'd never get out of rabbit period because I'd never be able to say all that. You had to go to your squad leader, your platoon sergeant, and then your platoon leader, and recite whatever they called upon you to recite. You couldn't go to your platoon sergeant until you'd perfectly recited it for your squad leader, and so forth. You worked your way up. My platoon leader was Jack Lancaster. And by the time I got to him, I was so scared I was shaking. Fortunately, he asked the things that I knew the best and I just lucked out. So, because of that, I was allowed to have a date, and my parents were able to come up for the first parents' weekend. Those who hadn't said their poop sheet did not get to see their parents, got no date, and didn't get to go to the dance.

As those stories indicate, to those not aware of the forces churning behind the scenes, it seemed as though things were rolling right along in time-honored fashion at the school on the Hill. In March of 1960, there was even a little incident remarkably similar to something that had happened in the '20s, when Gen. Baird H. Markham, an OMA regent who'd just had the campus' first barracks named after him, gifted the cadets with a working cannon—only to have its twice-daily booming silenced due to protests from the townspeople.

In the '60s version, the cadets had scored a 75-mm howitzer from the Army and had begun firing it to signal both reveille and retreat. On the morning of Tuesday, March 22, however, the cannon was silent. Word quickly spread that Governor J. Howard Edmonson had issued orders to gag the cannon after a woman complained; in response, the cadets lined up in morning formation but refused to go to classes. It fell to the ubiquitous Col. Bill Bess, then commandant of cadets, to explain what had really happened and break the 45-minute strike. As he explained to a *Tulsa Tribune* reporter, "It was knocking plaster off the walls in some homes and shaking windows."

* * * * *

An explosion of a different sort came a few months later from OMA President Col. Homer Ledbetter, reminding those who paid attention to such things that the fate of the academy on the Hill was never really secure. What set him off was a recommendation following a joint meeting of the Legislative Council Committee on Higher Education and the Governor's Commission on Higher Education, which revived the idea that OMA should be transformed into a regular two-year junior college. According to a Nov. 5, 1960, report in the *Tribune*:

> Fiery Col. Homer M. Ledbetter unleashed a few salvos today at a committee which has suggested turning Oklahoma Military Academy into a coeducational junior college.
>
> "We are trying to do our best," Col. Ledbetter said. "We think we are doing a damned good job. We will put our program up against anybody's any time. "If they think they can get something better, that is certainly up to them. I don't think they can…I say I believe Oklahoma needs desperately the type of school OMA represents."

Ledbetter also said that OMA had "the best damned military school in the country" and was adopting a new motto: "Kill us or support us." Seen in retrospect, those seem like remarkable statements for a man who knew, like no other OMA president, the value of publicity and politics. Perhaps he thought that his bold statements would swing public support the school's way. Or perhaps he was simply fed up with the constant battle to keep the academy what it had been when he had taken the reins: a state-supported military school. The state's appropriations to the school, he said in a later *Tribune* piece, only amounted to "20 to 32 percent of the OMA budget," and was used exclusively to pay salaries and utilities, with tuition, sales from campus stores and the rental of real estate properties owned by the school making up the rest. Apparently, Ledbetter felt as though the school was being shortchanged by the state.

Whatever his thoughts and motives, he kept the pressure up. A month later, he was handing out folders—titled "Kill Us or Support Us"—to members of the Oklahoma House Committee on Higher Education. By then, however, his tone was a bit more conciliatory. Wrote Joseph E. Howell in a *Tribune* story dated Dec. 5, "Ledbetter told the legislators it is 'true we could service more people' if OMA were made into a coeducational college as has been suggested.

"'We're not fighting the change, we simply want to point out that the state has here a tradition worth preserving,' he said. 'There will always be wars and rumors of wars. OMA believes that our state and nation needs to respect our flag, needs to develop leaders in the arts of living a disciplined life and adept in soldering.'"

Rev. Neal J. Harris, the rector of Claremore's Episcopal Church, supported Ledbetter and OMA with a priestly zinger, saying "to change to a coeducational college would be the most foolhardy thing the state ever did, and they've pulled more boners than anybody."

At that time, during the '60-'61 school year, enrollment at the institution was at an all-time high of 462 students. However, only 334 were actual full-time cadets, boarding on campus. The other 128 were day or night students. Perhaps that non-cadet enrollment, suggesting a pool of other types of students in the Claremore area, was one of the things the committees considered in making their recommendations.

For whatever reasons, the idea of changing Oklahoma Military Academy into a regular junior college was something that wouldn't go away. It came up again during the '61-'62 school year. "Although quick to point out that OMA is prepared to take on any mission assigned it by the legislature," wrote Mac Sebree in the Nov. 6, 1961, *Tulsa World*,

"Ledbetter has become alarmed at proposals to make OMA into a co-educational junior college. 'I would hate to see it. There still is a need for the traditional military school,' he said."

As befits a military institute with a long tradition, the article was devoted, at least in part, to linking the OMA of the past and the OMA of the present. Sebree wrote:

> ...Thirty years ago, Will Rogers played polo with the cadets on the fields of the Oklahoma Military Academy here. Today, the horses are gone and the cadets are more interested in helicopters, jets and other 1961 military technology.
>
> OMA has changed in other ways, too. But some things remain the same.
>
> "There still is a need for a military school in Oklahoma," says Col. Homer M. Ledbetter, the outspoken president of OMA. "Even with the ever-more modern Army, the value of OMA is enhanced. We must teach the fundamentals before the men can specialize." Eight to 10 per cent of the cadets at OMA go on to full-time military careers. The others benefit.
>
> "For those who intend to enter civilian life, the stiff discipline and enforced study patterns here made for academic distinction," said Ledbetter.
>
> Since OMA offers instruction only through the sophomore year of college, those going on to four-year colleges take with them healthy study habits. "And 88 per cent of our enrollees go on to finish college," Ledbetter said...

One of the biggest changes under Ledbetter's watch was dealt with obliquely in Sebree's story. In the summer of 1949, just after his first year as OMA president, the colonel had announced that only the "cream" of the applicants would be admitted to the school. Even given Ledbetter's tendency toward hyperbole, it seemed clear that the academy's standards had relaxed in the subsequent decade and a half. Wrote Sebree, "[A] military school still is an excellent boarding school for boys from broken homes, who need discipline and are likely to get into serious trouble. 'I've been here 15 years and have seen some severe disciplinary cases enter the school, but only three ever wound up in the penitentiary,' said the OMA president."

* * * * *

Meanwhile, forces were gathering on the other side of the world that would have a major effect on the ultimate closing of OMA. In 1961, President John F. Kennedy had begun sending military advisors to help with the internal conflict in Vietnam, increasing their number from 900 to 16,000 over the space of two years. In 1965, the first U.S. ground troops would enter that Southeast Asian war, and as more and more Americans began fighting and dying in a war that many of their countrymen didn't understand, anti-military sentiment in the country rose.

The brunt of that sentiment was directed toward President Lyndon B. Johnson, however, following President Kennedy's assassination in November of 1963. Like Pearl Harbor, Kennedy's death was one of those history-changing incidents that left a profound and lasting impression when news of it was first heard. Remembered former cadet James Elder:

> Everybody asks, 'Where were you when you learned the President had been assassinated?' Well, I can tell you that I was in the process of trying to get a military letter signed by the commandant—an authorization for a weekend pass. It was the weekend before Thanksgiving leave was to start, and I had an honor-roll weekend pass coming.
>
> I was getting a hard time from one of the assistant command-ants, who was telling me, "I really don't think you ought to go," etc. So I was on my way over to talk to the commandant. He happened to be in the office of the academic dean, Dean Tanner, at the time, and as I was trying to get in to see him, somebody rushed through the door and said, "President Kennedy's been assassinated."

The staff and cadets at OMA responded to the tragedy with con-siderable haste, remembered Elder.

> I don't know if it's still true or not, but at that time, no active military training could take place between the time of a President's death and his burial. All training operations were suspended. Well, they construed that to include military academies, and [OMA] was an Army honor school answering to Fourth Army headquarters. So all the cadets were quartered back in their barracks to receive further instructions. It was pandemonium.

I was in the band, and we were instructed to report to the band room and draw our instruments. In nothing flat, they had a parade scheduled. Homer Ledbetter came out, all the brass from the faculty and military departments were there, and we had to do the death march for President Kennedy.

We lined up as we would for a regular parade, but the cadence was cut in half, so you took steps half as fast. And the drums had a set death-march cadence we had to play, which we learned in about five minutes. We marched on the drill field, the same route as we would do for a Sunday afternoon parade.

Oh, by the way…Thanksgiving leave started at the end of the parade, so we left, and on my way out the gate, I waved at the assistant commandant who'd been giving me such a hard time.

The academy band also responded to another presidential crisis during the '60s, and while this one was far less serious than John F. Kennedy's assassination, it brought the cadets close to his successor—and, as Elder recalled, it was something that the band could hardly have prepared for.

There's an ordnance plant in McAlester that was built and dedicated while I was a cadet, and the OMA band was called upon to provide the music, because, I think, the band at Fort Sill was on another assignment. So we got on the buses and headed for the plant, where President Johnson was going to give the dedication speech. We were to precede his speech with "The Star Spangled Banner" and other music we'd play while the dignitaries were being seated. Of course, we were all in uniform, dress uniform, which was almost identical to the regular Army's.

Well, as we're playing "The Star Spangled Banner," two or three vehicles pulled up, and one had the presidential seal on it. I was band commander, and after we finished "The Star Spangled Banner," I was approached by a man who told me he was with the Secret Service and wanted to talk to me.

I thought, "Oh, my gosh, what has one of my people done now?"

So he took me aside and he said, "Some of our people are not here. We need uniforms—just for image, just for looks. Do you have suitable people that you can call upon to form a perimeter around the President?"

I said, "No question about it. No problem," because I had senior ROTC people in my unit. So we provided about a dozen of them to the Secret Service. I guess something had happened. A car had broken down, or their plane didn't make it. I never got a straight story out of the guy. It really wasn't any of my business. I'm sure, though, he was getting flack from his higher-ups.

So, as it turned out, just by happenstance or coincidence, some of the OMA band members provided security for the President of the United States. We did a parade-rest perimeter around him the entire time he was there.

* * * * *

The early '60s continued to be a time of both good and bad news for OMA. Cadets were happy and the administration proud when the Thunderbird Student Lounge was completed in '62; the same year, however, some legislators were once again challenging the way the institution was run. A committee at the state capitol had found that Col. Ledbetter's $1,200 a month salary—as well as the $900-plus salary of three of the faculty members—was well over the $866 per month paid to the president of Northeastern Oklahoma A&M in Miami, another state school offering a junior-college degree. In a Feb. 7, 1962, *Tulsa World* story, a couple of senators called the salary discrepancies between NEO and OMA "fantastic," especially considering that NEO had "two and a half times as many students."

A little over a year later, Oklahoma City-based Senator Cleeta John Rodgers, head of the Senate Higher Education Committee, told United Press International that "we want to determine whether Oklahoma can afford an institution of specialized study such as this." The article, syndicated to area papers in late March of '63, once again brought up the relative cost of attending OMA.

Rogers pointed to a report issued by Regents for Higher Education which stated OMA had the highest cost per student in the state for general administration and expense. He said this ranged from $44.36 per student at Central State College, Edmond, to $231.07 at OMA. On costs for educational and general functions, OMA showed $697.94 per student, compared with the state average of $688.69.

Ledbetter said OMA offered more services than the average

college and maintained a 24-hour, seven-day-per-week watch over its students, bringing higher costs.

Another part of the story told of a vintage Ledbetter response. The man who'd come aboard in the '40s as a tireless promoter of the school still believed that getting the word out about OMA was important— so important, in fact, that when the committee asked him what the school's "greatest need" was, he responded, "To continue a strong public relations program that the citizenship of our great state may be kept informed of the availability of OMA's program for our state's young men." Rogers and his committee, according to the article, responded by "questioning operating costs of Oklahoma Military Academy…including amounts spent for public relations."

* * * * *

Sports, of course, was an important public relations tool, giving OMA a chance to reach potential students by sending both high school and junior college teams across Oklahoma and, occasionally into surrounding states. In the early '60s, the school fielded teams in high school football (with junior college football, dormant for a few years, returning in 1963), wrestling, high school and junior-college basketball, high school and junior college baseball, and golf.

Although participation in varsity athletics was voluntary, some, like Timothy Malishenko, were recruited. "I'd never really participated in

The 1967 OMA Junior College Football Squad

sports at all," he said, "but the lower-weight classes of wrestling were really hard to fill. Given my size and weight, I was going to be lower-weight class for a very long time, so the wrestling coach came after me right away. I remember going to those initial wrestling meets and just getting beat to a pulp. That experience set me on a lifelong venture with athletics."

Malishenko persevered, becoming a member of the varsity wrestling team his sophomore year. As a letterman, he also joined the O Club, one of several fraternal organizations on campus. By that time, using paddles on rabbits had been banned for at least a couple of decades, but he believes "they kept the paddles around for some of the other pledging," creating a situation similar to fraternity pledging at non-military schools.

Malishenko

The O Club was the club for all varsity lettermen in whatever sport, and as a pledge, you had to get every member of the O Club to sign a paddle. But before they signed it, they got to hit you once with it. Some were easy, and some were not. I was president of the O Club my junior year, and I had the football players and all kinds of folks pledging to me. That was probably my big moment on campus. You never liked going through pledging, but you sure liked it when you were in charge of calling the rules.

General Malishenko also remembered that the rivalry between town boys and cadets continued during this time, although at perhaps a lower level than in previous days. "OMA increased the male population significantly," he explained, "and there weren't enough girls to go around. To the townies, you were moving into their turf, and they didn't like it.

"But it wasn't intense, you know," he added. "It wasn't bitter. People weren't going out and looking for it. I had a girlfriend down in Claremore, and we'd go to Saturday night dances downtown. We always had to wear our uniforms, so it was going to be pretty obvious who you were. But I never recall, personally, running into any problems. And the families there were always supportive."

Much of the reason for the relaxing of tensions between the academy and the town probably had to do with the rising number of day—and night—students attending OMA. The *Vedette* yearbooks of this period

The 1964 OMA Wrestling Team

show several guys in civvies among the college cadets, even though the day students also had the option of taking ROTC. Tom Seely was one of the early '60s town students who attended junior college classes on the Hill, returning to his Claremore home every evening.

When we were students at Claremore High School, I think there was a little jealousy or resentment on both sides. But once you were up there, you were all pals. When you get away from your high school group and go to college, you make new friends, and that's what we did. There were quite a few people there [as day and night students] from all around the Rogers County area. We had a lot of fun, and the classes were great. They were small, and the instructors were very, very good.

* * * * *

In March of 1964, only a couple of months before the end of a school year that had once again seen enrollment rise at OMA, Col. Ledbetter appeared before the school's Board of Regents and announced that he was resigning as president. He was 50 years old and had been in charge of the school on the Hill for 16 years.

The reasons for his leaving aren't readily apparent, although the continued pressure from state legislators had to be a factor. According to some reports, his wife had health problems as well. He may have been referring to both of those things when he made an atypically brief statement to the press, saying he was leaving "for business and personal reasons" and that he wasn't "ready to make an announcement as to my future except to say I am planning to enter private business."

It was a far less messy exit than that of, say, Capt. John C. Hamilton two decades earlier, but in some ways it was more curious. Col. Ledbetter was a man who loved to communicate, who always had something to say to the press, who tirelessly talked about the school. Yet, when it came to his exit, he was almost silent—at least publicly.

"I have enjoyed my years at OMA," he told a *Tulsa Tribune* reporter, and said little more to the Tulsa press.

On June 10, 1964, twenty days before Ledbetter's final exit, the OMA Board of Regents announced the school's new president. Like several of his predecessors, Major General John Farnsworth Smoller was a West Point graduate, where he'd later been an instructor and academic dean. At the time he took the OMA job, he was the commanding general of the Second Army Corps at Fort Wadsworth, New York.

In a *Tulsa World* story, Robert D. Lengacher, regent chairman, said that Smoller was "giving up a brilliant career in the armed services, but he feels in this new position he can spend his entire productive future being of service to the youth of the United States.

"Gen. Smoller," added Lengacher, "brings to OMA the prestige of West Point and a colorful army background. He also has led a distinguished career in the academic field, consequently the OMA board is extremely pleased with his qualifications."

Smoller took over on July 1, the day after Ledbetter left. The longtime OMA president left a final legacy on the Hill: In May, the regents had named the campus' newest building the Col. Homer M. Ledbetter Barracks.

* * * * *

Surely, Gen. Smoller knew something of the challenges of the job, many of which were not of the school's making. As the conflict in Vietnam, the first war brought into America's living rooms by television reporters, raged on, sentiment against all things military—including schools—continued to grow. Other social forces were in play as well. In 1965, the school was threatened with the loss of its ROTC program because it hadn't desegregated. However, OMA dodged that bullet when

Col. Elmer Tanner, the academic dean, pointed out that the institute had two full-time black cadets.

It was during the mid-to-late '60s that mandatory ROTC requirements were dropped at many campuses all over the country, another response to the country's divisions over Vietnam. For a time, it looked as though all of this might actually help OMA. In a lengthy article published on Sept. 28, 1966, *Tulsa Tribune* education writer Bill Sampson explained the situation.

> Oklahoma Military Academy's status as an officer training school, sometimes shaky when Uncle Sam has no shooting war on his hands, apparently is secure for a while because of Vietnam. The Army needs more officers than it is getting at present and OMA's Reserve Officers Training Corps program is highly valued by the Department of the Army. As a result, the state Board of Regents for Higher Education has decided not to tamper with OMA's program during "the present crisis" but may re-evaluate it later.
>
> The regents periodically examine OMA's function and wonder if it might not be better to turn it into a coeducational junior college or perhaps a four-year college with either limited or no military training…

Senior ROTC training on the Hill began at the start of the junior year of high school and ran through the final year of junior college. That meant a student who started at OMA in high school and graduated from the two-year college would get four years of ROTC training, which was then equivalent to what a regular student could get at a four-year college. In the past, a cadet had to transfer to a four-year college and graduate before being eligible for a commission. But, as Sampson's article noted, the Army decided to change all that in 1966:

> The Department of the Army last July notified OMA that cadets completing the ROTC course could apply for commissions as second lieutenants without having a baccalaureate degree.
>
> This is a new policy apparently brought on by the Vietnam war and the growing need for officers to meet U.S. military commitments throughout the world. The policy is retroactive to cover last year's OMA graduates…
>
> A graduate of the U.S. Military Academy, Smoller said the Army's present requirement is for 17,000 new second lieutenants

a year. He said West Point is producing fewer than 1,000 and that the rest must be obtained from ROTC and Officer Candidate School programs.

"It's my personal opinion Oklahoma, and every state for that matter, has an obligation to Uncle Sam to help meet those officer requirements," said the OMA president.

"The trend in state universities across the nation, I believe has been to de-emphasize the ROTC programs. They are not compulsory everywhere. I believe OMA has a definite mission to provide training which will qualify young men as officers." ...

By 1966, several former cadets were already in Vietnam; a few, like Capt. William D. Reynolds, had already died there. Meanwhile, four 1965 OMA grads became the first men from the Hill to apply for commissions under the Army's new policy.

General Smoller, however, knew better than to put all the school's eggs in one basket. The *Tribune* piece concluded with a Smoller quote about how the "discipline, character and leadership" learned at OMA would help a young man "become a leader in either military or civilian life."

"Our program is to train leaders," he concluded, "regardless of whether they ever become Army officers."

The story, and Smoller's observations, made the continued existence of the academy seem both right and necessary. But less than a month later, a powerful Claremore-based state representative would once again fan the flames of change, calling OMA too expensive and too specialized to serve the area.

* * * * *

In November of 1966, Representative Bill Briscoe of Claremore announced that he would introduce a bill in the upcoming session to turn OMA into a co-educational junior college. The *Tulsa World's* Mike Flanagan reported, in a Nov. 16 article, that Briscoe felt "the school could eventually become a branch of the University of Oklahoma as a four-year college." With America still in the midst of the Vietnam war, Briscoe was challenging the ruling of the Oklahoma Board of Regents, Flanagan noted:

The state Board of Regents for Higher Education, which sets policy for the school, decided in September that OMA should continue to function as a military school as long as the nation critically needs officers. However, the regents said that OMA's function should be reconsidered when the military emergency ceases. Briscoe said any college graduate can be turned into a top military officer with six months of military training. He said a general college would be better able to meet the needs of the area's students…

In the story, Briscoe said the idea to study new uses for the institution came "after 81 students in his district contacted him for financial aid or scholarships. He reported that he was able to help only 11."

By some accounts, that statement indicates a hostile relationship between Briscoe and the new OMA president, Gen. Smoller, a relationship that was the antithesis of the one that had existed between the representative and Smoller's predecessor, Col. Ledbetter. It has also been said that Smoller made some immediate and possibly ill-advised moves once he took over, which included recalling an OMA typewriter and OMA-produced letterhead paper from Briscoe's office.

At about the same time, the Tulsa Chamber of Commerce had asked the legislature to create and help finance a community junior-college system in the area, and it wouldn't be long before that group also set its sights on the Hill.

Meanwhile, OMA persevered, although some observers feel that the transition to a regular junior college had already begun in earnest by this time. It was something gradual, *de facto* rather than *de juris*, but real nonetheless. For one thing, more college day students, who did not have to take ROTC, began attending classes on the Hill, learning and working side by side with full-time cadets. This situation sometimes put the latter at a disadvantage, as late '60s cadet John S. Ross recalled in a written account:

In November 1966, during my second year of college, I was taking a land surveying course. On this particular day, the class was conducting a leveling project out on the old parade ground.

The weather, in the beginning, was warm, so the uniform of the day was lightweight blues. Unfortunately, someone at regimental HQ had not checked the forecast, because while my class was in the field, a cold front came in and the temperature dropped into the twenties.

The day students donned their overcoats while I, being the only cadet, did not have a coat to keep out the chill. After about five minutes of shivering, I decided that the sensible thing to do was to return to the barracks and retrieve a warm coat. I did just that and finished the course work in comfort and warmth.

A few days later, I was doing my routine check of the company's bulletin board for duty assignments when I saw my name on the "stuck" list. I immediately went to the first sergeant...and he said the sergeant major had reported me. I then walked up the company street to regimental HQ to confront the sergeant major. He said I was out of uniform on Tuesday. When I explained to him I was participating in a one-hour class out in the cold weather and needed to put on a coat due to the drastic change in the temperature, he responded that it did not matter. He continued to emphasize the uniform of the day was bravo without a trench coat. He went on to say that I should have worn a sweater or a sweatshirt under my uniform if I wanted to be warm.

I left HQ feeling that the sergeant major was a very unreasonable martinet! I went to the guard house, drew my "03," and walked off my points so I could get a weekend pass.

When I went home that weekend, I told my father about the ludicrous incident. To my amazement, my father took up for   the cadet sergeant major! He said the same thing used to happen at the San Antonio Air Cadet Center during WW II. When my father was officer of the day, he would report aviation cadets for the same infraction and would give them the same advice when they objected. He then gave me an olive drab sweater that his mother had knitted for him for just such an occasion.

After hearing this, I was devastated for being wrong when I just knew I was right! My only consolation consisted of the sweater and being put on the same level as B-17 pilots.

The summer before that incident happened, the OMA campus opened for the first time to female day students—something else presaging the eventual change to a co-educational institution. About 50 young women from the Claremore area attended OMA's first co-ed summer session. There would also be female students in the night school program; a couple of years later, in the fall of '68, two made the jump to full-time-student status.

By the time Mrs. Alessa Ann Barrow and Mrs. Clara D. Walker—both former summer and night-school students—made their first classes of the 1968-69 school year, Gen. Smoller was gone. In 1967, he'd dealt with a negative report on OMA's books by the State Examiner and Inspector, as well as with a substantial hike in the school's fees, implemented by the Oklahoma Regents, that he felt was unfairly higher than those at other state junior colleges. And even though America's continued presence in Vietnam made OMA's continuance a necessity in the eyes of many, the swell of anti-war feeling was beginning to work against it. By the late '60s, when campuses were aflame with protests, even the school on the Hill wasn't exempt. As Alan Phillips, who arrived at the institution in 1967, remembered:

We had our little bits of it here. There were a few who voiced their opposition, but they weren't real popular. It wasn't a popular view when you were in the military.

On the other hand, if you left the Hill, the majority of the public seemed to be against the war. We didn't catch it as bad as some of the regular military. But, you know, we'd go into town or go home in uniform, and people would treat us funny. They'd ask us if we were in the Army, or if we were in Vietnam. You could tell that they were looking at you.

* * * * *

Col. John E. Horne was 48 years old when he became Oklahoma Military Academy's seventh and final president. The Chickasha, Oklahoma native would also be the only former OMA cadet to take the helm of his alma mater. An Air Force colonel and graduate of the Air Force Academy, he'd been working as deputy chief of staff for personnel at the Colorado-based school. Recalled Horne:

I was stationed at the Air Force Academy, finishing a career, and Carl Brasier who'd been a college freshman at OMA when I was a high school sophomore, came by and picked me up for golf one Saturday morning. He showed me his copy of the *Claremore Progress* and said, "I see Joe Smoller is retiring, and they've put out a national search for an OMA president."

He said, "You ought to do that. You ought to apply for that. After all, you talked about it earlier." Well, I had talked about it a *little* earlier—29 years or so earlier.

So I went home and talked to my wife, and then I filled out

a resume and sent it in, and I was called for an interview. It was down at one of the state lodges, with the board. They interviewed two other people, I believe—an English professor from someplace and another candidate.

*Horne's rabbit year
1934-35*

At least one other ex-cadet also figured that Horne was the man for the job. "I read in the newspaper where Smoller had resigned," recalled Donald Ruggles. "Johnny Horne and I had been roommates at OMA, and I'd maintained contact with him, so I picked up the phone real quick and called him at the Air Force Academy. I told him there was an open place at OMA for a new president. And I guess they showed good interest in him."

In an April 20, 1968, interview with the *Tulsa World's* Jim Henderson, the newly designated OMA president not only explained the benefits of a military education, but also confronted head-on America's deep divisiveness about the war in Vietnam.

"You learn a lot from the barracks life of a military school that you don't always learn in a civilian school," he said. "You learn how to get along and live with other people.

"There is a closeness there that you don't have in a civilian school."...

Despite anti-draft activities throughout the country in recent years and reports of a decline in the military's popularity, Horne said he does not believe that military schools will be affected.

"All the furor may cause some drop in enrollments," he said, "but I don't think it will be very noticeable.

"The ones who are demonstrating against the military are not the ones who would have applied anyway. And those who are interested in a military school probably will not be influenced by the demonstrators." ...

"There have been a lot of changes since I left," he added, "and I'll need to jump in and get acquainted with things."

Among the changes Horne confronted was the increasing presence of day students on campus, whose numbers were overwhelming those of the cadets. By fall of 1969, according to a report by the *Tulsa Tribune's* Mandell Matheson, OMA's student population consisted of "227 high school students, 330 day college students, 53 boarding college students and 159 attending night school. Day college students include 76 women, with 48 women in night classes."

As Vietnam wore on, also, fewer and fewer potential new cadets arrived each year, a pattern that Horne believes always occurred in wartime. "Look at the enrollment during World War II, when you'd think everyone would want to go to a military school to get a commission, and it didn't happen," he said. "And about the time they built up again, we had Korea and enrollment went down again. You can see it from the inception of OMA. So we had Vietnam, and it was down. The war was unpopular, and I just couldn't attract cadets."

Because room and board for the cadet corps—which, of course, didn't apply to the day and night students—paid a big chunk of the school's expenses, Horne found it harder and harder to make ends meet during his years as president. That situation only added fuel to what seemed to be a growing fire among legislators to change the school. In May of 1969, Rep. J. Fred Ferrell of Elgin, head of a special committee, recommended that OMA cut its high school program and become a liberal arts college with a new name by the fall of '72. A couple of weeks later, members of the state Board of Regents for Higher Education revived the notion of making the institution a part of a Tulsa-based junior college system. That didn't go over very well with the Claremore business leaders and others who gathered in an open forum, sponsored by the town's Chamber of Commerce, to talk about the academy and its future.

According to a Mike Zacharias article published in the May 16 *Tulsa World*, *Claremore Progress* editor and Chamber president Donn Dodd set the tone by announcing that some people were already referring to the academy as "The Port of Tulsa Junior College at Claremore."

Some 80 people, including Col. Horne, attended the open meeting— "which delved," wrote Zacharias, "into the school's functions, facilities, finances and future." The idea of getting rid of the high school was tossed around, as was the notion of actively recruiting more female students. But by the end of the forum, pride in the institution and its cadets took center stage.

One parting comment was voiced by Fred Gilbert, a member of the Tulsa public defender's staff who is also an Army Reserve

Special Forces officer who recently directed a weekend field problem at Camp Gruber involving some 270 OMA cadets and about 60 Green Berets.

"I never heard a whimper from any cadet. Some of them weren't as big as the M-1 rifles they carried, they were in the right place at the right time, and my Special Forces people would rather train with those cadets than any other reserve outfit in the state of Oklahoma."

It was a ringing endorsement, and an echo of the pride and honor that still existed on the Hill, as well as in the hearts and minds of cadets past and present and those who knew them. But these were different times, and just about two years to the day after Gilbert made his powerful statement to the Claremore forum, OMA would graduate its final class.

OMA Soars through the '60s

Junior College Basketball ~ 1960

The 1960 OMA Divot Diggers

The same drill...
different drill teams.
Above 1953 ~ Below 1963

OMA's 1961 College Baseball Team

1963 ~ Porter Officer
Mess Hall Manager

Busch Stadium ~ 1965

Grand March ~ 1966

Mardi Gras in New Orleans ~ 1966

Bivouac ~ 1967

Machine Gun Range, Summer Camp ~ 1967

Baseball ~ 1969

1969 Junior College Basketball

Col. John E. Horne, President
1968 ~ 1971

The 1970s

In these days of barefooted professors and permissive school administrators, the tough structured environment of OMA is an oasis of discipline amid the shifting sand of educational experiment.

The decision that Oklahoma's Military Academy would remain a traditional military school brought a sigh of relief to the many Oklahomans who want and understand the 24 hour a day discipline for boys.

"There will be no barefooted professors at OMA," the commandant Col. John Horne said. "And there will be no unshorn-unshod students either.

"The purpose of a military school is to educate the whole boy and we do that on a 24 hour basis, which is what makes cadet experience so much more than just classroom education..."

—Yvonne Litchfield
"Cadets Caper, Cram 24 Hours a Day"
Tulsa World, November 15, 1970

In his 1992 doctoral dissertation, *Eighty Years of University Preparatory Education on College Hill*, Larry Dean Rice listed four interconnected reasons for the demise of OMA: the "arrival and subsequent social revolution of the 1960s," during which all things military fell into disfavor with much of the country; a decline in enrollment; financial difficulties; and "the rapid decline in the caliber of students attending the institution."

Certainly, as Litchfield's story indicates, the school did its best to continue the practices and traditions it had always maintained, even as the winds of change swirled tirelessly around it. The late '60s and early '70s, indeed, were a time for kids of cadet age to go barefoot on campuses across the country. It was an era of rebellion and experimentation by America's youth, and for many of them, a military school not only represented unreasonable discipline, but an unpopular war.

On the Hill, the summer of '66 was noteworthy for being the first time female students were allowed to take day classes on campus. Across the nation, that same summer would become the Summer of Love, when the American media discovered the "hippies" of San Francisco's Haight-Ashbury district, and uncounted thousands of kids migrated westward in search of new freedoms, new thrills, and a new way of life.

Surely, then, changing times had much to do with the decline and ultimate fall of OMA. A bit more debatable, however, is Rice's contention that the quality of students dropped off during this period. In his dissertation, Rice helped make his point with statements from former OMA high school registrar Shirley McClurg, who said that while the students in the early '60s "could in general be described as gentlemen," by 1971 a better description would have been "ruffians, [who] were kids that their parents sent because they didn't know what else to do with them." She added:

> I was always angry because I would get a phone call, and the first thing they would start out with was, they "couldn't do anything with [their] son. Can you take him and keep him?" I always wanted to say, "We don't have walls around this place."
>
> [The school had the] reputation that we were babysitters to take care of kids that nobody else wanted to mess with.

Former cadet Alan Phillips, who graduated from high school at OMA in 1970, agreed with at least some of that assessment. "I don't really know what the classes were like back in the '30s and '40s, he said. "But there were a lot of people sent there for problems—disciplinary problems, social problems. There may have been more of that in later years."

Col. Horne, OMA's final president as well as one of its '30s graduates, wasn't so sure about all of that, though. In fact, he said he thought the idea of students being worse in the final years of OMA was "a very big misconception."

The Obstacle Course - 1971

Some kids' parents realized, "This guy needs some self-discipline," and some kids rebelled pretty bad. But there weren't any more problem kids than when I was there [as a cadet]. I couldn't see a whole lot of difference. I got a lot of statistics about the cadets, so I could see what we were lacking, what we had the most of, where they came from. And the first thing that jumped out at me was that we had an unusual number of truck-drivers' sons. I checked, and truck drivers made good money and were away from home a lot. So the natural thing was that the mother couldn't control the teenagers, probably, and wanted them to go to military school.

In the fall of 1970, the first of another kind of cadet showed up on the OMA campus. Debbie J. Garner, a then-recent graduate of Pryor High School intent on a career as a military nurse, became the first female military-science student in the history of the institution. The history-making event was recorded in a short *Tulsa World* piece on Sept. 12, 1970, which read in part:

> Military science personnel at OMA said Miss Garner will be exempted from the academy's three-day bivouacs and from drill periods, but otherwise will be a full-fledged military student.
> She will learn to march as a member of the school's proposed "Powder Puff Drill Team." She plans to try out for the rifle team to learn marksmanship.
> More than a dozen junior college students have indicated a desire to join the women's drill team...

"They were the best members of the rifle team we had," said Col. Horne with a chuckle, recalling the female cadets. "They'd never shot a rifle before, so they hadn't developed any bad habits. So, when we told 'em to squeeze, hold, breathe, squeeze, they'd do it—and make *excellent* scores. The boys knew how to do it, you know. They'd shot squirrels."

By the beginning of OMA's 1970-1971 school year, there were enough women in the junior college, recalls former student Wayne McCombs, that OMA added a women's basketball team to its varsity sports program. "The number of female students wasn't real large," he said, "but I'll bet it was 15 to 20 percent of the junior college."

Debbie Garner (bottom left) & the Rifle Team

A Claremore High School graduate, McCombs was one of the many male junior-college day students on the Hill. As was the case with many other members of OMA's population, Vietnam had something to do with his being there. "The year of my birth, 1952, was the last birth year subject to the draft," he explained. "They were taking the first 100 in the draft, and my number was 46. So I thought if they looked at my record and saw I was 17 and in a military school, they might pass me by. I was not drafted, so I'm guessing they saw I was attending college at a military school and said, 'Well, let's move on.'"

As a day student, he added, "I went to all my classes in street clothes. My military classes were in the afternoon, so after lunch I'd change into my uniform. You'd eat lunch, change clothes, and then you had your drill and your military classes and your rifle range, all of that."

By that time, the day and night students had been in the majority for at least a couple of years. Col. Horne said that in OMA's final semester, "we had somewhere in the neighborhood of 350 in the boarding school, and probably another 500 day students—we had a summer school for them and everything." Even though the numbers weren't bad, he knew that the school couldn't continue to exist that way.

The accreditation people had come around and said, "Look, you're going to have to make up your mind what your objective is.

Are you going to be a military school *and* a junior college *and* this *and*...? What's your mission here?"

Before we had girls and day students in such large numbers, of course, everybody knew what our mission was.

Ultimately, as Larry Dean Rice indicated in his dissertation, a lack of finances, brought about by the changing nature of the student body, did OMA in. There was, for one thing, a $675,000 bond debt on barracks built in the '50s and '60s during a period of rising enrollment. Now, with more day students than full-time cadets, there were plenty of empty bunks in the campus buildings, which translated to a continuing loss of operating funds. To OMA, which had always received much of its funding from room and board, uniform, and other cadet expenses, those empty beds represented a big drop in revenue.

Financial issues provided a convenient peg for those who wanted to see the school changed, and their numbers had grown—even in the city that had housed the institution since 1919. Claremore Representative Bill Briscoe continued to press for a new school, joined by other lawmakers, and, as Col. Horne remembered, even regular citizens began choosing up sides.

"They'd circulated a petition downtown, to make it a co-educational junior college, but I didn't know who'd signed it or how many or anything," he said. "The town was split about half in two. Half the town loved the cadets and liked having them around. But it was a bad year."

Horne realized just how bad it could get in the spring of 1971 when he attended a meeting presided over by E. T. Dunlap, the state's Chancellor for Higher Education in Oklahoma City.

I used to get tickled at him. He'd call meetings of the presidents of all the junior colleges and four-year universities, and he'd say, 'You gentlemen have your own Boards of Regents. I don't work with the internal workings of your colleges. I just control the budgets.' I thought that was really something. That's how he told you who was the boss.

On this particular day, he'd asked my regents to come with me. And on the agenda, at one point, was an OMA paper to be read. And he read the recommendation that the place be closed. It was a complete surprise.

One of the state regents turned to me and said, 'You know, you have 90 days to prepare an objection to this.' And I looked at my regents and said, 'I don't think we've got a chance.'

As one of the generals I used to work for used to tell me, we were OBE—overtaken by events. My wife had driven me up there. I read her the message, and I guess I cried from about Chandler to Sapulpa. It broke my heart. First alumni president, and I was going to close the place.

By the time Horne got back to the OMA campus, the cadets had just assembled in the mess hall for their evening meal. Horne read them the message and assured the ones who weren't graduating in '71 that he'd help them with transfers to other ROTC schools, so they wouldn't have to lose their upcoming commissions. "Then," he recalled, "I said, 'I can't tell you very much more now, because all I know is what I've read to you.'"

He knew, however, it was the end of Oklahoma Military Academy. The demise became official when a bill authored by Representative Briscoe and another Rogers County lawmaker, Senator Clem McSpadden, won passage through the Oklahoma legislature, changing both the name and the mission of the school. A few months after Horne's meeting with Chancellor Dunlap, that legislative action would turn the school on the Hill into a co-educational institution renamed Claremore Junior College.

* * * * *

A little more than 50 years ago, 40 young cadets pitched tents on the one-building campus here and Oklahoma Military Academy was in business.

Since then thousands of young men have formed a Long Blue Line and trod the 500-acre campus, absorbing the skills and disciplines of military life along with their academic training.

No more.

Bugles, boots and bellowing sergeants were silenced Tuesday by Regents for Higher Education who voted to change OMA to a comprehensive junior college, beginning in September. Regents asked the Legislature to change the name to Claremore Junior College…

Some of the blame for the change is laid to lack of public support for military schools in recent years, which created financial woes for OMA.

And part is based on bickering about the school's status for several years. This made it difficult for the school to recruit high school cadets because parents could not be assured the school would be operating the next year.

Whatever the causes, a piece of Oklahoma's life has passed into history...

—Mandell Matheson
"Decision Sounds 'Taps' on OMA's 50-Year History"
Tulsa Tribune, March 24, 1971

"I'm not bitter," said OMA Board of Regents Chairman Bob Lee Kidd in a *Tulsa World* article, also published on March 24th. "I'm just mad as hell."

So were many others. "There were a lot of rumors that the cadets were going to burn the place down," remembered Horne. "A couple of the cadets took some of the signs [on campus] down and put them right up in front of the Will Rogers Hotel. They'd painted things on the back of them like, 'This is the last you'll ever see of this.'

"It was quite an emotional thing for the cadets, particularly the ones that were upper class ROTC. They were a year away from getting a commission, and they were bitter about it."

Wayne McCombs, who continued going to the Hill after the changeover, saw a Vietnam analogy in OMA's situation. "The war stuff was in the news every day, and you didn't know if President Nixon was going to end it," he said. "It was an uncertainty, and what was going on at OMA was an uncertainty. You wanted to ask, 'Which way is it going?' I could go either way. I could see us keeping the military aspect of the school, or not. And I could see us either going all out in Vietnam, or leaving the situation."

Vietnam would go on for another few years. But OMA ended on May 29, 1971, following the graduation ceremonies for its last class. "It closed right after graduation—that's how quickly we pulled the flag down," said Horne, who stayed on as president of the new institution, Claremore Junior College. "I didn't bring it down. I had my commandant of cadets do it. To be quite frank with you, I was in my office. I was brokenhearted.

"I didn't think I could do it, and I didn't want the cadets to witness that," he added with a chuckle. "I just didn't think it would be good for 'em."

The Baird Markham Barracks

The End

The Oklahoma Military Academy Museum, occupying the second floor of what was once Meyer Barracks on the campus of Rogers State University, is a repository of photos, publications, and other memorabilia from every decade of the school's history. Here, a visitor will find everything from oil paintings of OMA's presidents to cadet uniforms, *Vedettes* and *Guidons* full of youthful faces and high spirits to sobering lists of alumni who died in America's wars. It's a place packed with intriguing links to the school's still-living heritage, with at least one item that acknowledges the finite life of that heritage. It's a bottle of *Grand Vin DeChateau Latour*, bottled the year the academy closed, resting in a display case affixed to the wall with a plaque that reads, "to be presented to the last living cadet, at a suitable ceremony."

As this is being written, the youngest graduate of OMA's final class has likely passed the 50-year mark in his life. The boys of the Hill are aging now, all of them middle-aged men and beyond. Many are retired, following working lives full of achievement and even fame in their chosen fields.

The dozens of alumni interviewed for this book did many different things after they left OMA. Some rose high in military rank; others excelled in areas ranging from psychology to politics, business and finance to journalism and novel-writing. Although our purpose with the interviews was to find representative voices from each era of the school, what those voices told us were not only representative but unique, as individualized as each of the thousands of students who passed through the Hill on their journey to adulthood. Former cadet Bud Inhofe summed it up nicely when he said, "I can't say that my experiences were anything different from everybody else's, but they were in one respect. They were mine. And OMA was probably the greatest thing that ever happened to me."

His latter statement was echoed by virtually every former cadet we interviewed. No matter how long or when they attended the school, they invariably mentioned how much of a factor their OMA experiences were in setting their lives on the right course. Many of them mentioned the school motto of Courage, Loyalty and Honor as the principles that shaped their lives and guided them, long after their few years as students. In fact, as the following quotes indicate, from the '30s through the '70s the life lessons taken away from the Hill were remarkably similar.

Had I not come to OMA, I undoubtedly would have been a juvenile delinquent. Instead, I got discipline and responsibility and everything was different for me. Everything flowed from the fact that I got straightened out, without intending to. Without OMA, I probably would have ended up behind bars.
—Lt. Col. Edwin D. Ramsey, Class of '37

OMA changed my life—in matters of personal discipline, personal appearance, practical living. I didn't realize it until later on, but a lot of the things I learned at OMA were useful in my civilian life. OMA taught leadership. You got a chance to exercise it. You had a chance to make decisions that you had to be responsible for.
—Joe McBride, Class of '49

As a Rabbit, I realized the upperclassmen were guided by a code: Courage, Loyalty and Honor. Within a short time, I realized as well that the code was applicable to every aspect of life, military or otherwise. Of equal significance, I became a part of something larger than myself—the tradition and brotherhood of the Corps. The upperclassmen instilled in me the attribute that has served me all my life—the attribute of discipline.
—Matthew Braun, Class of '53

I didn't have to go into the service. I was 4F. I mean, I was free and clear. But there was something that made me want to go in when everybody else was trying to get out. It was the courage and the loyalty and the honor I was taught. In 33 years of teaching, I've tried to teach that, too—courage, loyalty, and honor, and doing the right thing.

—B.G. Jones, Class of '64

When I left OMA, I went to college on a full scholarship, and it's all because of that place, I guarantee. The way I had been headed wouldn't have resulted in that. The discipline you learn, the self-discipline—it's amazing the difference it makes in your life and how you carry it on.

—Alan Phillips, Class of '70

These men, and thousands more like them, took the lessons learned and the discipline instilled at Oklahoma Military Academy out into the world, spreading the values of courage, loyalty and honor to friends and family and co-workers, applying them in every situation and making things better because of it. And when that last lone cadet sits down with his bottle of *Grand Vin DeChateau Latour* '71 and considers the ghosts of all those who've gone before him, he'll know that while he may be their final physical representative, as long as those principles exist in the life of our nation and our world, the voices from the Hill will never be stilled.

The Legacy: Today & Tomorrow

In May, 1971, after its last graduation ceremonies and the final lowering of the colors, Oklahoma Military Academy ceased to exist, and a new institution replaced it atop College Hill—Claremore Junior College. Many of the things that had been living symbols of the school instantly became artifacts and memorabilia, much of it stored away like old memories in a vault in the basement of Preparatory Hall —interestingly, the only building on campus that predated OMA, having been built for Eastern University Preparatory School only a few years after the beginning of the 20th Century.

But the material didn't stay there long. In 1974, a group of alumni contacted Claremore Junior College President Dr. Richard S. Mosier, to discuss the OMA material that was still on campus. "From that day forward," said Dr. Danette Boyle, Rogers State University Vice President for Development, "the bond has continued to strengthen between this institution and its predecessor on the Hill. We developed a mailing list of OMA alumni and started paying attention to what they'd like to do, which included building a museum and creating a relationship with this institution. All credit goes to the OMA alumni, who raised money and gathered memorabilia for the museum, and former RSU President Dr. Richard Mosier. I've been the one fortunate enough to work with them over the years."

As Claremore College metamorphosed into the four-year Rogers State University, OMA and its alumni took on increasing visibility, not only because of the yearly weekend-long reunions—which have expanded over the years to include a golf tournament and Hall of Fame and Distinguished Cadet ceremonies—but also in the first-rate museum that now occupies the entire top floor of RSU's Meyer Hall (formerly

Meyer Barracks).

With an alumni association and a newsletter—dubbed *The Guidon* in a nod to former OMA publications—many graduates are making their presence felt on campus in another profound way. It began when Tony Massad, Class of '47, came up with the idea of establishing a scholarship endowment at Rogers State. Known as the "Troop 40 Oklahoma Military Academy Cavalry Endowment," it is supported by former cadets from the '40s and earlier and provides scholarships to Rogers State University students.

"The cadets of the '50s have also started one," said Boyle, "and the people from the '60s are just beginning their own. In addition, several alumni have established personal endowments. Hundreds of RSU students," she added, "have benefited from the contributions of these ex-cadets. The OMA alumni are an integral part of RSU; the backbone of our support base. They're helping us move forward, and our desire in turn is to pay respect to the thousands who came here as boys and left as men."

Because the OMA-affiliated scholarships come from endowments, they are funded by interest income, leaving the principal untouched. "That really puts OMA on this Hill in perpetuity," noted Boyle. "OMA lives on through the museum, and the cadets live on through the students. The history and tradition really will be here forever."

Those who'd like more information on these scholarships can contact Dr. Boyle at the RSU Foundation Office, 1701 W. Will Rogers Blvd., Claremore, OK 74017. She can also be reached by telephone at (918) 343-7773, or via e-mail at dboyle@rsu.edu.

OMA

OKLAHOMA MILITARY ACADEMY

Contributors

V oices *from the Hill: The Story of Oklahoma Military Academy* would not have been possible without the generous contributions from the following supporters of the Oklahoma Military Academy. Each of them has our deepest appreciation and gratitude.

Ronald G. Acree

Lee A. Adams, Jr.

Alex K. Adwan

Euel Avon Barber

Morris G. Barber

Jim Barker

G. O. Bayless

Lew Beach

Marcuss Beauchamp

Angel Beltran, Jr.

David L. Bennett

Clyde W. Beson

Ben F. Boyd

Danette Boyle

Gerald L. Breeding

Gary M. Breneman

Joseph Briggs

Robert C. Bruner

Herbert N. Burghart

William Burke

James Burt

Larry W. Burton

Joel Card

R. Alan Chase

Dick Cline

Arthur F. Cochran

Zorus Patterson Colglazier

Kenneth C. Colley

John Copeland

Charles Corbett

Bob Corlett

Steve Cowen

Nance G. Creager	*Jack E. Harris*
Jim Curtis	*Bill B. Harris*
Joe Cecil Daniel	*James Hilton*
Richard D. Darnell	*Ted Hine*
Roy W. Davis	*John E. Horne*
Jack Dempsey	*Homer H. Hulme Jr.*
William C. Denney	*Arthur Blaine Imel, Jr*
Daniel Duggan	*J. Downing Johnson*
James R. Elder	*William J. A. Johnson*
Allan Ephraim	*Thad M. Keenan*
John C. Estes	*George V. Keith*
James E. Ferneau	*J. K. Killion*
Melvin Foster	*Robert E. Killion*
Ralph B. Foster	*Kenneth D. Kirkland*
Fred L. Friend	*Don Kuebler*
Ted Frizzell	*Jack W. Lancaster*
Carlos E. Galvez	*Robert B. Lewis*
Duane Gibbs	*Gene Little*
Phil Goldfarb	*Jerry R. Long*
Robert Gomez	*Court E. Loomis*
James E. Graalman	*Timothy P. Malishenko*
D. P. Hall	*Paul J. Manning*
Ralph Carr Hall	*John E. Martin*
Roger W. Hamilton	*Anthony M. Massad*
DeAtley Hampton	*C. J. Masters*
Willis Hardwick	*Ronald & Eileen McGee*

Curtis E. McMenamy	*John Sawyer Ross*
William D. Medford Jr.	*Donald K. Routh*
Hugh Miller	*Henry Kenneth Sanders II*
Louis A. Miller, Jr.	*Tom Sherer*
Robert T. Motter, Jr.	*Jack E. Short*
Vernon Mudd	*Robert Sibley*
Orlin Mullen	*Thomas I. Simpson*
Andrew R. O'Connor	*Stewart L. Stover*
David A. Orndorff	*Robert K. Sumner*
John Osborn	*Robert L. Tayar*
Paul D. Overton	*Charles F. Toegel Jr.*
Harry H. Poarch	*R. C. Van Nostrand*
William D. Poteet III	*Randy Vierling*
William E. Potts	*Lew Ward*
Walter E. Price	*Carl E. Ward*
Edwin P. Ramsey	*Noel Weeks*
Edward Reif	*Wilton C. Westbrook*
Craig Reynerson	*Sam Whitehill*
Thomas M. Robinson	*Bryan Wilkinson*
Stanley Rogers	*Harold T. Wright*
Bert J. Rosson	*Bob Wright*

Killed in Action

World War II

J.F. Albright

Jack C. Altam

Jack M. Baker

Kyle E. Ball

William A. Barrett

Robert W. Bartlett

Jackson G. Berryhill

Roy L. Booth

Marvin E. Bradley

Claude A. Brasier

Nolan B. Cargile

Joseph L. Carnell

Lloyd F. Cathy

Wayne W. Christian

Dean H. Corbett

Woodrow L. Dick

Vincent L. Dixon

Paul H. Dolman

Walter E. Downs, Jr.

Fritz W. Eisenlohr

Richard T. Ellison

Alva L. Fisher

Jay W. Gold

Jermone M. Hacker

George M. Hale

Walcott R. Hall

Gayle H. Harmon

John R. Harris

William K. Hester

Wilber Hill

Frank C. Howk

Stuart M. Jenkins

Edward L. Jillson

Glen C. Johnson

Charles C. Kigelman

Billy A. Krowse

Leroy L. Lette

Howard F. Liddell

Charles W. Locke

Garrett H. McCallister

William D. McLennon

Clabe C. Mackey

Thomas W. Mackey

Jack C. Maxey

Killed in Action

World War II

Eugene F. Moriarity

Moran S. Morris

Harry A. Patterson

Peter W. Perrier

Marvin Phiefer, Jr.

John D. Pizarro

David Presnell

Clyde A. Pulse

John T. Resler

William S. Richardson

Edwin L. Ross

William E. Schleuter

Walter J. Schmidt

James D. Scott

William W. Smith

John T. Swais

Ralph E. Tidwell

Wayne E. Turk

Clark G. Turner

Bob F. Unverferth

Richard E. Vensel

Foster L. Walker

George R. Walker

Elmer C. Weinrick

Harlod B. Wright

Korea

William R. Badgett

Frank L. Brown

William B. Castle

Carey S. Cowart

Jack R. Durant

Roger L. Fife

William C. Gates

Emery M. Hickman

George W. Kimbrell

Daniel W. McKinney

Gordon A. Moore

Thomas E. Taylor

Jim A. Trimble

Killed in Action

Vietnam

Stephen C. Beals

John E. Black

Bradley D. Bowers

Michael D. Casey

John Egger, Jr.

James R. Fortenberry

Harold A. Grass

Donald O. Hartman

Michael D. Hyatt

Daniel A. Idsardi

Howard K. Kerney

Ronny L. Kinnikin

George W. McDonough

Lionel E. Parsons

William D. Reynolds

Drew D. Shipley

John B. Stizza

John R. Stockdale

Sam R. Trizza, Jr.

Frank C. Vasser

Theodore D. Ward

Robert F. Warren

Victor D. Westphall

William R. Wilson

Craig M. Yancey

Daniel W. York

Cadets Who Became Generals

Throughout the years, many Oklahoma Military Academy cadets have gone on to proudly serve their country. The following cadets are among the OMA's most distinguished graduates.

Brig. Gen. William A. Hamrick ~ 1932

Brig. Gen. N.P. (Preston) Wood ~ 1933

Maj. Gen. Rollen H. Anthis ~ 1934

Lt. Gen. William E. Potts ~ 1941

Maj. Gen. William A. Burke ~ 1941

Brig. Gen. Judson F. Miller ~ 1942

Brig. Gen. Clifford A. Druit ~ 1954

Brig. Gen. Timothy P. Malishenko ~ 1961

Brig. Gen. Orlin L. Mullen ~ 1961

Brig. Gen. Michael A. Kuehr ~ 1968

Oklahoma Military Academy Alumni Association

Hall of Fame &
Distinguished Alumni
Honorees

Mr. Alex Adwan
Class of 1948
Distinguished Alumni 1990
Hall of Fame 2002

Mr. Ron Acree
Class of 1954
Distinguished Alumni 2005

Maj. Gen. Rollen H. Anthis
Clsas of 1934
Hall of Fame 1993

Speaker Jim Barker
Class of 1955
Hall of Fame 1988

Mr. Lew Beach
Class of 1953
Distinguished Alumni 2005

Col. Ben F. Boyd
Class of 1943
Distinguished Alumni 1997

Col. Bob Brashear
Class of 1950
Hall of Fame 2001

Mr. Matthew Braun
Class of 1953
Hall of Fame 2001

Col. Glen Burke
Class of 1953
Distinguished Alumni 2002

Maj. Gen. William Burke
Class of 1941
Hall of Fame 1990

Mr. Larry Burton
Class of 1963
Distinguished Alumni 2002

Mr. Jarold B. Casey
Class of 1929
Distinguished Alumni 1999

Col. A. Frank Cochran
Class of 1945
Hall of Fame 2002

Mr. Bob Corlett
Class of 1962
Distinguished Alumni 2003

Mayor Dale Covington
Class of 1954
Distinguished Alumni 1996

Capt. Walter E. Downs, Jr.
Class of 1940
Hall of Fame 2000

Brig. Gen. Clifford A. Druit
Class of 1954
Hall of Fame 1991

Col. Daniel E. Duggan
Class of 1953
Distinguished Alumni 2000

Mr. James R. Elder
Class of 1967
Distinguished Alumni 1984
Hall of Fame 2004

Mr. Charles Wayne Ellinger
Class of 1953
Hall of Fame 1999

Mr. Dave T. Faulkner
Class of 1934
Distinguished Alumni 1983

Lt. Col. Barry H. Grabel
Class of 1964
Distinguished Alumni 1988

Brig. Gen. William Hamrick
Class of 1932
Hall of Fame 1990

Mr. Bill B. Harris
Class of 1954
Distinguished Alumni 2003

Mr. Jack E. Harris
Class of 1955
Distinguished Alumni 2004

Mr. Joe Hedrick
Class of 1948
Hall of Fame 2005

Mr. Gary Henry
Class of 1950
Distinguished Alumni 1996
Hall of Fame 2003

Col. John E. Horne
Class of 1939
Distinguished Alumni 1991
Hall of Fame 1995

Mr. George Hudman
Class of 1953
Distinguished Alumni 1991

Mr. A. Blaine Imel
Class of 1941
Hall of Fame 1989

Mr. P.D. "Bud" Inhofe
Class of 1950
Distinguished Alumni 2003

Mr. B.G. Jones
Class of 1964
Distinguished Alumni 2004

Col. Charles Kegelman
Class of 1934
Hall of Fame 2001

Col. Robert B. Lewis
Class of 1940
Distinguished Alumni 1994
Hall of Fame 1997

Mr. Leon Lloyd
Class of 1943
Distinguished Alumni 1992

Brig. Gen. Timothy Malishenko
Class of 1962
Hall of Fame 1997

Mr. Anthony M. Massad
Class of 1947
Distinguished Alumni 1997
Hall of Fame 2000

Mr. Jack W. McMichael
Class of 1941
Distinguished Alumni 1995

Mr. Hugh Miller
Class of 1953
Distinguished Alumni 2005

Brig. Gen. Judson Miller
Class of 1942
Hall of Fame 1988

Mr. James H. Morrison
Class of 1952
Distinguished Alumni 1990
Hall of Fame 1996

Dr. Richard H. Mosier
Honorary (non-alum)
Hall of Fame 1997

Brig. Gen. Orlin L. Mullen
Class of 1961
Hall of Fame 1993

Mr. William O'Brien
Class of 1941
Hall of Fame 2003

Mr. Joel Owens
Class of 1940
Hall of Fame 2003

Mr. Harry Poarch
Class of 1953
Distinguished Alumni 1997
Hall of Fame 2005

Lt. Gen. William E. Potts
Class of 1941
Distinguished Alumni 1987
Hall of Fame 1984

Lt. Col. Edwin P. Ramsey
Class of 1937
Distinguished Alumni 1992
Hall of Fame 1994

Mr. David Raper
Class of 1965
Distinguished Alumni 2000

Mr. Carroll A. Reddic, Jr.
Class of 1936
Distinguished Alumni 1989

Mr. Dale Robertson
Class of 1942
Hall of Fame 1992

Mr. Bert Rosson
Class of 1954
Distinguished Alumni 2005

Dr. Donald K. Routh
Class of 1955
Distinguished Alumni 2004

Col. John W. Russell, Jr.
Class of 1943
Distinguished Alumni 1998

Mr. Norma Shaw
Class of 1953
Distinguished Alumni 2003

Mr. Jack Short
Class of 1959
Hall of Fame 2005

Col. James Spurrier
Class of 1938
Distinguished Alumni 1993
Hall of Fame 1998

Mr. Herbert Standeven
Class of 1953
Distinguished Alumni 1998

Mr. John Tatroe
Class of 1939
Distinguished Alumni 2001

Mr. Sam Trizza, Jr.
Class of 1963
Distinguished Alumni 1999

Mr. Randy Vierling
Class of 1963
Distinguished Alumni 2001

Dr. Carl E. Ward
Class of 1960
Distinguished Alumni 1986

Mr. Lew Ward
Class of 1950
Distinguished Alumni 1993

Mr. Robert Wright
Class of 1953
Distinguished Alumni 2002

Mr. Ted Wright
Class of 1952
Distinguished Alumni 1995
Hall of Fame 2003

Mr. Daniel York
Class of 1965
Distinguished Alumni 2002

SCHEDULE OF CALLS

			Daily	Sat.	Sun.
REVEILLE	1st Call	AM	6:15	6:15	6:40
	March		6:30	6:30	6:50
	Assembly		6:35	6:35	6:55
BREAKFAST	Immediately following assembly for reveille.				
SICK CALL			7:00	7:00	7:30
SCHOOL	1st Call		7:55		
	Assembly		8:00		
SUN. SCHOOL	1st Call				8:45
	Assembly				8:55
CHURCH	1st Call				10:00
	Assembly				10:10
INSPECTION—					
Barracks	1st Call			8:25	
	Assembly			8:30	
Field	1st Call			9:25	
	Assembly			9:30	
DRILL	1st Call		11:45		
	Assembly		11:50		
	Recall	PM	12:40		
DINNER	1st Call		12:55	11:55	12.25
	Assembly		1:00	12:00	12:30
SCHOOL	1st Call		1:45		
	Assembly		1:50		
ATHLETICS	1st Call		3:55	1:00	
	Assembly		4:00	1:10	
	Recall		5:00	5:15	
RETREAT	1st Call		5:45	5:45	4:20
	Assembly		5:50	5:50	4:25
	Retreat		5:55	5:55	4:30
SUPPER	Mess Call—Immediately after retreat.				
CALL TO QTRS	1st Call		6:55		7:55
	Assembly		7:00		8:00
	Recall		9:30		9:30
TATOO			9:55		9:55
TAPS			10:00		10:00

Punishment tours will be served on Fri & Sat afternoons as prescribed by the Commandant.

CLASS PERIODS	1. 8:00-8:50	4. 10:45-11:35
	2. 8:55-9:45	5. 1:50-2:40
	3. 9:50-10:40	6. 2:45-3:35

From the 1943 *Rabbit Manual*. This schedule remained relatively consistent throughout OMA's years. For reference see 1928 version on page 13.

GLOSSARY OF CADET SLANG
From the 1943 *Rabbit Manual*

A.W.O.L. — Absent without leave. To leave the Academy without official permission.

AS YOU WERE — To disregard, skip it.

B.S. — Bull session. A gathering for the purpose of borrowing cigarettes and discussing sundry subjects. Superfluous talk. British Science.

B.A. — Busted aristocrat. A cadet officer who has been reduced to the ranks for some flagrant violation of the regulations, or inefficiency.

BLEAT — To object, to moan, to explain (badly).

BUCK — A cadet private. To work against, to oppose.

BULL RING — That oblong path upon which members of the Corps who have deviated from the rules and regulations are requested to pace and muse over their many sins.

BUNK — Those padded slabs upon which cadets recline during the hours between Taps and Reveille.

BUNK FATIGUE — A soldier's dream—his idea of a perfect drill. Loafing or sleeping during daylight hours on one's bunk. True definition unknown—has it ever happened?

BUST — To revoke the appointment of a cadet commissioned or non-commissioned officer. To demote, reduce in rank. To bestow the B.A. Degree.

BUTT — A short—a snipe—reminder of a cigarette.

BRACE — The correct military carriage for a rabbit. An exaggerated position of attention imposed upon new men. Chin and stomachs in, chest arched, shoulders back and dropped, fingers straightened.

CANTEEN — That dispensary of cold drinks and colder coffee, located in the basement of the Auditorium.

C.C.C. — The hospital's most powerful medicine—a local female admirer of cadets.

CELLS — Our spacious, luxurious and comfortable rooms—apartments—quarters.

CHECK IN OR OUT — Official notice of one's comings and goings.

CHEESE KNIFE — A saber—a much coveted but useless piece of equipment carried by officers for parades and when on guard.

CHEVRONS, OR BUTTONS — A token worn on the sleeve, or shoulder graphically depicting the degree of rank one has.

CHICK — A modern Simon Legree—usually one who is stripe conscious. Generally used when referring to First Sergeants.

CHICK BOOK — A stick pad, notebook carried by chicks for keeping a record of forbidden acts.

CIG — Cigarettes, nic-stick, coffin nail, weed or fag.

CIVIE — A free and happy civilian—that fortunate person representing the civilization we return to during furloughs. A man with pockets in his trousers and hair on his head.

CIVVIES — Civilian clothing, glad rags.

C & P — Cleaning and pressing—turning one's uniform over to a civilian concern for the purpose of having it mutilated.

C. O. — Commanding Officer.

C. Q. — Call to Quarters—charge of quarters.

COLD BOTTLE — One who gets no joy from living.

COLD JUG — One who has a sober air.

COM. — Commandant of Cadets. Allah's prophet, who himself can do no wrong, but who catches all who do.

CON. — Confinement to quarters, as a punishment for breaches of discipline. Loss of all pass privileges by reason of excessive demerits or for some grievous sin.

CRAWL — To correct a first year man, to rebuke.

DEADBEAT — An easy time. One who believes in as little work as possible. To get out of a disagreeable duty.

DEMERITS — Degrading marks awarded by the Commandant, seriously affecting our liberties and conduct.

DINKY OR DINKY SHEET — That grim sheet of paper appearing on the Bulletin Board each evening and reporting the sins of those who have done wrong the day before.

DODO — An ignoramus—a recruit—a rabbit—a new man.

DOOGIE BAND — A conglomeration of tin horns and hat boxes played at formations by those who aspire to be musicians. Drum and bugle corps.

DOUGHBOY — Infantryman—a poor misguided member of the Bunion Brigade.

FROG STICKER — Sergeant Major's sword.

F. T. — A particularly forward and persistent C.C.C.

FURLOUGH — Official permission to go home. The key which the Commandant holds to our happiness.

GENERAL LIBERTY — A condition rarely existing, where every cadet may go to town—even those on Con.

G. I. — Government Issue. Property of Uncle Sam.

GOLD BRICK — One who enters or attempts to enter the infirmary for purposes of rest and meditation only.

HERMIT — One who has no wife—no roommate.

HOP — Formal dance.

KAMPUS KID — Cadet who should have remained in a civilian institution.

K. P. — Kitchen Police—cadets who serve us "mess" in the "food" hall.

MAKE SHEET — A published list of promotions among cadets.

N. C. O. — Non-commissioned officer. One who flaunts chevrons.

O. A. O. — One and only. HER.

O. C. — Officer in Charge.

O. D. — Officer of the Day.

OPEN HOUSE — Informal hops on Saturday nite in the Canteen.

PATCHES — Cloth insignia worn on the blouse or shirt.

PEGS — Riding breeches.

PLUGS — Those spirited animals on which we spend many hours of slow trot without stirrups. The G.I. horses.

P. M. S. & T. — Prof. of Military Science and Tactics.

PICCOLO PLAYER — A member of the band.

POOP SHEET — A penalty sheet—a dinky.

POST EXCHANGE — That modern crossroads Emporium where we buy everything from shirts to Shinola. Abbreviation: P. X.

R. H. I. P. — Rank hath its privileges (as well as obligations).

RABBIT — That ignorant, insignificant specimen of O.M.A. school life, who is in his first year of attendance. A plebe.

ROOMIE— A cadet's "wife" for nine months, whom we take for better or for worse. Generally some one we loan sox to, borrow money from, etc.

S. C. C. — A telegram saying "Sorry, can't come." Usually received from a femme the Saturday noon before the hop.

SCURVE — A member of the band, a piccolo player.

SHAVETAIL—A second lieutenant—cannon fodder—The most expendable thing in the Army.

SNIPE — See butt. Also a worthless person.

S. O. S. — Chipped beef on toast.

SOUND OFF — The ultimate development of one's vocal cords. A quick reply to a remark.

SOUPIE — Mess call—the only bugle call ever welcome to the ears of a cadet.

STICK— To report one for a delinquency. The report itself.

STOOGE — An understudy—an assistant—a substitute.

T-TOWN — The metropolis some thirty miles from the Academy.

TOUR — One hour spent in walking the Bull Ring.

WEEKLY WIPE — Our home town newspapers. Usually contain items of interest such as Tax Sales, Church Bazaars, Dandruff Cures, and a few clippings from other papers.

WIFE — A roommate, etc.

"X" — Abbreviation for "Absent."

YEARLING — A second year man.

Faculty & Staff

The former cadets of Oklahoma Military Academy would like to recognize the dedication, wisdom, patience, and knowledge of the faculty and staff members who devoted many years of their lives to teaching and mentoring the students. We salute each of you!

Lt./Lt. Col. Ralph E. Baird
Mathematics, Dean, Administration ~ 1943-1965

Dr. Bill Beson
Geology 1960-1971

Lt./Lt. Col. William Bess
Assistant Commandant, Commandant ~ 1951-1960

Captain/Col. W. S. Bryan
Latin, English, Acting President, Dean Emeritus/Chaplain Dean, Registrar ~ 1920-1949

Captain James B. Burruss
Physics & Mathematics ~ 1961-1971

Lt./Maj. Eldon R. Bushong
Mathematics 1959-1969

Major Jesse C. Bushyhead, M.D.
School Physician, Chief of Medical Staff ~ 1928-1942

Captain Virgil E. Caldwell
Languages, Librarian & Publicity 1929-1940

Captain John T. Cline
History 1925-1939

Captain Murl A. Cline
Coach, Director of Athletics 1928-1945

Staff Sgt. Frederick Crowell
M.S. & T., Calvary ~ 1932-1943

Mrs. Marian Cunningham
Registrar, Secretary to the Dean ~ 1958-1971

Captain/Major Clyde F. Deaton
Humanities, History, Social Studies ~ 1958-1971

Colonel Walter E. Downs
President ~ 1925-1940

Lt./Major Jerry M. Evans
Social Studies, Mathematics, Physical Education,
English, Dean of Activities ~ 1958-1966

Cpt./Major R. E. (Robert) Flynn
Band/Music ~ 1923-1933

Staff Sergeant Frederick H. Funk
Cavalry, M. S. & T. ~ 1931-1940

Mrs. Sue Fuston
Manager of Post Exchange ~ 1947-66 & 1970-71

Cpt./Lt. Col. Lee F. Gilstrap
Adjutant, Instructor, Coach ~ 1927-40 & 1946-47

Dr. M. E. Gordon
Physician ~ 1947-55, 1960-62, 1971

Colonel Howard Hart
Dean, Social Sciences ~ 1954-1965

Captain Sherman Albert Huffman
History, Mathematics, Government ~ 1920- 1946

Cpt./Major Truman Johnson
Director of Athletics, English ~ 1955-58, 1961-71

Mr. Kermit Jones
Science ~ 1962-1971

Captain P. H. Kelley
Band Director, Head of Music ~ 1933-1952

Lt./Major Warren King
English, Humanities, Assistant Dean ~ 1955-1971

Cpt./Major Warren S. Kleinsteiber
Public Relations, Speech, English ~ 1956-1971

Cpt./Colonel Homer M. Ledbetter
President ~ 1949-1964

Lt./Major Hoyt Lessley
Academic Staff ~ 1952-1968

Lt./Major A. N. Loshbaugh
Science ~ 1944-1968

Miss Dorotha Majors
Business Manager ~ 1943-1953

Mrs. Catherine Michael-Raymond
Secretary to the President ~ 1951-52 & 1953-66

Mr. Porter Officer
Mess Hall Manager ~ Pre-1951 & 1954-66

Captain Gordon Paine
Mathematics, Administration, Dean ~ 1937-1948

Captain Henry Clay Park
Mechanical Drawing & Building Trades, Vocational Arts,
Mathematics, Aviation ~ 1922-1941

Captain Cecil Parkinson
Science ~ 1955-1971

Mrs. Violet Patton
Business Manager ~ 1952-1966

Cpt./Major John C. Resler
Science, Principal, Commandant of Cadets
Biology, Mathematics, Physics ~ 1920-1943

Captain H.G. Riggs
Registrar, Librarian ~ 1938-1949

Captain Glen O. Rinearson
Finance, Aviation, Registrar ~ 1927-1937

Lt./Major H. J. Shirk
Eng., Mech. Drawing, Industrial Arts ~ 1944-1970

Mr. John Spann
Mess Hall, Watchman, Custodian ~ 1938-1956

Miss Joy Talbert
Secretary, Bookkeeper ~ 1945-1955

Maj./Colonel Elmer Tanner
Dean of Student Activities & Dean of Academics ~ 1959-1969

Mrs. Joan Tanner
Secretary, Business ~ Various 1951-1965

Mr. George Thompson
Laundry, Maintenance Supervisor ~ 1958-66 & 1970

Lt./Captain Beryl Ward
Foreign Language ~ 1941-47, 1949-50

Mr. Harry Webb
Superintendent of Bldgs. & Grounds ~ 1944-51 & 1955-64

Mrs. Imogene White
Librarian ~ 1951-1966

Mrs. I. H. Whitewater
Nurse ~ 1945-1954

Lt. Donald R. Wofford
English ~ 1963-71

Please Note:
Best efforts were made to ensure that all long-serving faculty were recognized on this list. Please accept our sincere apologies if any worthy individuals were inadvertently omitted.

Index of Photos

{Year shown refers to the OMA Guidon or Vedette in which they originally appeared.}

Index of Photos

{Year shown refers to the OMA Guidon or Vedette in which they originally appeared.}

Index of Photos

{Year shown refers to the OMA Guidon or Vedette in which they originally appeared.}

Index of Photos

{Year shown refers to the OMA Guidon or Vedette in which they originally appeared.}

Oklahoma Military Academy Students 1919-1971

Harry Abdo
Jesse V. Abel
Don Abercrombie
Alan V. Abernathy
John W. Abitz
William J. Ablett
Sam E. Aboussie
Joe L. Abraham
Louis B. Abraham
Jack S. Abrams
Johnnie C. Abramson
Mike Abramson
William Abrego
Hans M. Acher
Robert N. Ackerman
Ross M. Ackerman
Lloyd A. Acosta
David W. Acree
Ronald G. Acree
Edwin Adair
Everett Adair
Joe Adair
L. G. Adair
Melinda M. Adair
Robert C. Adair
Robert Adair
William Adair
Robert Adam
Albin L. Adams
Dale M. Adams
Earl F. Adams
Jeffrey Adams
John R. Adams
Lee Adams
Margie Sue Adams
Phillip Adams
Raymond R. Adams
Richard C. Adams
Roy E. Adams
William Y. Adams

Paul W. Aday
James G. Adcock
James L. Adcock
Roland K. Adcock
John E. Addington
Michael J. Addington
Kenneith F. Addison, Jr.
John J. Adelman
Lee Adkinson
Willis Adkisson
Alex Adwan
Jack C. Adwon
Jimmy L. Agee
Cesar A. Aguilu
Guillermo A. Aiken
Bruce Ailstock
James Aimsworth
Paul Ainsworth
Boyd Airhart
James Aitcheson
Robert L. Aitken
Gary J. Aker
Bruce D. Akin
Carol J. Akin
Ray Akin
John A. Akin, Jr.
Robert Akin, Jr.
Richard Albert
James J. Albertson
Warren L. Alberty
Edith M. Albrecht
Charles R. Albright
George W. Albright
J.F. Albright
Charles R. Albright, Jr.
Duane B. Alder
Warren L. Aldridge
Belle Alexander
Henry M. Alexander
Jerry L. Alexander

Jim L. Alexander
Joseph D. Alexander
Philip Alexander
Russell Alexander
Shelby T. Alexander
Chris N. Alexander III
Robert J. Alfrey
Claude O. Allbritton
Charles E. Allen
Charles W. Allen
Chester K. Allen
Curtis Allen
Donald E. Allen
Fay Allen
Frank M. Allen
Franklin Ellsworth Allen
George William Allen
Greg Allen
Harrison B. Allen
James P. Allen
John Allen
Richard R. Allen
Timothy D. Allen
William R. Allen
William E. Allen, Jr.
Walter E. Alling
Thomas R. Allison
William R. Allison
Maurice R. Allman
Luther Allphin
Fred T. Allsop
John R. Allspaugh
Charles Allton
Joe Allton
Richard C. Almack
David M. Almquist
Jessie F. Alsobrook
Robert L. Alspaugh
Gerald L. Alsup
Michael L. Alt
Bill Altman
Jack Altman
Charles V. Alton
Dick Alton
Francis Alton
Stephen A. Alvarez
Perry L. Amerine
Billie June Amos
Dennis S. Amos
Forrest Anders
Clyde Anderson
David S. Anderson
Douglas Anderson

Elmer Anderson
Freddie L. Anderson
Gary Anderson
Gaylon R. Anderson
George Anderson
Guy R. Anderson
Jack L. Anderson
James Anderson
Jim L. Anderson
Joe Anderson
John A. Anderson
John R. Anderson
Kenneth Anderson
Laura L. Anderson
Michael D. Anderson
Neil L. Anderson
Ralph Anderson
Robert E. Anderson
Robert M. Anderson
Ronald A. Anderson
Roy E. Anderson
Thomas W. Anderson
Tim M. Anderson
Vernon L. Anderson
William C. Anderson
William L. Anderson
Austin F. Anderson, Jr
Peter Anderson, Jr.
George A. Andre
Jerry E. Andress
Calvin Byron Andrews
Carrie Jo Andrews
Charles Andrews
David A. Andrews
David T. Andrews
Frank Andrews
Homer M. Andrews
James I. Andrews
Michael E. Andruss
Claude J. Ansel
Frank N. Ansel
Gary R. Ansorge
Rollen Anthis
Ernest Anthis, Jr.
James E. Anthis, Jr.
George Anthony
Samuel E. Anthony
Thomas F. Appel
Charles Apperson
Timothy C. Arango
George A. Arbuthnot
Albert R. Archer
Jack Archer

Tuck A. Archer
Linda Jean Archerd
Paul H. Archerd
Bob F. Archibald
James Argentos
Bob Armstrong
James E. Armstrong
Kenneth Lee Armstrong
Robert L. Armstrong
James M. Arnall
Michael F. Arnett
Charles Arnold
Donald E. Arnold
Paul D. Arnold
Perry L. Arnold
Rickey W. Arnold
Warren D. Arnold
Jesse C. Arnold, Jr.
Robert Arredondo
Joe B. Arric
Mrs. Darrell R. Arrowwood
Earl D. Arthur
Elizabeth M. Ary
Carroll M. Asbell
Henry E. Ashby
Jackie L. Ashby
Carolyn Sue G. Ashley
Virgil Ashley
Michael J. Ashmore
Tom Ashmore
John E. Ashworth
George J. Asimos
Marvin L. Astell
Dewitt Aston
Charles Atchison
Robert J. Atchison
Clanton R. Athey, Jr.
Bruce L. Athon
Melvin J. Atkin
Charles R. Atkins
Earl L. Atkins
Ernest Atkins
Jack E. Atkinson
James L. Atkinson
James W. Ator
Logan W. Atteberry
Renee J. Attebury
Derek R. Audley
James Ault
John E. Ault
O.T. Austin
Stacker L. Austin
William D. Austin

Jim D. Avery
Thomas R. Avery
James Edward Averyt
Carl T. Avey
Gary Lee Axley
Donald J. Ayres
Charles Babb
James Patrick Babb
Joe Babb
Danny Babcock
William P. Babcock
Joseph Baber
Rodney Bachelder
Charles Bacon
Donald C. Bacon
George Baconrind
John P. Badami
William R. Badger, Jr.
William R. Badgett
Gary R. Baergen
Harry A. Bagby
Everett J. Baggett
Phillip Jeffrey Baggett
Richard S. Bagwell
Brett Bailey
Joe E. Bailey
John D. Bailey
Larry Bailey
Marvin T. Bailey
Ray A. Bailey
Ray Bailey
Robert E. Bailey
William Bailey
Bill Bain
Dwight S. Baird
George G. Baird
John C. Baird
John E. Baird
Randall F. Baird
Barry Baker
Billy O. Baker
Carl L. Baker
Don M. Baker
Douglas D. Baker
George Kevin Baker
George L. Baker
Harry M. Baker
Henry L. Baker
Homer Baker
Jack M. Baker
James W. Baker
John E. Baker
Kenneth W. Baker

Martin M. Baker
Michael R. Baker
Mickey R. Baker
Orville L. Baker
Revelle Baker
Robert M. Baker
Roger Baker
Russell W. Baker
Sarah L. Baker
Terry Baker
Theodore B. Baker
Charles C. Baldridge
Janice M. Baldridge
John R. Baldridge
Robert Carl Baldridge
Thad C. Baldridge
William E. Baldridge
Elbert E. Baldwin
George W. Baldwin
Glenn Baldwin
Guy E. Baldwin
J. W. Baldwin
James L. Baldwin
Kenneth H. Baldwin
Stephen W. Baldwin
Thomas P. Balentine
Bill M. Bales
Howard Claude Bales
Jack W. Bales
Janice M. Bales
Edwin L. Balkham
Charles O. Ball
Dorothea C. Ball
John W. Ball
Kyle E. Ball
Randolph H. Ball
Virginia Ann Ball
Benny R. Ballard
Ron Ballard
Ronald P. Ballard
Rowland R. Ballard
Sam P. Ballard
Tommie Ballard, Jr.
Jack Ballew
Frank Balliet
Steven K. Bamber
Monte B. Bamford
Leon S. Bancroft
Kenneth Banes
Julian E. Banker
Lawrence E. Banks
Roger L. Banning
Charles Banther

Jack Banther
Lewis Foster Barb
Don C. Barbee
Alan R. Barber
E. Avon Barber
Morris Barber
Richard Barber
Van Barber
Calvin Bard, Jr.
Lynn M. Bardo
Harry T. Bare
Newell Barefoot
Robert W. Barkeen
Ben Barker
Jim Barker
George N. Barlas
Chas Barnard
William Barnard
Bennett A. Barnes
Betty J. Barnes
Boyd Barnes
Charles J. Barnes
Delbert W. Barnes
Jim Barnes
John W. Barnes
Jon A. Barnes
Kenneth E. Barnes
Larry J. Barnes
Lewis E. Barnes
Mickey Barnes
Mike D. Barnes
Nelda Lois Barnes
Ronnie Barnes
Thompson Barnes
Paul David Barnes, Jr.
Beverly Barnett
Buford Barnett
Harry Barnett
Lionel W. Barnett
Byron L. Barnhart
Robert W. Barnhill
Michael F. Barno
James P. Barnum
Tom Barnwell
Moss L. Baron
Charles F. Barr
Jimmie D. Barrack
Jon W. Barrack
Wayne Barrack
Earl Barrett
Eugene Barrett
Jack Barrett
Jon Barrett

Lenna M. Barrett
Marian W. Barrett
S. M. Barrett
Stephen R. Barrett
William Barrett
William Barrett, Jr.
William E. Barrett, Jr.
William Barringer
John B. Barritt
Phillip W. Barritt
Allesa A. Barrow
William E. Barrow
Bill B. Barry
Robert Barry
William R. Barry
Worley J. Barry
Larry J. Barthel
Jeffrey M. Bartlett
Lawrence A. Bartlett
Robert W. Bartlett
Anderson ". Bartlett II
George Barton
Michael R. Barton
Rita Barton
Robert J. Barton
Robert L. Barton
Roger J. Barton
Suezan Coylene Barton
Bruce A. Bartovick
Jeffrey D. Bartz
DeWayne W. Basham
Jerry Dale Basks
Debbie L. Basore
Bill L. Bass
Eva S. Bass
Neil A. Bass
Bert Bassett
David L. Bassett
Verne S. Batchler
Donald J. Bateman
Larry Alvin Bateman
Becky A. Bates
Burwell Bates
Charles S. Bates
Robert Frank Bates
Rockne B. Bates
Claude L. Bates, Jr.
Writ Batis
Gary Battenfield
Reginal A. Baughman
Billie Bauldridge
William E. Bauldridge, Sr.
Elfrieda Baumann

John S. Baumert
Eugene Bavinger
Gary Baxley
Gordon H. Bayless
Guy O. Bayless
John Bayless
Paul Bayless
R. M. Bayless
Solomon H. Bayouth
Craig D. Bazzle
Lewis C. Beach
Chris W. Beale
Brent W. Beals
Stephen C. Beals
Jack E. Beam III
Thomas Beaman
William Beamer
Dow Bean
Joe L. Bean
William Brent Bean
Frank C. Bear
Jamison N. Bear
George L. Beard
Glynda L. Beard
Ron W. Beard
Virginia A. Beard
John Lee Bearden
Frankie E. Bears
John T. Beasley
Lyal Beattie
Jessie Dean Beaty
Marcus S. Beauchamp
Donald P. Beaulieu
Chas J. Beaver
Ernest Beaver
Robert Beaver
Rufus Beaver
Kenneth Beavers
Don M. Beck
Jessie Beck
Kathy Gail Beck
Steve O. Beck
Steven DeWayne Beck
Kurt Charles Beckelman
Daniel O. Becker
Donald E. Becker
Richard Becker
Yvonne M. Becker
James Beckham, Jr.
Carroll W. Beckman
John P. Beckner
Marvin R. Beckwith
Chalen Bacsom Bedford

William C. Bednar
Daniel A. Bednarski
Byron D. Beeler
James L. Beeman
Rusty G. Beeman
Don A. Beene
Gloria Irene Beesley
Linda Kay Beeson
Joe Beeton
Robert B. Beezley
Thomas P. Behm
Troy L. Belcher
Edwin L. Belkham
Alden C. Bell
Billy T. Bell
Billy W. Bell
Bob Norris Bell
Bob Bell
Clyde E. Bell
Dickie Bell
Gregory Lee Bell
Jerry L. Bell
John P. Bell
Kirk Daniel Bell
Mark Bell
Michael W. Bell
Morris Bell
Patrick C. Bell
Robert C. Bell
Wiley W. Bell
Robert J. Bell, Jr.
Michael G. Bellatti
Jerry H. Beller
Lonnie D. Beller
Burney Belletini
Angel Beltran
William R. Bender
Carl DeWain Bennett
Charles Bennett
David Eugene Bennett
David L. Bennett
David Randall Bennett
Fairfax Bennett
Jack A. Bennett
Jim G. Bennett
Oletha C. Bennett
Paul A. Bennett
Robert Bennett
Steven Wayne Bennett
William F. Bennett
Bill Bennett, Jr.
Richard L. Benningfield
Robert A. Benningfield

Roy A. Benson
William R. Benson
Dan E. Bentley
Eph Bentley
Mack Bentley
Kenneth R. Benvenuto
Donny W. Berg
Randall G. Bergtholdt
Henry H. Berman
Dan Bernardy
William R. Bernell
Robert L. Bernhardt
Joe Berrian
Carol L. Berry
Carolyn M. Berry
David L. Berry
Denzel Berry
Donald Berry
Frank G. Berry
George M. Berry
John Douglas Berry
Margaret Ann Berry
Robert Berry
Ronald Berry
William E. Berry
William L. Berry
Jackson G. Berryhill
Mathew Berryhill
Robert E. Berryhill
Timothy W. Berryhill
William S. Berryhill
Matthew Berryhill, Jr.
William Berryman
Ed Beshara
Wadea Beshara
Arthur Beshears
Clyde Beson
James W. Beson
Joe L. Beson
John Robert Beson
Clyde William Beson III
W. Bess, Jr.
Thomas Bess, Sr.
Carl A. Bessier, Jr.
Dolores Marie Best
Virgil Best
Albert Bettes
Lawrence W. Bevins
John H. Bevis
Gregory Bewley
Kirby Michael Bickel
Larry J. Bickel
William Bickell

Gary Arlen Bickford
Robert Miles Bickham
Charles Lee Bicknell
W. S. Bicknell, Jr.
Gerald O. Bidwell
Jerry D. Biernat
Joe L. Biffle
Don Big Elk
Donald G. Biggerstaff
Edmund L. Biggs
Lloyd W. Biggs
Walter G. Biggs
Virgil P. Biggs, Jr.
J.R. Bigheart
Tom D. Bigler
William G. Bigley
Cecil Bilbo
Gerald L. Bilby
Harold D. Bilby
Charles Bilderback
James A. Bilderback
Glynn Billings
Joe Billings
Kent Billingsley
Thomas L. Billingsley
Marilyn S. Bingham
Richard W. Bintliff
William Keen Bippus
Jonathan E. Bird
Mike Bird
John T. Birden
Thomas G. Birdsong
Patti A. Birkes
Mitchell T. Bisanar
F.R. Bishop
Lewis S. Bishop
Ronnie E. Bishop
Nick C. Bitsis
Danny L. Bivens
Thomas M. Blachly
Carl L. Black
Eugene Black
Keith R. Black
Michael A. Black
Ronnie Reve Black
William G. Black
Ernest M. Black, Jr.
Donna S. Blackard
James Blackbird
George A. Blackburn
Hurschel Blackburn
James A. Blackburn
Robert Blackburn

Bill J. Blackstone
John R. Blackwell
Kenneth R. Blackwell
Robert G. Blackwood
Michael L. Blagg
Lorean L. Blaine
Bill B. Blair
Bill W. Blair
Jimmie H. Blair
Phillip Blair
Julian Blake, Jr.
Daniel V. Blakemore
Fred R. Blakemore
Loy D. Blalock
Gerald E. Blancett
Donald Blanchard
Paul Blanchard
Geneva B. Bland
James R. Bland
Richard Bland
Bill E. Blankenship
David L. Blankenship
Lonnie M. Blankenship
William E. Blankenship
Billy F. Blansett
Raymond Blass
Joseph H. Blass, Jr.
Clifton L. Blaylock
James E. Bledsoe
Allan W. Blessman
David Blevins
Jerry Blevins
Larry G. Blevins
Toni Lee Blevins
William M. Blevins
Julian Bleyer
Charles Bliss
Russell E. Bliss
Wayne L. Blissit
Roy Blizzard
Elliott G. Bloch
Claude Lee Blood
Shirley Diane Blood
Eugenia Faye Bloom
Jeffery R. Bloom
Ernest F. Bloss
R. Bloss
Oscar Bluemal
Charles Blunt
Orval W. Blunt
Allen R. Boatright
Alfred G. Bobo
William K. Bodine

Milton Boehm
Randall Thomas Boehm
John Boersma
Brent Edgar Boes
Carl Bogdahn
Don H. Bogdahn
Mary Inez Bohannon
Phillip Bohart
William O. Bohnefeld
Alfred Boisseau
Ronald A. Boisseau
James T. Boland
Quinton Boland
Ken Bolenbaugh
Wayne R. Bolin
Theodore Bolling
Don G. Bollinger
Frank Bollinger
James C. Bollinger
Robert C. Bollinger
Daniel Bolt
Donald Bolt
John Bolton
Larry J. Bomar
Baxter Bond
James Greig Bond
John Bond
Don R. Bone
John E. Bone
Bob K. Bonebrake
Gerald R. Bonen
Dan H. Bonham
Dan F. Boone
George F. Boone
Hashell Boone
Larry H. Boone
Walker Boone
Jerry R. Booth, Jr.
Roy Booth
Ervin L. Boots
Brad Borchardt
William J. Borden
Delores A. Boren
Homer L. Boren
Frank Borglund
Michael M. Bosch
Howard Boss
John Boss
Barbara J. Boston
Beverly N. Boston
James I. Boston
Michael T. Boswell
Sue N. Boswell

Vol Boswell
Nelson Bott
Francis C. Botz
Charles H. Boudreaux
Claude E. Boudreaux
Cuynthia A. Boudreaux
Donna L. Boudreaux
Gary Boudreaux
Mary G. Boudreaux
Don Boulton
James R. Boulton
John W. Boulton
Jon C. Boulton
John W. Boulton, Jr.
James M. Bouquet
Joe W. Bourland
Amos D. Bouse
Eugene K. Bouse
Kenneth N. Bousum
Steven A. Boutwell
Carl Bowden
Jack E. Bowen
James Bowen
Kelley D. Bowen
Thomas A. Bowen
Ralph H. Bower
Robert W. Bowerman
Bradley D. Bowers
Bryan Kirsten Bowers
Marcus J. Bowers
Thomas G. Bowers
John R. Bowie
Charles E. Bowlby III
Chessar Bowles
Ferman Bowles
Carvin L. Bowline
Larry Bowlware
Beverly G. Bowman
Charles C. Bowman
Edward P. Bowman
James Bowman
Nancy L. Bowman
Ronald Bowman
Thomas D. Bowman
Jim Bowman, Jr.
David A. Box
Frank Box
Michael D. Boyce
Barry Boyd
Ben F. Boyd
Bob G. Boyd
Carl F. Boyd
Charles Boyd

Damon R. Boyd
Dan Boyd
David M. Boyd
Don Boyd
Edward Earl Boyd
Ella Boyd
Gerry K. Boyd
James C. Boyd
Jess A. Boyd
Jesse Doyle Boyd
Robert Boyd
Tom R. Boyd
Wallace Neil Boyd
Walter C. Boyd
Wilbur Boyd
Joe M. Boydston
Keith E. Boydston
Tom Boydston
James J. Boydston III
Darrell E. Boyer
Paul E. Boyer
William L. Boyington
Charles G. Boyle
Johnnie J. Boyle
Fred Boynton
Robert D. Bozarth
Walter Bozarth, Jr.
Mozell Wilma Bracke
Harold M. Bradbury
Clint Braden
Glenn Braden
Jack Braden
Norman D. Braden
Jeff L. Bradford
Richard K. Bradford
Robert Bradford
Ben Bradley
Holley D. Bradley
Lee Bradley
Marvin E. Bradley
Ronney Bradley
David Bradshaw
Kenneth L. Bradshaw
Phillip Bradshaw
Wm. C. Bradstreet
J. M. Braffett
Bryan Brainard
Helen Maria Brainard
Larry K. Brainard
Ralph B. Brainard
Steve Brainard
Tommy R. Brainard
William M. Brainard

Ralph B. Brainard, Jr.
Joe W. Braley
Malcolm H. Branch
Virginia M. Branch
Gene Brandenburg
Lilyan L. Brandenburg
Luther G. Branham
Ralph L. Branham
John P. Braniff
Phillip A. Brann
C.C. Branstetter
James M. Branstetter
Jerry D. Brasel
B. J. Brashear
John N. Brashears
John M. Brasher
Carl Brasier
Claude A. Brasier
John P. Brasier
Phillip W. Brasier
James L. Brassfield
Joe R. Brassfield
William C. Bratton
Kenneth Braudway
James M. Brauer
Clifford Braughton
Murray Grant Braum
Matt Braun
Bill Bray
Danny Leon Brazeal
Gary Lee Brazeal
Jerral R. Brazeal
Michael Alan Brazeal
Phyllis Jean Bolch Brazeal
Jerral R. Brazeal, Jr.
Breaner
Harold Brecht
Charles Breeden
George W. Breeden
Joe Breeden
Steven Turner Breeden
Gerald L. Breeding
Jack Breedlove
Frank Breen
Jim O. Breene
Joel M. Brehm
Neville Brehm
Dalma C. Breland
Gary M. Breneman
Ed Brenneman
Arthur Brenner
Beverly A. Brewer
Jim M. Brewer

Paul M. Brewer
Timothy L. Brewer
Jack C. Brewster
Robert W. Brewster
Richard A. Bridge
Michael F. Bridges
Michael W. Bridges
Cecil Brien
Lowell K. Briggs
Marvin E. Briggs
Robert L. Briggs
Thomas C. Briggs
Thomas M. Briggs
Joe Briggs, Jr.
Levy L. Briggs, Jr.
Dan L. Brigham
Bob J. Bright
Joe L. Bright
Leonard Brightwell
Frank Brindel
Michael J. Brink
Robert A. Brink
James H. Brinkman
Garland Brinlee
Nikki Sue Brinlee
Ray K. Brinley, Jr.
Miller Briscoe
Powel Briscoe, Jr.
Richard P. Bristow
Rodney D. Bristow
Fred M. Britain
Roger E. Brittain
Robert N. Brittan
Shawnee Brittan
Dudley Britton
Horace Britton
William E. Broaddrick
Sidney Broaddus
Barton Broadhead
Wheeler E. Brock
Carl R. Brocksmith
James Brogan
Claude Bronaugh
William Bronson
John A. Brooke
Donald Brookhart
Bonnie Brooks
Bruce Brooks
Damond L. Brooks
David Brooks
Ralph D. Brooks
Ralph William Brooks
Randal G. Brooks

Randy Brooks
Robert E. Brooks
Roger A. Brooks
Steve B. Brooks
Hardy O. Brooks III
Donald Broome
Jerrel D. Broshears
Lawrence C. Brotherton
Jack Browder
Arnold W. Brown
Bill Brown
Bobby D. Brown
Calvin Brown
Carl L. Brown
Carol D. Brown
Charles S. Brown
Charles Brown
Charles Brown
Cliff Brown
Clyde E. Brown
Deanna S. Brown
Donald M. Brown
Ed Brown
Eric D. Brown
Floyd Brown
Frank L. Brown
George A. Brown
George M. Brown
Glendon Brown
Guy Brown
Hayden Brown
Henry P. Brown
Jack P. Brown
James E. Brown
James M. Brown
James Marion Brown
James R. Brown
Jerrell M. Brown
John E. Brown
John R. Brown
Kenneth Anderson Brown
Larry Kent Brown
Lawrence J. Brown
Lee F. Brown
Lewis F. Brown
Margaret A. Brown
Merwin H. Brown
Nelda P. Brown
Paul C. Brown
Paul S. Brown
Preston S. Brown
Randall L. Brown
Rickey D. Brown

Robert Patrick Brown
Robert V. Brown
Robert Brown
Ronald A. Brown
Ronald Mack Brown
Ronnie Brown
Sam E. Brown
Stanley Brown
Steven D. Brown
Terry Brown
Timothy C. Brown
Wayne T. Brown
James Brown
Steven Jay Brown
Charles Spencer Brown, Jr.
Louie W. Brown, Jr.
Louis A. Brown, Jr.
Walter Brown, Jr.
Wayne Brownewell
Fred L. Browning
Bob Bruce
Richard A. Bruce
Robert Bruce
Adelbert W. Bruce, Jr.
Dorothy Bruffett
Sally J. Brummett
Jack Brundage
John T. Brundage
Carl D. Bruner
Fred M. Bruner
Richard Bruner
Robert C. Bruner
Terry L. Bruner
Virginia Margaret L. Bruner
Bruner
Roland E. Bruner III
John C. Brunnemeyer
Mike Brunson
Bob Brunswig
Audrey R. Bruster
Curtis V. Bryan
David W. Bryan
Joe C. Bryan
Joe M. Bryan
John P. Bryan
Pat Bryan
Robert A. Bryan
Robert J. Bryan
Steven R. Bryan
Leonard B. Bryan, Jr.
David T. Bryant
Don W. Bryant
Donald D. Bryant

Donna Mae Bryant
Essary V. Bryant
Jimmy Jack Bryant
Michael B. Bryant
Winston E. Brymer
Stephen S. Buchan
Robert Buchanan
Allen H. Buck
Clarence Buck
Dan Buck
LeRoy Buck
Albert W. Buckholz
William D. Buckley
Charles N. Buckman
Glenn Buckminster
Dan Buckner
Charles D. Budd
Marcus H. Budd
William L. Budd
George E. Buelke, Jr.
John B. Buell
Billy D. Buerger
James C. Buff
James W. Buff
Roy Buffalo
Homer J. Buffalohide
Philip S. Buford
Alvin Builderback
Gus Bullette
Charles Bullock
Roy A. Bullock
Robert W. Butler
Robert R. Bumgarner
Rufus Bumgarner
David A. Bunch
Phyllis J. Bunnell
Harold A. Buntt
Pamela M. Bunyard
Terry Burcham
Charles Burckhalter
Georgia N. Burd
Jerry W. Burd
No N. Burd
Thomas Burd
Theollon Burd, Jr.
Jack Sterling Burden
James Burdick
John Burdick
Howard Milton Burdick, Jr.
Richard Burdyn
Patricia Mozelle Burford
Edward Burger
Mike Kent Burgess

Thomas Jerome Burgess
Herbert N. Burghart
G. W. Burgin
Horace L. Burgin
Ray E. Burgin
Greg Burk
Phillip G. Burk
C. M. Burke
Doyle Burke
Frank E. Burke
Glen Burke
John Burke
Robert E. Burke
William Burke
Burke
Arthur E. Burke, Jr.
Walter P. Burkhall
Bobby D. Burkhart
Amy Joanne Burks
James Burks
Rubye Burley
Garry M. Burnett
John Burnett
Jon R. Burnett
Allen Burnham
Fred Burns
Harry K. Burns
John R. Burns
Newton Burns
Richard Burns
Tim C. Burns
William E. Burns
John Burnsed
Frank Burris
Phillip R. Burris
Sandor Stephen Burrough
Henry J. Burroughs
Bonnie K. Burrows
Harold C. Burrows
John H. Burrus
James B. Burruss
Rodney E. Bursom
William G. Burt
James E. Burt III
Charles O. Burton
Earl H. Burton
James W. Burton
Larry W. Burton
Patricia J. Burton
Ronnie L. Burton
John Busby
Ronald D. Busby
John w. Busey

Billy G. Bush
William W. Bush
Francis X. Bushner
Eldon Bushong
Florence G. Bushong
Dennis Bushyhead
George Bushyhead
James B. Bushyhead
Jesse Bushyhead
Kenneth E. Bushyhead
Don R. Bussey
Donald E. Bussey
R. F. Bussman
Kathy Ann Bussy
Richard L. Buster
Bill Butler
Billy B. Butler
Bobby G. Butler
Charles W. Butler
Curtis R. Butler
Donald R. Butler
James D. Butler
Leonard Butler
Nilburn Eugene Butler
Robert E. Butler
Roy A. Butler
William L. Butler
Thomas W. Buttrey
William Butts
Jimmie A. Buxton
Joe B. Buzan
David D. Byars
Joseph W. Byford
Larry J. Bynum
Richard Bynum
Walter Kent Bynunn
Tom Byrd
Ray Byron
Stephen D. Cadewell
Jerry W. Cadion
Gary D. Cagle
Billie B. Cahill
Larry R. Cail
William Cain
John C. Caldwell
Ralph R. Caldwell
Ross E. Caldwell
William A. Caldwell
T.J. Call
James D. Callahan
James E. Callahan
Patrick A. Callahan
Patrick W. Callahan

John E. Callan
Robert Callan
William F. Callan
Hugh J. Callery
Henry Rex Callison
James Floyd Callison
Bernard Calte
Marrion L. Calvert
William J. Camden
Robert F. Cameron
Tommy Cameron
Paul Cammack
William D. Cammack
Alvin W. Campbell
Billy F. Campbell
Billy L. Campbell
Clayton L. Campbell
Edmund B. Campbell
Herman Campbell
Jack M. Campbell
Jack Alan Campbell
James A. Campbell
James D. Campbell
James S. Campbell
Joseph Alan Campbell
Keith A. Campbell
Leonard B. Campbell
Milton C. Campbell
Monte R. Campbell
Oscar L. Campbell
Pansy Jo Campbell
Richard C. Campbell
Richard F. Campbell
Roland Campbell
Ronnie L. Campbell
Roy Campbell
Vann Campbell
Everett Campbell, Jr.
Karen Jean Campo
Leo J. Canavan
Robert J. Candill
Patrick D. Candler
Scott Candler
William Candler
Lawrence E. Canfield
Brownie Cannon
David B. Cannon
Dennis L. Cannon
Patrick Cannon
Harold Cantrell
John E. Cantrell
Raymond Cantrell
Roy J. Cantrell

Edward W. Caperton
Billie W. Capps
Roy A. Carbine
Joel Card
Jon Carder
Linden A. Carding
David A. Cardone
Charles A. Carey
Nolan Cargile
Thomas E. Cargile
Edward R. Carillo
John R. Carle
John R. Carleton
Gerald F. Carlile
Judy M. Carlile
Harold Carloss
Don Carlson
Joseph W. Carmack
Lee E. Carman
Leslie Carman
Peter Carman
G.V. Carmichael
Jack Carmichael
Thomas Carmichael
Tommy G. Carmichael, Jr.
Joseph L. Carnell
Dave Carney
Gary Michael Carney
Lance Carney
Terry R. Carney
Dale Carpenter
David A. Carpenter
Gary P. Carpenter
H.G. Carpenter
Johnny Doyle Carpenter
Orville Carpenter
Ralph Carpenter
Robert M. Carpenter
Ronald H. Carpenter
Ross Carpenter
Sarabeth Carpenter
Thomas R. Carpenter
Harry J. Carr
John Carr
Sammuel J. Carr
Michael J. Carrabba
James M. Carrell
Floyd E. Carrier
Dollie M. Carriger
Thomas J. Carriger
Paul N. Carris
James T. Carroll
Kraig L. Carroll

Arch Carroll, Jr.
Archie Carroll, Jr.
William E. Carrols
James Carson
William A. Carson
Charles Carter
Ed M. Carter
John E. Carter
John T. Carter
Keith R. Carter
Larry D. Carter
Larry G. Carter
Larry R. Carter
Randall Lee Carter
Ronald D. Carter
Warren Carter
William T. Carter, Jr.
George E. Cartwright
Max A. Carver
David Schneider Carwile
Gary E. Carwile
E.W. Case
Leo Case
Melvin Case
Barre P. Casey
Bill Casey
Colin C. Casey
Harry Casey
Jareld William Casey
Jarold B. Casey
Jerry Casey
John M. Casey
Leonard R. Casey
Michael D. Casey
Walter Casey
William Casey
Darrell Ray Cash
Fred Cash
Jerry D. Cash
LeMar Cashion
Bruce H. Casler
Clifford K. Cason
Connie M. Cason
Edward T. Cason
Larry J. Cason
Oren W. Cason
Robert Casper
Robert D. Cassel
George E. Cassity
Robert Castillo
Billy B. Castle
John R. Castle
John Castle

Donald H. Castling
Russell E. Casto
G. Caswell
Frank D. Cate
Timothy Cateon
Bryan D. Cates
Margaret J. Cates
Roy L. Cates
G.C. Cathey
Lloyd F. Cathey
Phillip A. Cathey
Drate Cathey, Jr.
Larry Caton
Ronald N. Caton
Kim L. Catron
Timothy L. Catron
Gerald Catterlin
George P. Caudill
Robert G. Caughron
Jon C. Cavalier
James Cavanaugh
Roy S. Cavener
Eugene Cavette
John M. Cawthon
James W. Caylor
Purcell Cecil
Shelby J. Cecil
Mike E. Celcer
Paul Chamberlain
Bob Chambers
Glenn N. Chambers
John Chambers
Kenneth Chambers
Lonnie Chambers
Robert Chambers
Sam L. Chambers
Vernon Chambers
Willard Dean Chambers
William W. Chambers
Jack Chamness
John P. Champlin
George Champman
Rex G. Chance
A.W. Chandler
Ann Elizabeth Chandler
Iola P. Chandler
Robert R. Chandler
William Chandler
Barbara N. Chaney
Douglas E. Chaney
Paul W. Chaney
Robert Chaney
John S. Channel

Keith B. Chapin
Owen W. Chapin
Charles Chapman
Gene Carlus Chapman
George Chapman
Herbert G. Chapman
Lindy Chapman
Melvin L. Chapman
Reynolds Chapman
Richard H. Chapman
Steve Chapman
William D. Chappell
William Charley
Gerald Duane Chartier
Jim Chase
Jon V. Chase
R. Alan Chase
Terry Chase
Thomas Chastain
Roland K. Chasteen
Jimmy G. Chatham
Lawrence E. Cheatum
Nickey L. Checkovsky
Alex Cheek
Harold Cheek
Henry Cheever
Neal H. Cheever
Charles W. Chenoweth
Francis Chenoweth
Bonnie J. Cherry
Claud H. Cherry
Earl K. Cherry
Juanita S. Cherry
Reginald C. Cherry
Richard Chesbro
Clyde R. Chew
Ernest Childers
Thomas W. Childers
Robert Chiles
Fred Chiles, Jr.
Ralph H. Chiles, Jr.
James R. Chilton
Larry C. Chinn
Ernest Chipman
Robert Chipman
Steve M. Chisolm
Errol D. Chittenden
William Chitty
Stephen K. Christenberry
John W. Christensen
Wayne W. Christian
James Royce Christie
Johnny K. Christie

William J. Christin
Frederick N. Christman
John P. Christman
Tommy E. Christman
Benny R. Chronister
Randy L. Chronister
Donald R. Chrysler
Charles Church
Clifford M. Claggett
Patrick Edward Clancy
D. Clanton
Anthony Clark
Brent M. Clark
Bryan Clark
Dana L. Clark
Darrell B. Clark
David K. Clark
Dean E. Clark
Doyle Clark
Dwight N. Clark
Earl J. Clark
Evelyn Mae Hovis Clark
Gary L. Clark
George D. Clark
Gordon Clark
Grant Clark
Isom P. Clark
Jack L. Clark
James C. Clark
James L. Clark
James Clark
Jeffrey A. Clark
Mark W. Clark
Michael Clark
Millard B. Clark
Richard E. Clark
Robert M. Clark
Robert Clark
Rocky Louis Clark
Stephen C. Clark
Stephens Z. Clark
Thomas C. Clark
William Clark
Richard E. Clark, Jr.
Robert J. Clark, Jr.
Arnet D. Clarkson
Forth Claunch
Fred E. Claunts
Betty L. Clawson
Cathye L. Clawson
Garland Clay
Henry R. Clay
Michael R. Clay

Christopher K. Claybaker
Thomas M. Claydon
A. Clear
Fred L. Clear
Larry J. Cleary
Charles H. Cleckner
Marion Clem
John T. Clement
Edwin Clements
Robert Clements
George N. Clemmens
John W. Clemmens
Lucille Clemmens
James Clemmons
Donald James Clemons
Eugene C. Clemons
Ray M. Clemons
William D. Clemons
Hildebrant C. Cleson
Ronald D. Clevenger
Fred L. Cliar
Homer Clifford
James F. Clift
Ralph M. Clift
Robby B. Clift
Charles W. Clifton
Glenn A. Clifton
Larry Clifton
Prentice A. Clifton
Bette L. Cline
Billy M. Cline
Charles Cline
Dick Cline
George Cline
John C. Cline
Murl Cline
Ted Cline
Charles Cline
Richard M. Clinkenbeard
Mike L. Clinton
Albert Cloninger
M. D. Close
Norma Jean Close
William A. Cloud
Thomas R. Clydesdale
Joe Coachman
Joseph H. Coachman
Kenneth M. Coatney
Alvin B. Cobb
Charles B. Cobb
Dan Cobb
David D. Cobb
Kristy Suzanne Cobb

Mary E. Cobb
Teddy Ney Cobb
Victor E. Cobb
William W. Cobb
Robert D. Coble
Arthur F. Cochran
Fred Cochran
Gerald O. Cochran
Harold J. Cochran
Harold W. Cochran
Jarold Cochran
John A. Cochran
Jon Lee Cochran
Lewis L. Cochran
Michael Paul Cochran
Thomas C. Cochran
Thomas P. Cochran
John R. Cockburn
Donald Cockrell
Rodger Howard Coday
Charles Codrey
Ernest Codrey
David Wayne Cody
James D. Cody
Billy Coe
Trilla Faye Coe
Tom Coebran
Charles Coffey
Joanne Christine Coffey
Larry W. Coffey
Robert C. Coffey
Thomas R. Coffey
Harold Wayne Coffman
Thurmon Coggins
B.G. Cogle
William Coglizer
Keith B. Cogswell, Jr.
Bob G. Cohen
Lee M. Cohen
Carroll Coke
Joseph R. Coker
Tommy T. Coker
Arliss Colbert
Dale Colbert
Murray D. Colbert
William C. Colcord II
Charles E. Cole
Frank Warren Cole
Frank Cole
Glen R. Cole
Irven G. Cole
James R. Cole
Larry M. Cole

Robert R. Cole
Ron Cole
Sam M. Cole
Victor R. Cole
William A. Cole
Wm. R. Cole
Alva L. Cole, Jr.
Carl K. Coleman
Jack Coleman
Richard A. Coleman
Richard B. Coleman
Rick Coleman
Robert D. Coleman
Roy Coleman
Virginia M. Coleman
Teresa Sue Coles
Dan Coley
Zorus P. Colglazier
Bill Colglizer
Irving R. Collard, Jr.
Kenneth C. Colley
David Lee Collier
George Matthew Collier
L. W. Collier
Roy D. Collier
Steven Collier
William Collier
Bill C. Collins
Catherine L. Collins
Drinda M. Collins
Homer Collins
Rue Collins
Terry L. Collins
Thomas Collins
John J. Collins II
Frederick L. Collins, Jr.
Milton R. Collum
Robert N. Colombe
Don E. Colston
Herman Colston
George M. Colton
Michael George Colton
Ernie D. Colvard
Gerald D. Colvin
Norman Daniel Colvin
Eugene Colwell
Arthur L. Combs
Clinton E. Combs
Don W. Combs
John Combs
Robert Combs
William A. Combs
William F. Combs

Ray B. Comer
Fred Comfort
Philip E. Compton
Paul B. Comstock
Leland Conard
Ava D. Conder
Bobby Cone
Maurice Conkle
David E. Conklin
William M. Conklin
Charlotte Ann Conley
Steven E. Conley
Albert Conn
Mary Irene Conn
Jerry L. Connell
Gary M. Connelly
Thomas Matthew Connelly
Lester Conner
James W. Connor
Don Conover
Kenny D. Conover
Donald R. Conrad
Patrick Conroy
Henry Conseen
John Coody
A.J. Cook
Bill Cook
D. H. Cook
Ed Cook
Edward Cook
H. L. Cook
Harry G. Cook
Irby Cook
Jackie L. Cook
James R. Cook
John C. Cook
Melvin R. Cook
Phillip Cook
Robert V. Cook
Ron L. Cook
Ronald O. Cook
Ronnie L. Cook
Russell A. Cook
Russell Cook
Stephen T. Cook
Terry L. Cook
Wendell Cook
Ben R. Cook, Jr.
William Howe Cook, Jr.
William R. Cook, Jr.
James W. Cooke
Thomas F. Cooke
David R. Cooley

Thomas Coon
Bill Wayne Cooper
Bobby Forrest Cooper
Charles A. Cooper
David Cooper
Edward Cooper
Estel Cooper
Hobbs H. Cooper
Mary Ellen Cooper
Robert Cooper
Roy Cooper
Rustie Cooper
Samuel W. Cooper
Sharon R. Cooper
Shelley Ann Cooper
Willa-Beth S. Cooper
James C. Cooper, Jr.
Roy Cooper, jr.
Larry W. Coor
John M. Copeland
W.A. M. Copeland
Jerry S. Copp
Thomas S. Copp
Ralph Coppinger
Gary R. Coppock
Charles R. Corbett
Dean H. Corbett
John Wayne Corbin
John Corbin
Lawrence Eric Cordray
Rick L. Cordray
William J. Core, Jr.
Joseph E. Corey
Max Corey
Rowland Corey
Bob Corlett
William Robert Corlett
Leroy Corley
Ricky L. Corley
Robert L. Corley
Betty L. Corn
C.C. Cornelison
Clemmel Cornelison
Jack Cornelius
John M. Cornelius, Jr.
Peter R. Cornell
George P. Cornwell
Danny D. Correll
John L. Correll
Allen B. Cortner
Walter Cory
Phillip C. Cosby
Danny E. Cosgrove

Ron Cosgrove
Sheryl Lynn Coston
Albert C. Cottingim
Deborah J. Cottingim
Robert A. Cottingim
George V. Cottom
Sam Cotton
William D. Cotton
Art Couch
Ernest A. Couch
Gordon A. Couch
James S. Couch
Kirk A. Couch
Richard Couch
Tommy J. Couch
Curtis L. Coughran
Philip A. Coulter
James Counts
Moses L. Courington, Jr.
Don L. Coursey
James L. Coursey
Frances Courtney
Jeffery Wood Courtney
Dean G. Cousparis
Richard J. Covey
Dale Covington
Beverly F. Cowan
David A. Cowan
Murl Cowan
Paul Cowan
William R. Cowan
Carey S. Cowart
Steve Cowen
Murrell E. Cowherd
George M. Cowles
David Cowsar
Ricky W. Cowsar
Betty B. Cox
Betty Sue Cox
Charles Cox
Eugene B. Cox
Floyd L. Cox
Jack Cox
James L. Cox
James S. Cox
Jean Marie Cox
John R. Cox
John R. Cox
Larry Cox
Mary J. Cox
Patrick A. Cox
Reid A. Cox
Stanley M. Cox

Tide Cox
Tom Cox
William F. Cox
William G. Cox
Jesse G. Cox, Jr.
Stephen B. Coy
Everett Coyne
Reece J. Crabtree
J.T. Craig
Pete Craig
Ray L. Craig
William B. Craig
Wm. H. Craig
Robert E. Craighead
N. Richard Crain
Joel W. Crain Jr.
Glen Crane
Justin T. Crane
Henry L. Crank
Roger H. Crank
Charles D. Cravens
Charles D. Cravens
Barbetta J. Crawford
Charles Crawford
Paul Crawford
Ronald Crawford
Frank Crawley
Jerry Crawley
Lee Crawley
Rev Crawley
Stanley L. Crawley
Sara Crazy Thunder
Nance G. Creager
Gene Creighton
James Edward Crenshaw
Keith Crew
Lonnie Ray Crews
James D. Cribbs
Harley Crichton
Ralph E. Crigler, Jr.
Donney W. Criner
Thomas Richard Crisman
Donnie R. Criswell
Thomas O. Criswell, Jr.
Jack L. Critchfield
Michael R. Critchfield
James Crocker
Clydene Crockett
Luther Crockett
Phillip L. Crodus
Curtis V. Crofford
Donald Croft
William F. Croft

David C. Croninger
Ken Cronk
Billy Crose
Gene Crose
Billy H. Cross
Bobby Jean Cross
Neil C. Cross
Neil Cross
Tom D. Cross
Ed J. Crossland
Thomas M. Crossland
David Allen Crossley
David S. Crosslin
Daryl Crotts
Marshall Crotts
Delbert Crouch
John S. Crouch
Harry P. Crow
Thomas Crow
John L. Crow II
Carl F. Crowder
George F. Crowder
Harold Lee Crowder
Phillip L. Crowdus
Clifford Crowe
Stanley Crowe
Frank Crowley
Tommy Crowson
William J. Crume
Wm. H. Crume
Woodrow Crume
Margie Crump
Robert W. Crump
W.B. Crump
William M. Crutcher
David L. Crutchfield
Donnie L. Crutchfield
Harold J. Crutchfield
Mary Frances Crutchfield
Neil W. Crutchfield
Richard David Crutchfield
Phillip T. Cruzan
Samuel J. Cruzan
Bobby M. Cubitt
Lewis Culbertson
Courtney D. Culley
Alden Culp
Charles Culp
Joe Culp
Frank Culpepper
Sherwood F. Culpepper
James R. Culver
Leo V. Culver

Edgar M. Culwell
John W. Culwell
Mike Cumiskey
George Cummings
Howard J. Cummings
Ronnie W. Cummings
Charles C. Cummins
Leroy W. Cummisky
Ramon K. Cundiff
Allen Cunningham
Coburn C. Cunningham
David A. Cunningham
Eugene Cunningham
Larry D. Cunningham
Marian M. Cunningham
Newt Cunningham
Robert F. Cunningham
Roy Cunningham
Andrew M. Current
Kenneth G. Currie
Leon W. Curry
Richard N. Curry
Robert N. Curry
Frank Curtis
Jack Curtis
James Faulkner Curtis
James P. Curtis
Jim Curtis
Joseph R. Curtis
Robert D. Curtis
Roger E. Curtis
Tommy D. Cutsinger
James E. Cyr
Jim Cyrus
Albert G. Dabney
Jerry R. Dacus
Franklin F. Daggs
Ronald C. Dahl
Jack R. Dailey
Dick M. Daily
James H. Daily
Pat Daily
Paul I. Daily
Roger I. Daily
Harold Dake
Joe Dake
Edward E. Dale
Harold W. Dale
John L. Dale
Richard S. Dale
Richard Dale
Robert M. Dale
John H. Dalgarn

John Dalgarn
John Dalgarn
Ted E. Dalton
William P. Dalton
Charles R. Dancer
Gilmore Daniel
Hugh H. Daniel
Joe C. Daniel
John B. Daniel
Michael F. Daniel
Reginald E. Daniel
Robert C. Daniel
Carl U. Daniels
Everett H. Daniels
Jerry D. Daniels
Robert R. Daniels
Michael L. Darby
Charles D. Darks
Charles Darling
Richard Darnell
Robert Darnell
William L. Darnell
Raymond W. Darrah
Long Jamk Darrell
James B. Darrough
Hiawatha Darrow
William Allen Darrow
John Datrick
Oce Daugherty
Thomas Daugherty
William J. Daugherty
J. C. Daugherty, Jr.
Otto H. Daugherty, Jr.
Daniel W. Davenport
Ginger K. Davenport
Glenn Davenport
Grover T. Davenport
Ira G. Davenport
Jimmy L. Davenport
Joe L. Davenport
Phillip Daves
Bob E. Davidson
Carroll P. Davidson
Glen A. Davidson
James F. Davidson
Russell Davidson
Sydney L. Davidson
Thomas J. Davies, Jr.
A. D. Davis
Billy J. Davis
Bradley K. Davis
Clay Davis
Dan Rodney Davis

Denton E. Davis
Edward E. Davis
Floyd Davis
Gary Allen Davis
George E. Davis
George Kenneth Davis
Gordon L. Davis
Gordon L. Davis
Hale V. Davis
Howard E. Davis
Hugh B. Davis
James W. Davis
Joe E. Davis
Joe Davis
John C. Davis
John R. Davis
Johnnie Davis
Judyth Ann Davis
Lawrence S. Davis
Linda K. Davis
Paul Edward Davis
Paul J. Davis
Ray L. Davis
Reginald L. Davis
Robert A. Davis
Robert C. Davis
Robert M. Davis
Robert Y. Davis
Roy W. Davis
Thomas E. Davis
Tom Davis
Walter B. Davis
Warren Davis
William L. Davis
William Davis
Claiborne W. Davis III
Joe T. Davison
Richard F. Dawes
Donald D. Dawson
Donald Y. Dawson
Harry Dawson
Kaye D. Dawson
Alan Lee Day
David E. Day
George Day
Gilbert C. Day
Jean A. Day
John N. Day
Joseph E. Day
Michael G. Day
Phillip R. Day
Gilbert C. Day, Jr.
Barry F. Dayton

Patrick N. Deal
Bob Dean
Howard L. Dean
Robert L. Dean, Jr.
Theodore E. Dean, Jr.
William S. DeArman
Rick DeArmond
Clyde Deaton
James D. Deaton
Leo R. Deaver
Jimmie L. Debo
Albert M. DeBolt
John J. DeCandelaro
Roger W. Deeba
Clint Deel
M. Josephine Davis
Marcus A. DeFever
Theodore Deffeyes
Michael R. Deford
David L. DeFriese
Claude L. DeHart
Walter del Pinal
Louis Deldrier
Okay Delman
William L. DeLong
James L. DeLozier
Louis DeLuce
Charles Demaree
Gene H. DeMarsh
Dean R. DeMerritt
Thomas E. Demmitt
Charles Dempsey
Eddy M. Dempsey
Jack Dempsey
Delayno Denbo
Jack Denby
Duane R. Denham
Leonard P. Denham
H. W. Denison
Janice Darlene Denison
Frank Denker
Sean Denmark
Gary R. Denney
William C. Denney
Brian W. Dennis
Daniel W. Dennis
David Dennis
Inise M. Dennis
Gene P. Dennison
Hilliard Dennison
Andrew E. Denny
Paul K. Denny
Willard L. Denny

Rawley J. Dent
Richard O. Dent
Charles J. Denton
Frank Denton
Jim Denton
Edward Merle Deplois
Lucille Derby
Walter L. Derby
Wanda L. Derby
Grant W. Derfelt
Larry A. DeShane
John G. DeTar
Douglas Deter
Dennis Wayne Detherow
Delores A. Devers
Robert J. DeVoy
Jess Dew
John N. Dew
Bob Dews
Ernest R. Dick
Jimmy J. Dick
William H. Dick
Woodrow L. Dick
Billy G. Dickenson
Michael W. Dickerson
Ted J. Dickey
Bryan Dickinson
Warren Dickinson
Daniel Dickison
Dudley Dickson
Robert B. Dieter
Carroll J. Dikeman
Gary Dikeman
William B. Dikeman
Henry A. Dilbeck
Glen Dill, Jr.
Ernest E. Dillahunty
Charles Dillard
Don O. Dillard
Floyd Dillard
Jack Dillard
James H. Dillard
Sam Dillion
Carl Dillon
Gene D. Dillon
Sam H. Dillon
W.O.(Jack) Dillon, Jr.
Chester T. Dirck
Jeanette A. Dirck
Charles Dirickson
John C. Dirickson
Marjorie Dirickson
Dorothy I. Dishman

Robert R. Ditto
Jerry A. Dixon
Joe M. Dixon
L. Dixon
Richard Dixon
Vincent L. Dixon
Wilma L. Dixon
Howard Doak
James W. Doak
Lindell Trent Dobson
Beverly L. Dodd
Victor Dodge
William Dodge
Aubrey K. Dodson
Kenneth N. Dodson
Nick D. Dodson
Phyllis A. Dodson
Ted D. Dodson
Thomas D. Dodson
William A. Dodson
Clarence B. Doebber
Harry R. Doerner
Phillip Doerner
Albert Y. Doggett
Bobbie Doggett
Daniel F. Doggett
Harve A. Dolan
Billie H. Doler
Charlie Dollard
John A. Dollard
Paul H. Dolman
Paul W. Dolman
Jack A. Dolman, Jr.
Thomas L. Dome
Forbest M. Donaho
Michael O. Donathan
Robert M. Donley
Edwaard T. Donnelly
Lowell L. Donnelly
Jim H. Donohue
Richard Michael Donohue
William Edmond Donohue
Timothy Donovan
William J. Donovan
Charles L. Dooley
Christopher B. Dooley
Daniel N. Dooley
Daniel N. Dooley
C. K. Doran
Larry A. Doran
Robert S. Dorn
Glenn Dorsey
Joel C. Doss

Tony Dossett
Hugh Dossey
William Dost
Carol A. Dotson
Bruce P. Dougherty
Robert F. Dougherty
J. C. Dougherty, Jr.
Bobby R. Douglas
Chris W. Douglas
David Douglas
Doug Douglas
Gary D. Douglas
George Douglas
J. Charles Douglas
Marcellus Douglas
Novelena Douglas
Ray Douglas
Stephen A. Douglas
Stephen B. Douglas
David Douglass
Denny J. Doutaz
Jack Dowd
John G. Dowd
Roy L. Dowden
Don Dowell
H. L. Dowell
Vern B. Dowell
Waymon G. Dowell
Waymon Dowell
Carol A. Dowers
Charles L. Dowland
John H. Dowling
Johnny L. Downard
Nile R. Downer
Jeffrey B. Downing
Michael Earl Downing
William E. Downing
John Downs
Ronald E. Downs
William M. Downs
Walter E. Downs, Jr.
Darrell R. Dowty
Patrick J. Doyle
William P. Doyle
Doyle
Gary L. Drafger
Bob Drake
Curtis T. Drake
Donald A. Drake
Garland J. Drake
Robert L. Drake
Emmitt L. Drane
John V. Drane

James M. Dresser
Robert Dresser
Bill Drew
William E. Drew
Clifton Driggs
Jay Driskill
Clarence F. Driver
Stuart A. Droms
Alan J. Drover
Clifford Druit
Don C. Duckering
John S. Duckering
Joseph P. Dudley
Frederick L. Duerr
Torrence S. Duff
Bob E. Duffner
Richard L. Dugan
Bonnie M. Duggan
Daniel Duggan
Rick J. Duggan
Stratford B. Duke
William S. Duke
Charles Duller
William W. Dumas
Gerald Edgar Dunahay
Roy L. Dunahay
David Frank Dunaway
Donald R. Dunaway
Frances Dunaway
Taylor Dunaway
Wayne Dunaway
Robert J. Dunbar
Kelly Duncan
Kent B. Duncan
Ronald L. Duncan
John H. Duncan, Jr.
Arthur Dunham
Fred Dunham
Steven H. Dunham
David Morris Dunlap
Morris Dunlap
Pamela J. Dunlap
Richard Dunlap
Roger Dunlap
Roy Dunlap
Walter Dunlap
Paul O. Dunlop
Carolyn J. Dunn
Joyce Elene Dunn
Keith E. Dunn
Robert L. Dunn
Toby Dunn
Robert E. Dunnam

Diane Susan H. Dunning
Frank Dunning
Guy R. Dunning
Geoffrey B. Dunsmoor
Mike Dunwoody
Jim Dupre
Charles E. Dupree
Roger A. Durall
Jack R. Durant
R. B. Durant
Richard Durant
David M. Durham
George M. Durham
LaMoyne Durham
Max Durkee
Sondra Lynn Durr
Sherman D. Durrett
Francis Durrum
Johnny R. Dusenberry
John Duston
Jack G. Dutton
Kenneth DuVal
Richard Duvall
Jack A. Dwyer
Robert Dwyer
Peach Dye
Barbara K. Dyer
Jack P. Dyer
Jack P. Dyer
Linda S. Dyer
Timothy M. Dyer
Ronnie S. Eads
Joe B. Eagleston
Judy F. Eagleton
Ira Eaker
Michael K. Eakin
Lonnie Eales
Larry W. Earl
Mike J. Earley
Kenneth Earling
David M. Earnhart
Charles L. Easley
Gary Easley
Donald E. Eason, Jr.
Gerry G. East
Bobby Easter
Daniel J. Easterling
Gerald W. Easterling
Marvin M. Eastman
Robert Eastwood
James Eaton
Terry D. Eaton
John L. Eaves

Marcus Ebenhack
Patsy A. Eby
Charles R. Eddy
James F. Eden
Jim Eden
Raymond M. Eden
Curt D. Edgerton, Jr.
Joe R. Edgington
Marvin W. Edgmon
James M. Edmiston
Carroll Edmonds
George Edmonds
N. Edmonds
Allen Edmondson
Arthur Gerald Edmondson
Robert Edward
Boppy Edwards
D.H. Edwards
Fredrick L. Edwards
Irwin Edwards
John D. Edwards
Ray R. Edwards
Reese Edwards
Roland Edwards
Ronald H. Edwards
Robert D. Edwards.
Ron Eells
Roxie Jan Eesley
Thomas Egbert
J.C. Egger
Donald L. Eggerman
Terry B. Egleston
Harold Egolf
Darrell B. Ehmke
Joe D. Eichling
A.E. Eidson
Edsel Eidson
Jesse Eisenhauer
Fritz Eisenlohr, Jr.
Ina Lou Ekstedt
Leroy J. Elam
Theodore M. Elam
Don Elder
Hoyt Elder
James D. Elder
James R. Elder
Clarence Eldridge
Neal Eldridge
Theodore M. Elem
Pat Jeanne Elgin
James Elkins
John W. Elkins
Harvey Elkouri

James D. Elledge
Oscar Elledge
David Ellenburg
John L. Eller
Ralph Ellinger
Wayne Ellinger
James W. Ellington
Paul Ellington
John W. Elliot
Mack Mathis Elloit
Bob Elliott
Charles Elliott
Gail K. Elliott
Jimmy R. Elliott
John C. Elliott
Robert J. Elliott, Jr.
Thomas R. Elliott, Jr.
Gene Ellis
James H. Ellis
Larry D. Ellis
Melton E. Ellis
Michael D. Ellis
Edwin P. Ellison
James O. Ellison
John W. Ellison
Richard Ellison
Robert E. Ellison
Carl N. Elmore
Clarence B. Elsey
Francis Elston
James A. Embrey, Jr.
Jack Emerick
Bruce Emerson
Charles Emerson
Timothy K. Emerson
Charles Emmerson
Thomas W. Emmert
James L. Emmons
Steve G. Emmons
Tony W. Emmons
Henry Enders
Clifford W. Endicott
Timothy J. Endres
Albert B. Engel
William Engel
James Edward England
Janice Kay England
Michael W. England
Jerry L. Engle
William J. Engler
Bill C. English
Steve English
William Stephen English

Mark Engskov
John R. Enselman
James Eoff
Jerry G. Eperson
Allan Ephraim
G. S. Ephraim
Dale D. Epperson
Gary N. Epperson
Danny L. Epple
James Eppler
James Erickson
James E. Erixon
Jack Ersking
Dennis W. Ervin
Billy Erwin
Claude C. Erwin, Jr.
Carl Eschbach
Charles R. Eslick
William A. Eslick
Franklin Jackson Estes
Gary L. Estes
James M. Estes
John C. Estes
Lee Estes
Alfred R. Etchison
Joseph Etheridge
Robert Q. Etsel
John W. Etter
Jack D. Eubank
Curtis F. Eugene
Toby D. Eugene
Claude Eurton
Bradford Eutsler
Charles Evans
Don R. Evans
Donald F. Evans
Donna Lou Evans
Estel J. Evans
Everett Evans
Gay Evans
Hal Evans
J.S. Evans
Jerry Evans
Lewis E. Evans
Mary F. Evans
Perry Evans
Robert Evans
Terry L. Evans
Walter Evans
William T. Evans
John R. Evans, Jr.
Jerry W. Evatt
Michael D. Everett

Rex M. Everett
Max Evory
James E. Ewing
John A. Eyberg
George Failing
Robert G. Failing
Elwood Fain
Gary R. Faine
Jerry L. Fair
William R. Fairbanks
Otto Bror Falk
Denny W. Falkenburg
Bob Falling
Joe C. Fambrough
Thornton Fankhouser
William L. Farbro
Stephen S. Farha
Barbara H. Farley
Earl L. Farley
Howard Farley
London J. Farley
Loren Farley
Robert Farley
Roy L. Farley
Jimmie B. Farmer
John Farmer
Larry Farmer
Robert A. Farmer
Robert A. Farmer
George C. Farr
Leo A. Farr
William Lanier Farrell
David Lawrence Farren
Robert L. Farrill
John Farris
Mark B. Farris
Scott Farris
Carl A. Fast
Danny L. Faught
Janet Elaine Faught
Stanley C. Faught
Steven L. Faught
Chester Eugene Faulconer
Dave Faulkner
K. D. Faulkner
Melvin C. Faulkner
Taylor Faulkner
Faulkner
Clay Faust
Dick Faust
Joseph R. Faust
Lee Faust
LeRoy J. Faust

John Fawcett
Michael E. Fawks
John W. Fearing
Gregory C. Featherston
Ward D. Fec
Jewel Dean Feeback
Craig V. Felber
Mark D. Felber
Clarence W. Fell
Curtis E. Fell
George Fell
Gwynne E. Felton
George T. Felts
Enos Fenderson
Thomas Fenderson
John R. Fenly
Dorothy V. Fenton
Howard Fenton
Richard E. Fentress
Barbara Lee Fergeson
John Fergus
David Ferguson
Donald R. Ferguson
John H. Ferguson
Mark D. Ferguson
Michael A. Ferguson
Patricia E. Ferguson
Richard L. Ferguson
Robert W. Ferguson
Jim Ferneau
George Ferry
Howard Fertig
Francis S. Fickling
O. V. Field
Robert Field
Robin Field
William A. Field
Michael L. Fielding
Paul D. Fielding, Jr.
Glenn Fields
Lawrence Fields
Roger L. Fife
Oran W. Fifer
David R. Fike
Sheila B. Fikes
Irwin C. Files
Paul Finiher
Bob Fink
Charles Finklea
Harold M. Finks
Eugene A. Finley
Glenn Finley
Marion Lou Finley

Wallace Finley
Arthur Finn
John G. Finney
Marshall Finney
Robert Finney
Robert Finnigan
Eugene V. Firth
Arthur J. Fisch
Joseph L. Fish
Alva L. Fisher
Carl E. Fisher
Charlie Fisher
Darrell Channing Fisher
John Fisher
Larry L. Fisher
Rob Fisher
Walter W. Fisher
Harry C. Fisher, Jr.
Larry E. Fishpaw
Eugene Fitch
John Fitterer, Jr.
Charles Fitzgerald
Don Fitzgerald
James Fitzgerald
William J. Fitzgerald
Dale F. Fitzgibbon
Michael G. Fitzhugh
Earl E. Fitzjerrell, Jr.
John J. Fitzstephens
Johnny L. Fivecoats
Timothy A. Flaig
Jerome T. Flammger
James R. Flanagan
Tom Flanagan
Malcolm Flanary
Burt Fleeger
Carlisle M. Fleetwood
Kipton E. Fleming
Thomas Fleming
Irene M. Fletcher
Roy R. Fletcher
James G. Flickinger
Charles W. Flint
Charles Flint, Jr.
Samuel Flood
Richard W. Flora
Robert Florence
Robert J. Flow
Andy Floyd
Ronald D. Fluke
Augus Fluty
Larry I. Flynn
Robert Allan Flynn

Robert W. Fobes
Harold Folkers
Ernest R. Fondren
Daniel Fonvielle
Bill Foote
Leo C. Footer
William W. Forbes
Don P. Ford
Frank M. Ford
Henry W. Ford
Holland C. Ford
John M. Ford
Lee Ford
Nannie M. Ford
Virgil C. Ford
Paul R. Ford, Jr.
Helen Lenora Foreman
William Darrell Forest
Stanley Forman
Joseph R. Forner
Charles B. Forrest
Frank R. Forrest
Jon Forrest
Thomas Forrestal
Larry G. Forsgren
John Forster
James R. Fortenberry
Gerald R. Fortner
Morrison V. Fortson
Loyd Fortune
Charles W. Foster
Charles Foster
David J. Foster
Earl Foster
Eddie S. Foster
James R. Foster
James R. Foster
Jim Foster
Joe T. Foster
Mel Foster
Orval Foster
Ralph Foster
Reavis Foster
Robert E. Foster
Frank G. Fotenoculos
Michael L. Fought
Robert W. Foulks
Max Fountain
Van Foutch
Allan R. Fowler
Charles M. Fowler
Daniel F. Fowler
James G. Fowler

Lawrence W. Fowler
Richard L. Fowler
Robert Fowler
Ronald L. Fowler
William A. Fowler
Allan R. Fowler, Jr.
Jerry Fowlkes
Clifford Fox
Dwight Fox
Irwin C. Fox
John E. Fox
Michael D. Fox
Raymond Fox
Sharon Fox
Wilma Jean Frailey
David C. Francis
Peter B. Franckum
Keith B. Frank
Robert H. Frank
Robert T. Frank
Chester Franklin
David L. Franklin
Earl A. Franklin
Kenneth Franklin
Patty L. Franklin
Prentiss Franklin
Wanda Franklin
Claude Franks
Deborah Ann Franks
Tommy F. Fraser
Robert Frayser
Laddie L. Frazel
William C. Frazier, Jr.
Christopher J. Frederick
Carl W. Freed
Charles D. Freeman
Durcie E. Freeman
Hal K. Freeman
Harry C. Freeman
Michael P. Freeman
Norman L. Freeman
Richard J. Freeman
Roger Freeman
William O. Freeman
Wilmot Freeman
Ferris C. Frees, Jr.
Bennie M. French
Harold French
Robert B. French
Robert W. French
Joe R. Frensley
Joe Frensley
Gaines R. Friar

Mervin L. Friedman
Freddy Friend
William Friend
William F. Friend III
William J. Frier
William A. Frisbie
Ronnie Fritts
Gregory T. Frix
Sharon Marie Frizzell
Ted Frizzell
Larry Froese
Lloyd R. Froese
Vernon S. Frogge
Freddie D. Fruechting
Allen F. Fry
Esther G. Fry
Maxwell Fry
Rex A. Fry
William Fry
Harold E. Fudge
Jack Fudge
Gary J. Fugitt
Thomas S. Fujiyoshi
William Fulghum
David L. Fulkerson
Carol L. Fuller
David Fuller
G. H. Fuller
G.M. Fuller
Kenneth Fuller
Joseph W. Fullerton
Tom P. Fullilove
Clifford Fulp
Gerald F. Fultz
Harold Fultz
Imogene Fultz
Kevin Virgil Fultz
Glen B. Funk
Paul A. Funk
Paul Furgerson
John Furrow
Loyal W. Furry
J. M. Fuser, Jr.
Joseph L. Fusselman
Edgar Futrell
Stanley J. Gaberlavage
Carl Gadberry
Bradley J. Gaddis
Hal Gage
Thomas B. Gage
Craig Gahring
George Gahring
Roger R. Gahring

Stan Gahring
Earl E. Gaines
Stephen F. Gainor III
Dale E. Gallimore
Jess S. Gallion
John W. Gallion
David Gallman
David Galloway
Thelmar Galloway
Gene Gallupe
Dean F. Galutza
Carlos E. Galvez, Jr.
Paul S. Gamble
Anthony Ray Gan
Clarence Gander
James R. Gann
Kenneth W. Gann
Wesley L. Gann
Roderick L. Ganus
Lloyd O. Ganus, Jr.
Bruce M. Garbade
Fred L. Gardner
Fred Gardner
Robert N. Gardner
Ramon S. Gargantiel
Jack L. Garland
Deck Garman
Debbie J. Garner
Homer D. Garner
Nelson Garner
Robert L. Garner
Nelson V. Garner, Jr.
Robert L. Garnett
Wayne Garretson
Bert L. Garrett
Gregory A. Garrett
Joe P. Garrett
Larry J. Garrett
Robert L. Garrett
Gale L. Garringer
Michaele Ann Garrison
Robert J. Garrison
Frances E. Garroutte
Dorothy Garth
James Garth
James Garth, Jr.
Francis Garton
Terry G. Gartside
Harold T. Garvin
Mark J. Garwin
Hubert L. Gary
Jack Gaskill
Donald E. Gaskins

Ronald C. Gaskins
Bird M. Gaston
Robert S. Gaston
James K. Gatchell
Frederick A. Gateka
Francis Gates
Frederick E. Gates
John J. Gates
George Gates, Jr.
William C. Gates, Jr.
John R. Gatewood
Malcolm E. Gatewood
Ritchie G. Gatewood
Richard A. Gatlin
Robert Gatlin
Thomas G. Gault
Barry D. Gay
Karen K. Gay
James Larry Gean
James Eugene Geary
Jim E. Geary
Wood A. Gebhardt
Kenneth W. Gee
William L. Gehrs, Jr.
Andy Geisler
James A. Gentry
Jan C. Gentry
John P. Gentry
Blu Gentry, Jr.
Bluford M. Gentry, Jr.
Elizabeth D. George
James A. George
James E. George
Jay B. George
Charles B. George III
Desmond Gerard
Larry L. Gerber
James A. Gerdes
Giles E. Gere
Dan German
Rodney Germany
Gary H. Gettings
Jack Getty
John Gex
Joe V. Gfeller
Lennart T. Giannast
James Gibb
George L. Gibbons
Murray F. Gibbons
Bill E. Gibbs
Duane Gibbs
Frank C. Gibbs
Gorham K. Gibbs

Bruce A. Gibson
Don E. Gibson
Dorsey Gibson
Emmett W. Gibson
John R. Gibson
Kelly Gibson
Ralph Gibson
Ron L. Gibson
Stanley T. Gibson
David C. Gideon
John L. Gier
Harry R. Giesey
Jimmy Giesey
Wesley Leroy Gifford
William J. Gignac
Daniel Alan Gigoux
Earl R. Gilbert
Walter K. Gilbert
Roy Giles
Thomas H. Giles
Katherine A. Gilkeson
Wayne Girard Gilkeson
James P. Gillaspie
Glenn C. Gillespie
Jack E. Gillett
Emmett N. Gilliam
Howard Gilliam
Thomas J. Gilliam
Howard Q. Gilliam, Jr.
Terry D. Gilliland
Charles T. Gillis
Jackie F. Gilmore
Steven Campbell Gilmore
Ronald E. Gilstrap
William H. Gilstrap
Don D. Gish
Donald R. Gish
John Z. Gish
Michael F. Gladstein
Arthur Glass
Gary M. Glass
John Glass
Michael J. Glass
Robert Glass
William C. Glass
Frederick A. Glassco
Thomas C. Glasscock
Wallace Glasscock
Paul Glassgow
Carlos E. Glaves, Jr.
Robert F. Gleason
Belmont L. Glenn
Dave L. Glenn

Joe D. Glenn
Morris L. Glenn
Saul J. Glenn
Richard Glikes
John P. Gloeckler
Bonita Glover
Vernon P. Glover
Willard T. Glover
Charles A. Goad
Newton M. Gober
Roy Goddard
Richard Gode
Norman E. Godfrey, Jr.
Crawford W. Goff
Paul E. Goforth
James C. Gohn
William J. Goike
James W. Going
Jay W. Gold
Johnn Gold
Daniel Ernest Golden
Gregory Golden
Joe N. Golden
Robert Golden
Russell Daniel Golden
Phil Goldfarb
Joe Goldfeder
Juniuo W. Goldham
Cliff Goldsmith
Jimmy W. Goldston
Pete Goltra
Guillermo E. Gomez
Robert Gomez
Ruben Antonio A. Gomez
Bill Gooch
Joseph C. Gooch
Robert Lee Gooch
Charlie Good
Gary Good
Hall E. Good
Hugh C. Good
Edward E. Gooden
Doug W. Goodhue
Douglas W. Goodhue
David L. Goodin
Mike J. Goodin
Dale L. Gooding
Joseph H. Goodman
John A. Goodpaster
Clara Goodsell
Elwin Goodson
James R. Goodwin
Kenny W. Goodwin

Sammy R. Goodwin
Wayne Goodwin
William H. Gooldy
William T. Gooldy, Jr.
Douglas L. Goostree
Benny R. Gordon
David Guy Gordon
Dennis Gordon
Elizabeth Gordon
Elliott Gordon
Michael M. Gordon
Mike Gordon
Minor William Gordon
Minor Gordon
Pat S. Gordon
Terry M. Gorham
Nelson Gorom
John R. Gorrell
William A. Gossett
Paul Gotcher
Robert B. Gotcher
E. A. Gould
George H. Gould
Grant Gould
Edgar Gourd
Venson L. Gourd
James E. Graalman
Barry H. Grabel
Morris Grabel
Larry Grable
Chester Grace
Eric S. Graf
John C. Grafton
Johnnie Gragg
Leo Gragg
Richard E. Gragg
Gary M. Graham
Gene Graham
Jefferson M. Graham
Leon Graham
Olan Graham
Robert E. Graham
Robert Scott Graham
Scott L. Graham
Tommie Graham
Virgil A. Graham
Wilbur Graham
Robert E. Grammar
Joe D. Grandstaff
Joe Grandstaff
Clarence Granes
Cary Grant
Gary B. Grant

James D. Grant
James Grant
Fait H. Grantham
John Grantham
Mike J. Gras
Harold A. Grass
Ben Graves
Clarence E. Graves
Claude D. Graves
Jack Graves
Janice Graves
Ben C. Graves, Jr.
Charles E. Gray
Donald J. Gray
Gary L. Gray
Gary W. Gray
John F. Gray
Laverne Gray
Michael Gray
Pat C. Gray
Richard V. Gray
Robert R. Gray
Ronald Gray
Clarence Gray, Jr.
Woodrow E. Grayson, Jr.
Daryl Grazier
Joe W. Greathouse
Larry Greb
Bill A. Green
Clarence F. Green
Claudia Jane Green
David L. Green
Delbert Green
George Green
James K. Green
Jess D. Green
Lawrence T. Green
Lynell W. Green
Michael W. Green
Pearl L. Green
Ronald Lee Green
Tom R. Green
William R. Green
William T. Green
William Green
James Green, Jr.
Jess D. Green, Jr.
John W. Green, Jr.
Woodrow Greenback
Jeffrey F. Greenberg
Richard Leon Greene
Douglas R. Greenwald
Kenneth W. Greer

Dallas Greeson
Joe W. Greever
Bernard Gregory
Judson L. Gregory
John W. Gregory III
Wm. C. Gresham
O.A. Griffey, Jr.
Barbara B. Griffin
Billy D. Griffin
James Griffin
Jefferson D. Griffin
Richard T. Griffin
Willard Griffin
Everett L. Griffith
George Griffith
Howstin Griffith
Juan Griffith
Robert H. Griffith
Rolla Griffith
Terry F. Griffith
Tommy Griffith
Ron Griggs
James Grigsby
Walter W. Grigson
Otto Lewis Grimes
Ernest W. Grimm, Jr.
Earnest Grimms
Edna L. Grisham
Jon L. Grissom
Milton Griswald
Richard W. Groh
Marshall S. Groom
Worth Gross
Glenda M. Grossman
Howard Groth
William M. Groth
Gordon L. Grotts
Perry Ground
Charles K. Grounds
John H. Grove
Larence H. Grove
Earl H. Groves
Robert L. Groves
Rex Grozier
Timothy D. Grubaugh
Albert A. Guadagno
Michael K. Guard
Joel E. Guerin
M. T. Guerra
Jerry D. Guhl
Howard Guild
Leroy Guild
James H. Gungoll

Robert R. Gungoll
Judith A. Gunn
Thomas J. Gunn
George M. Gunter
Larry Gunter
Gary L. Guppy
Robert Gilman Guptill II
Richard C. Gust
Charles M. Gustafson
Dennis C. Gustafson
Billy G. Guthrie
John A. Guthrie
Elwyn F. Gutzman
John R. Gwynne
Jack Haberlein
Charles Hackbarth
Jerome M. Hacker
Joe A. Hacker
Robert E. Hadady
Vernon L. Haddon
Cordell Hadley
Patrick T. Hadley
James C. Hafer
Ned Hagan
Brenda Hagebusch
Darrel L. Hager
David Dwayne Hager
John F. Hager
Waldon Hager
Patrick Haggerty
William P. Haggerty
Ellen E. Hahn
Jim J. Hahn
James T. Haigh
David Michael Haines
John R. Haines
Roy D. Haines
Richard Lee Hakel
Lee F. Hakestraw
Dorothy V. Hale
Earlene F. Hale
George M. Hale
Loren Hale
Roy N. Hale
Tommy Darrell Hale
Warren H. Hale
Grady Haley
Terry R. Haley
Charles Halk
Alfred Hall
Allen H. Hall
D.P. Hall
Eldon M. Hall

Frank Hall
J. C. Hall
James D. Hall
Jim R. Hall
John M. Hall
John M. Hall
Kenneth Hall
Marion Hall
Nelson Hall
Olney Hall
Ralph C. Hall
Richard Hall
Robert D. Hall
Robert L. Hall
Robert L. Hall
W. E. Hall
Walcott R. Hall
Walter P. Hall
Warren Hall
Clifford E. Hall, Jr.
Roger Said Hallaway
Ernest Haller
David Halley
Harry Halley
Louis D. Halley
Stanton M. Halley
Stuart Halley
Roger Hallifax
William E. Hallmark
Darrell D. Halsey
Kirk W. Halsey
Harvey Haltom
Cheavest E. Ham
Welborne Hamble
John E. Hamblin
William R. Hamblin II
Charles E. Hambrick, Jr.
Eddie Hamilton
Jack W. Hamilton
Jerry Hamilton
John F. Hamilton
Kay Hamilton
Marsha K. Hamilton
Maurice Hamilton
Millard Fillmore Hamilton
Raymond Earl Hamilton
Roger W. Hamilton
Wayne T. Hamilton
Bruce L. Hamlin
Joseph H. Hamlin
Ronald W. Hamm
Fred R. Hammer
Carl Hammond

James Hammond
Peter H. Hammond
Robert E. Hammond
DeAtley Hampton
Robert W. Hampton
Ambrose Hamrick
William Hamrick
Brent Trevor Hancock
James A. Hancock
James R. Hancock
Kathleen R. Hancock
Robert Hancock
Roy E. Hancock
William A. Hancock, Jr.
Vernon Hands
Bill Handshy
Emmett Hanes
Mike D. Hanes
Cecil M. Haney
Donald F. Haney
Gary Haney
Ralph E. Haney
Rita M. Haney
Robert J. Hanigar
Mary A. Hankins
Ronald E. Hankins
Roger G. Hankovich
Bill Hanna
Francis Hanna
H. E. Hanna
Nequita Kay Hanna
Thomas M. Hanna
William E. Hanna
Barbara A. Hannah
Charles Hannah
Gail A. Hanoch
John W. Hanoch, Jr.
David G. Hansard
Robert Hansbro
Daniel G. Hansen
Donald Hansen
Joe K. Hansen
Leonard Hansen
Richard F. Hansen
Robert L. Hansen
Leonard Hansen, Jr.
W. G. Hanson
Randy Haralson
Calvin E. Hardage
Gordon T. Harden
Robert D. Harden
John Martin Harder
Joseph R. Harder

Lee P. Harder
Charles M. Hardesty
Neal Hardesty
Verlan Hardin
Fred Harding
True Harding
John S. Hardwick
Willis Hardwick
Carl Hardy
William R. Hardy
Earl H. Hargis
James Hargis
Tom B. Hargis
Tom E. Hargis
Amon Harjo
Sylvia Harjo
Sam E. Harlan
Clyte K. Harlen
John R. Harlin
Larry Harlin
Levi Harlin, Jr.
Jay P. Harlow
Riley Harlow
Warren Harlow
Ben Harmon
David Harmon
Gayle Harmon
James L. Harmon
Johnny Harmon
Jon B. Harmon
Mark Alan Harmon
Phillip L. Harmon
Bill Harned
Mike Harned
Chockpichai Harnsongkram
Alan G. Harper
Barbara Harper
Bruce Harper
David Harper
Don E. Harper
Ford D. Harper
Forest D. Harper
Howard Harper
James Harper
Marilyn Harper
Owen Harper
Randle E. Harper
William F. Harper
Robert L. Harpool
Jerry E. Harrell
Steve Harrell
Charles D. Harrelson
Patrick K. Harrelson

Averial Harrill
Robert E. Harrill
Ronald D. Harrill
Bill B. Harris
Bobby L. Harris
Carmon C. Harris
Carol Lynn Harris
Charles H. Harris
Edgar H. Harris
Edgar H. Harris
Gaylon B. Harris
Gene Thomas Harris
Harold Harris
Hugh V. Harris
Jack E. Harris
James J. Harris
Jamie H. Harris
Jefferson W. Harris
John R. Harris
John S. Harris
Linda L. Harris
Michael T. Harris
Paul C. Harris
Richard W. Harris
Rose M. Harris
Steven G. Harris
Ted L. Harris
Albert A. Harrison
Ben Harrison
Joe B. Harrison
John F. Harrison
Joseph H. Harrison
Mary E. Harrison
Percy L. Harrison
Ralph Harrison
Roger Harrison
Nobel S. Harrison, Jr.
R. L. Harrison, Jr.
Gary J. Harrod
Oran Harrod
Ben Harrover
Charles Hart
Chris Hart
Harvey C. Hart
Paul Hart
R. M. Hart
Lana S. Hartig
Kelly Hartley
Barbara L. Hartman
Donald O. Hartman
Kim Dwayne Hartman
Valroy D. Hartman
Jimmy W. Harvey

Lonia Harvey
Warnock Harwell
Don E. Hashagen
Ralph W. Haskins
Charles D. Haskins, Jr.
Ronald Hass
Kenneth J. Hassinger
Boyette S. Hasty
Jewell R. Hatch
Fred M. Hatcher
John Hatcher
Ed Hatcher, Jr.
Charles Hatfield
Mark W. Hatfield
Clark A. Hathcoat
Madge L. Hauenstein
Harley Haug
Mark E. Haught
Mary Michelle Haught
Maxine V. Haught
John L. Hausam
Larry J. Hauser
Thomas J. Hauser
Bernard R. Havard
Thomas R. Havelaar
Terry E. Havins
Robert Hawden
Lewis C. Hawes
Michael R. Hawk
Gary L. Hawkins
Jeffrey A. Hawkins
John Charles Hawkins
Robert R. Hawkins
Charles Hawks
Jackson D. Hawks
Donald Haxel
William Hayden
Barry Hayes
Belinda Darlene Hayes
Ben Hayes
Bill Hayes
Charles N. Hayes
Gary L. Hayes
Jeffery Paul Hayes
Lester C. Hayes
Wilkie H. Hayes
William C. Hayes
Harold A. Hayes, Jr.
Joe Hayhurst
Douglas A. Hayne
Phillip G. Hayne
Frank L. Haynes
Joe H. Haynes

Mable Crownover Haynes
Elmer T. Haynie
Norris W. Haynie
Paul G. Hays
Stokely D. Hays
Eugene S. Hays, Jr.
Ronald J. Hazday
Allan R. Hazelrigg
John C. Hazelrigg
Donald Hazelton
Gary R. Hazen
Herbert Hazzard
Allen Head
Frances Lynn Head
David Headrick
Herman Headrick
Michael Don Headrick
Arthur Heaney
Patrick Heard
William Hearne
David Scott Hearon
Robert Heatley
Joseph Heberlein
Doyle G. Heddins
Jack Hedge
Jack R. Hedge, Jr.
Tommy A. Hedgepath
Don R. Hedgpath
Marvin Hedgpath
David Hedrick
Joe Hedrick
Phylliss R. Hedrick
Patrick J. Heenan
Billy H. Heeter
Phillip Heffner
Roy E. Heffner
Delores C. Hefner
Flint Heide
Bille L. Heilgman
Richard Heiligman
Thomas A. Heilman
Bob Heiman
Gerald Heisler
Grant Heisler
John M. Heithaus
Jim Helbing
John E. Helbing
Ricky A. Heldenbrand
Stephen Everett Heldenbrand
Dicky L. Helm
James C. Helm
Randolf E. Helm
Michael R. Helms

Richard J. Helms
Virginia Ann Helton
William E. Hembree
John A. Henderson
Sammy D. Henderson
John T. Hendricks
Judith A. Hendricks
Marcus J. Hendricks
Richard Hendricks
Tim Hendricks
Vincent Hendricks
Barney Hendrickson
Bruce Hendrickson
James E. Hendrickson
Larry E. Hendrickson
Donald Ray Hendrix
Jesse H. Hendrix
Jewell R. Hendrix
Enoch A. Henley
James K. Henley
Kirk L. Henley
William L. Hennebergar
Charles W. Henning
Albert L. Henninger
Joseph L. Henrie
Clyde L. Henry
Fred Henry
Gary W. Henry
Horace Henry
Johnny David Henry
Paul P. Henry
Ronnie F. Henry
William F. Henry
Harold E. Henshall
Robert C. Henshaw
Dennis Hensley
James Ross Hensley
Pete Hensley
Frank Hensley, Jr.
Bobby J. Henson
Carl R. Henson
Charles W. Henson
Donald C. Henson
Glen Henson
Jack Henthorn
Warren L. Henthorn
Cloyse A. Hepler
Robert H. Hepp
Robert E. Hepworth
Cary B. Herbert
James C. Herbert
Janice Hereford
William A. Heritage

R. R. Hermes
William Hermes
David Michael Hermsdorfer
Mark Allen Hermsdorfer
Luis A. Hernandez
Avon Herndon
Jack H. Herndon
James R. Herndon
Dewey R. Herndon, Jr.
Thomas Herold
Ronald O. Herr
Donald Herrin
DeJarnett Herring
Ivan L. Herring
Jack Herring
Clifford D. Herrington
Ivy P. Herrington
James W. Herron
William H. Herron, Jr.
Max Herschberger
Ivan M. Hersh
James W. Hershberger
Gilbert Hess
Laurence A. Hess
Michael J. Hess
Norman B. Hess
Robert Hess
Norman B. Hess II
John M. Hestbeck
Clyde E. Hester
Don V. Hester
Kelley Hester
Neil D. Hester
Ted Hester
Verl Hester
Randy W. Hetherington
David A. Heuglin
Arthur G. Hewett
Pat B. Hewett
David P. Hewitt
Jim Hewitt
Kenneth H. Hewitt
Leonard D. Hewitt
William O. Hewitt
Woodrow Hewlett
Robert Heydt
L.R. Hiatt
Winston R. Hiatt
Hilbert A. Hibbs
Emery Hickman
Jeffrey P. Hickman
N. O. Hickman
C. D. Hicks

Craig H. Hicks
Lyndall Hicks
Robert R. Hicks
Ronald R. Hicks
John M. Higbee
Billy J. Higeons
Cathey A. Higgins
James E. Higgins
John E. Higgins
William R. Higgins
Glenda S. High
Mr. Jack E. Highers
John E. Highland
John Highland
Clyde C. Hightower
James Hightower
Bill Higley
Coy W. Hildebrand
Maloy Hildebrand
Floyd Hilderbrandt
James Melbourne Hildy
Archie B. Hill
Bill M. Hill
Bob K. Hill
Charles J. Hill
Charles W. Hill
Don Hill
Garrett L. Hill
Gary Hill
Giles A. Hill
Helen C. Hill
J.R. Hill
John D. Hill
John R. Hill
Larry J. Hill
Loretta Janice Hill
Norman Hill
Paul T. Hill
Philip Hill
Phyllis Jane Hill
Robert C. Hill
Robert K. Hill
Robert Hill
Ted W. Hill
Wilbert B. Hill
Bud Hillhouse
Charlie Hillhouse
Walter R. Hillhouse
William B. Hillman
James Hilton
Seth C. Hilton
John hinch
Robert Hinchee

Thomas J. Hinchey
James Hindman
Joseph Hindman
William M. Hindman
Ernest Hinds
Paul H. Hinds
Tom Hinds
William Hinds
Joseph T. Hine
Ted Hine
Blaney E. Hines
Carson D. Hines
Jon J. Hines
William B. Hines
William K. Hines II
George Hinkle
Keith Hinkle
Vickie S. Hinkle
Roy Hinman
William Hinton
Richard L. Hirsch
Albert Hirschfield
Kenneth R. Hirst
Albert D. Hirzel
Bobby J. Hise
Lloyd V. Hise
Lynn Hise
Steve E. Hiser
Richard E. Hisey
Edward Hitt
Jay T. Hitt
Michael D. Hix
Hal J. Hixon
Mark H. Hixson
Judy M. Hoag
Margaret Catherine Hoag
William D. Hoag
Clyde Hoagland
Lyle Hobble
Jesse Bryant Hobbs
Mary A. Hobbs
Thomas H. Hocker
Jack Hodgden
Lawrence D. Hodgden
Paul A. Hodge, Jr.
Ernest Hodges
Gilbert Hodges
Joe Hodges
Larry L. Hodges
Lloyd L. Hodges
Loyd L. Hodges
Mark Hodges
Richard M. Hodges

Robert L. Hodges
Lloyd L. Hodges III
Allan R. Hoegg
Bruce Hoffman
Charles M. Hoffman
Clarence Hoffman
George F. Hoffman
Jack A. Hoffman
Jack C. Hoffman
Margaret Ellen Hoffman
Mikel Hoffman
Robert Hoffman
Richard Hofschulte
Campbell Hogan
Ralph S. Hogan
Robert L. Hogan
G.W. Hogue
John A. Hohenstein
John D. Hohmann
Randolph A. Hoke
Terry R. Holaday
James Holbird
Carl D. Holbrook
Carl Holbrook
Lester W. Holbrook
Gary Holcomb
Billy Holdeman
George Holden
John L. Holden II
Charles A. Holden, Jr.
Richard L. Holder
Steve Holderby
Willard W. Holderby
Charles L. Holderman
Donald E. Holding
Kenneth L. Holeman
Leonard L. Holeman
Kirk H. Holiman
John D. Holiway
John K. Holland
Larry F. Holland
Robert Holland
Theodore Holland
Leslie R. Holland, Jr.
Thomas Hollands
Charles D. Holler
John V. Holley
Kruse M. Holliday
Paul A. Hollingshead
Alton E. Hollingsworth
Jerry M. Hollingsworth
Jerry Hollingsworth
Robert B. Hollingsworth

Stanley D. Hollingsworth
Leslie J. Hollis
Mark Howard Hollis
Ernest Hollopster
Bart Hope Holloway
Donald R. Holloway
John C. Holloway
O. Ray Holloway
Ray W. Holloway
Gerald L. Holm
Joe Holman
William S. Holman
Dennis L. Holmes
George Holmes
Gordon Holmes
Harry D. Holmes
James S. Holmes
Michael W. Holmes
Ronald F. Holmes
Steve R. Holmes
Gary Holmstead
Stephen Holoviak
James A. Holston
Charles M. Holt
Gordon Holt
Joanna Holt
John W. Holt
Johnnie R. Holt
Lawrence Holt
M. T. Holt
Major T. Holt
Michael A. Holt
Michael B. Holt
Tommy M. Holt
John E. Holton
Richard Frederick Holtszchue
Lenoy Holzemer
John Homer
Robert Donald Homer
Jack Homra, Jr.
Danny Leon Honeycut
Warren L. Hood
Nick R. Hood, Jr.
C.R. Hooker
Paul W. Hooker
James E. Hooper
John K. Hooper
Jon Hooper
Ted Hooper
Jack P. Hoopes
Mervyn E. Hooten
Charles M. Hoover
James Hoover

John R. Hoover
Max Hoover
Richard L. Hopeman
Samuel Hopkins
Rick L. Hopper
Stanley J. Hopper
George Horany
Oscar L. Horany
Hugh Horn
William L. Horn
Donna Sue Hornbeak
William Hornbeck
John E. Horne
Rex Horne
Carl J. Horner
Jack Horner
Theodore Horner
Barbara J. Horton
David Horton
Dick Horton
Charles Hoskins
James V. Hoss
Claud L. Hostetter
James F. Hostler
Charles R. Houck
Rocky Houdek
Ernie J. Hough
George C. Hough
Graydon M. Hough
Grover Houghton
William J. Houliston III
Tom Houser
Woody A. Houser
Trent Housley
Harold T. Houston
Jack E. Houston
Richard T. Houston
Michael L. Houtz
Earl Howard
Eugene C. Howard
Frank Howard
Gene Howard
George J. Howard
Guy O. Howard
James D. Howard
James E. Howard
John R. Howard
John Howard
Kenneth Howard
Lee R. Howard
Martin B. Howard
Michael Howard
Prentice C. Howard

Ralph C. Howard
Vincent M. Howard
Walter Howard
Stephen L. Howarth
Charles L. Howe
Michael L. Howe
Ted Howe
David Howell
Donovan E. Howell
George K. Howell
James R. Howell
Juanita K. Howell
Maurice Howell
Robert Howell
Robert R. Howell, Jr.
Witcher C. Howenstine
Frank C. Howk
Roy Howland
L. Hoxsie
Charles R. Hoyle
Harry Hoyt
Kenneth Hoyt
Larry S. Hrdlicks
John Hron
Pete Hronopulos
Homer H. Hubbard
Jim Hubbard
Kim Hubbard
Ralph W. Hubbard
Stanely Hubbard
Dennis G. Huchteman
Ralph Huchteman
William R. Huckleby
Creed T. Huddleston
Pleasant J. Huddleston
Donald P. Hudgins
Bobby J. Hudiburg
George Hudman
Calvin Hudson
Gerald W. Hudson
Herbert Hudson
James R. Hudson
Lytle Hudson
Orville D. Hudson
Perry E. Hudson
Ralph O. Hudson
Ralph Hudson
Ray C. Hudson
Richard A. Hudson
Richard E. Hudson
Richard N. Hudson
Rodney P. Hudson
Steven H. Hudson

Tommy Hudson
Reed O. Hudson III
Bob L. Huff
Carroll E. Huff
Howard S. Huff
Leon H. Huff
Ralph R. Huff
Robert Huff
Sherman Huffman
Tony Huffman
Leslie Tilden Huffman, Jr.
Charles R. Huggins
Peter Huggler III
Evelyn E. Hughes
Harry A. Hughes
Huber Hughes
James D. Hughes
James R. Hughes
Lloyd M. Hughes
Michael G. Hughes
Paula J. Hughes
R. P. Hughes
Carla M. Huisman
Bryon L. Huitt
Michael H. Hulings
David C. Hull
Terry L. Hull
Homer Hulme
Sam I. Hulse
Joe Hulsey
Charles Humbird
Glen D. Humes
Harvey C. Humes
Mervin L. Hummel
Robert Hummer
Gary R. Humphrey
Buel H. Humphreys
Robert H. Humphreys
William H. Humppi
Thomas C. Hundley
H. R. Humphrey
Don R. Hunsaker
Olive M. Hunsaker
Albert C. Hunt
Alonzo J. Hunt
Dan W. Hunt
Gregory Murray Hunt
John G. Hunt
Richard Hunt
Rudolph N. Hunt
Thomas Hunt
Walter L. Hunt
Warren J. Hunt

Woody Hunt
Vernon G. Hunt III
Arthur A. Hunter
Charles W. Hunter
Clinton A. Hunter
Dean H. Hunter
Frieda J. Hunter
Jerry M. Hunter
John S. Hunter
Larry M. Hunter
No N. Hunter
T. Hunter
Taylor V. Hunter
Dean E. Hunziker
Steve R. Hunziker
William C. Hurelson
John A. Hurlburt
Billy M. Hurst
Noel Hurst
Robert Hurst
Eugene C. Huss
Jack E. Husted
Jack L. Huston
Walter L. Hutcheson
Charles R. Hutchings
Charles F. Hutchinson
Gayle Hutchinson
William R. Hutchinson
James M. Hutchison
Patricia R. Hutson
Donald E. Hutto
James R. Hutto
Warren D. Hutton
Michael D. Hyatt
Douglas S. Hyde
Thomas C. Hyden
Jack A. Hyfield
Oscar Hyland
Inge E. Ibex
Dan A. Idsardi
John P. Iglehart
Donald J. Igou
Anthony S. Igwe
Robert D. Iliff
A. B. Imel
Nancy Ince
Terry Wayne Ince
William Walter Ingersoll
William R. Ingle
Albert Ingram
Duane G. Ingram
Jerry S. Ingram
Perry D. Inhofe

Thomas L. Irby
Eugene Iron
Gary L. Irons
Joe D. Irons
John H. Irving
Herbert G. Irwin
John R. Irwin
David Isaacs
Elwyn Isaacs
Ernest W. Isom II
Lonnie Ison
Henry D. Israel
Richard C. Israel
Bert Ives
Steven C. Ives
Don Ivey
Frank Ivy
Lee F. Ivy
C.J. Ivy, Jr.
Bill C. Jackman
Janie Ann Jacks
Brack E. Jackson
Bruce D. Jackson
Carrol Jackson
Dixie Jackson
Don Jackson
Flora R. Jackson
Glen A. Jackson
Grant W. Jackson
John H. Jackson
Kerry D. Jackson
Laurence C. Jackson
Murrell Jackson
Randy Dale Jackson
Richard T. Jackson
Robert W. Jackson
William G. Jackson
Thomas O. Jackson III
Sylvester Jackson, Jr.
Ula F. Jackson, Jr.
Alberta J. Jacobs
Brian Michael Jacobs
Frank J. Jacobs
Gloria L. Jacobs
John Jacobs
Mark Christopher Jacobs
Russell L. Jacobs
William G. Jacobs
Russell Jacobson
Walter W. Jacoby
Freeda Jaggers
Arthur James
Clarence W. James

Harry James
Morris E. James
Thomas H. James
William J. James
John Jarvie
Gary Jarvis
Richard E. Javine
Edward C. Jay
Lloyd R. Jeffern
Oscar Jeffers
Richard L. Jeffers
Roy Jeffers
William T. Jeffers
Clarence Jeffress
Joseph H. Jeffress
Marvin L. Jeffries
David Jeffs
Richard Jelama
A. L. Jenkins
Allen W. Jenkins
Andrew L. Jenkins
Asa Lee Jenkins
Charles Jenkins
Darrell Jenkins
David A. Jenkins
Ernest Jenkins
Larry R. Jenkins
Lawrence L. Jenkins
Stuart W. Jenkins
Walter Jenkins
Arlie E. Jenks
Bill P. Jennings
Dan Jennings
Dave Jennings
Frank Jennings
George H. Jennings
Jeff Jennings
John R. Jennings
John Jennings
Larry D. Jennings
M.R. Jennings
Mary M. Jennings
Raymond Jennings
Stephen Jennings
Raymond J. Jennings, Jr.
John Jeppson
George T. Jepsen, Jr.
Roscoe M. Jernigan
Philip L. Jerome
Bob Jessup
Stewart L. Jessup
Jack W. Jessup III
Jack Jessup Jr.

Bill L. Jeter
Ronnie D. Jett
Michael L. Jewell
Edward Jillson
Robert L. Jinks
Larry Joe
Larry C.Johns
Lawrence Johns
Patsy C. Johns
Harvey B. Johns, Jr.
Bobby G. Johnson
Carl Johnson
Carol E. Johnson
Charles W. Johnson
Claude J. Johnson
Dale H. Johnson
Darwin Johnson
David A. Johnson
David M. Johnson
Dewey Johnson
Edward F. Johnson
Ernest Johnson
Frederick Johnson
Gene R. Johnson
George H. Johnson
Gerald F. Johnson
Gerald L. Johnson
Gerald W. Johnson
Gerry Leroy Johnson
Glen C. Johnson
Greg K. Johnson
Gregory L. Johnson
Harold J. Johnson
Homer F. Johnson
Hugh L. Johnson
Ima L. Johnson
J. D. Johnson
J. G. Johnson
J. T. Johnson
James A. Johnson
James H. Johnson
Jerry A. Johnson
Jerry D. Johnson
Jerry R. Johnson
Jimmy E. Johnson
Joe N. Johnson
Joe Johnson
Johnny Johnson
John W. Johnson
Keith Leon Johnson
Kenneth L. Johnson
Lawrence Johnson
Leroy H. Johnson

Lewis Johnson
Lila J. Johnson
Lindsey L. Johnson
Michael E. Johnson
Mike Johnson
Nelda Maria Johnson
Pat Johnson
Paul E. Johnson
Richard L. Johnson
Ronnie Lee Johnson
Sam Johnson
Shirley Evelyn Johnson
Steve Johnson
Thomas Johnson
Travis Johnson
Troy G. Johnson
Troy O. Johnson
Truman Johnson
Vern L. Johnson
William B. Johnson
William D. Johnson
William J. Johnson
Willie Johnson
John C. Johnson, Jr.
Pat Johnson, Jr.
Arlus W. Johnston
Bill S. Johnston
Billy B. Johnston
Burl Johnston
Hugh L. Johnston
John E. Johnston
Mont Johnston
Paul Johnston
Ralph K. Johnston
Russell C. Johnston
William W. Johnston
Aubrey Jones
B.G. Jones
Bill Jones
Buford M. Jones
Cary D. Jones
Charles E. Jones
Charles Jones
Clarence Jones
Clifford Jones
David S. Jones
David W. Jones
Donald Ross Jones
Doris Elaine Jones
Duncan R. Jones
Earl C. Jones
Eugene Jones
Fred I. Jones

Fredric B. Jones
George M. Jones
George William Jones
Gerald W. Jones
Harold R. Jones
Harold Jones
Howard M. Jones
Hugh D. Jones
James R. Jones
James T. Jones
James Jones
James Jones
Jerry L. Jones
Jo K. Jones
Joann Jones
Kenneth R. Jones
Laura E. Jones
Leonard Jones
Lillian E. Jones
Malcolm D. Jones
Malcome L. Jones
Marvin Jones
Mavis L. Jones
Monte P. Jones
Norman N. Jones
Paul Jones
Preston Jones
Richard E. Jones
Richard P. Jones
Riley L. Jones
Robert B. Jones
Robert D. Jones
Robert J. Jones
Robert R. Jones
Robert W. Jones
Robert W. Jones
Robert Jones
Ronald C. Jones
Royce H. Jones
Ruth G. Jones
Sherman R. Jones
Steve F. Jones
Steven L. Jones
William C. Jones
William E. Jones
William Jones
U.V. Jones II
Robert Jones Jr.
Harold Jones, Jr.
Kenneth E. Jones, Jr.
Roy L. Jones, Jr.
William R. Jones, Jr.
John P. Jonte

Arthur J. Jordan
Johnny L. Jordan
Laurence Jordan
Patrick G. Jordan
Mark T. Jordan III
Don F. Jordan, Jr.
Carl A. Jorski
Duane L. Josephson
Danny W. Joslin
Jack Joyce
James L. Joyner
Russell M. Joyner
Charles Judd
Alan G. Judkins
Herbert Melvin Judkins
Lewis Jump
Ronald W. Jungling
William P. Junk, Jr.
Detler Justus
Lawrence Kahl
Sam Kahn
Mary J. Kaho
Lee Kalivoda
William R. Kambs
Kevan M. Kamer
Loyal Kamm
Jack R. Kappler
Peter W. Karlak
Robert E. Karnes
Gary P. Karr
Ronald C. Kasl
James T. Kassick
John M. Kates
Phillip Kates
Raymond E. Kating, Jr.
Myron Katz
Richard Kauffman
Robert L. Kayser
Patti Karen Keadle
Howard Kearney
Leland Kearns
Jay L. Keefer
Jim Keels
Roland P. Keely
J.W. Keen
James W. Keen
Thad Keenan
Timothy D. Keeton
Charles C. Kegelman
Lew A. Keim
Elmo E. Keirsey
James C. Keirsey
Charles E. Keith

George V. Keith
James Keith
John E. Keith
N.A. Keithley
Clyde A. Keizor
Byron Kellehan
Alvin R. Keller
Elven W. Keller
William S. Keller
Allen R. Kelley
Carolyn S. Kelley
Dennis D. Kelley
Jim B. Kelley
John T. Kelley
Lawrence Kelley
Raymond Clay Kelley
Roy Kelley
Susan Y. Kelley
James M. Kelln
Tommy A. Kellogg
Billy D. Kelly
Charles Ray Kelly
Horst R. Kelly
Jack Kelly
John A. M. Kelly
Larry Kelly
Paul J. Kelly
Rady M. Kelly
Tom L. Kelly
Ulis B. Kelly
Don M. Kelsey
Henry E. Kelsey
Howland Kelsey
Paul G. Kelsey
Rue W. Kelsey
Dick H. Kelso
John A. Kemler
John E. Kemp
Michael J. Kemp
O.K. Kemp
Merlyn D. Kemph
Carl T. Kemsha
Clyde O. Kendall
Nancy G. Kendall
Sammy J. Kendall
William A. Kendall
Dennis C. Kendrick
Morris D. Kendrick
Vivian Kendrick
Eugene R. Kendrigin
Robert E. Kenly
Robert E. Kennamer
Marhsall E. Kennard

Garry P. Kennedy
Jack B. Kennedy
Max W. Kennedy
Stephen Kennedy
Julie Elizabeth Kennon
Troye B. Kennon
J.L. Kenslow
Ray P. Kent
Leland H. Kepford
Henry F. Keplinger
Hoyt Kerby
Edd Kerkow
Jack Kern
Jerry Kern
Harry Kerns
Ronald L. Kerns
David Kerr
Robert Mansel Kerr
John D. Kersey
Viron T. Kersh
Fred Kershner
Vernon L. Ketchum
Jon R. Ketzler
Michael A. Keuhr
George W. Key
Hugh B. Key
Robert G. Keys
Sam Keys
Robert L. Kidd
Robert L. Kidd, Jr.
James H. Kidder
Charles B. Kidson
Dennis W. Kiefer
Jimmy Kiener
William Kiesel
George V. Kieth
Blaine O. Kifer
H. T. Kight
Joe W. Kight
M. A. Kiken
Vernon L. Kiker
Bobby G. Kilgore
Denton Kilgore
Don R. Kilgore
Edward Kilgore
Melvin D. Kilgore
George R. Killam
Tom A. Killian
James K. Killion
Robert E. Killion
Ronald A. Killingsworth
Leonard D. Kimball
Gerald Kimbley

George W. Kimbrell
Leroy Kime
Ronald E. Kime
Charles Kimes
James H. Kincannon, Jr.
Carol Ann King
Frank Wayne King
Garland King
George F. King
Gregory C. King
Harold V. King
John M. King
John P. King
Julian King
Kennith L. King
Mary Belinda King
Michael R. King
Milam M. King
Phillip R. King
Rex A. King
Richard S. King
Richard King
Rico H. King
Ronald D. King
W.K. King
Warren King
Milam King, Jr.
Don D. Kinkaid
Alfred Kinkead
Gordon L. Kinley
Martin F. Kinnaman
Lawrence Kinnan
Milford E. Kinnard
Louis C. Kinnear
Michael G. Kinney
Robert L. Kinney
Ludie E. Kinney, Jr.
Robert L. Kinney, Jr.
Ronny L. Kinnikin
William R. Kinsey
Hoyt Kirby
Jimmy D. Kirby
Thomas G. Kirby
Thomas L. Kirby
William R. Kirby
Lewis E. Kircher
Albert R. Kirk
Sherron Kirk
Gary D. Kirkendall
Kenneth Kirkland
Robert J. Kirkland
Darwin Kirkman
W. Kisner

Gerry H. Kistler
Frank Emerson Kistler II
Bobby Kitchen
William A. Kitchen
Richard Kitching
Floyd Kite
Kenneth Ray Kittrell
Brad Klar
George E. Klein
James Klein
Dan Kleindorfer
Kermit C. Kleinsteiber
Stanley W. Kleinsteiber
John E. Klentos
Elton R. Kline
Walter Kline
Larry D. Klinefelter
Billy L. Klutts
Gary B. Klutts
George S. Knapp
Richard Knapp
Thomas J. Knapp
Thomas J. Knapp, Jr.
Sammy H. Kneese
Barbara A. Knight
David E. Knight
Edward Knight
James P. Knight
Janet Louise Knight
Kenneth S. Knight
Mark C. Knight
Melvin Thomas Knight
Walter Knight
Wilfred K. Knight
Dean B. Knight, Jr.
William P. Knisley
Clarence W. Knollenberg
A.M. Knothe
R. Knowles
Dwight R. Knowlton
James P. Knox
Peter J. Knox
Robert F. Knox
William R. Knox
James W. Knox III
Douglas R. Koch
Harlan Koch
Richard M. Koch
Michael P. Koda
George Koehne
Everett Koester
William Koester
Steven C. Kohler

Thomas Wayne Kohler
Jerome L. Kohn
J. L. Kohn, Jr.
William R. Kolb
Phillip Koons
Walter E. Koons
Paul T. Koontz
Luther H. Kopanke
Henry F. Koplinger
Herman Clay Korthala
James Korwin
Lawrence C. Kost
Martha S. Koster
Ersel J. Kostka
Thomas F. Koszarek
Leland G. Kozar
Norman Kraker
Edwin S. Kramer
Richard Kramer
Harry R. Kramp
Fred Krannig
Carl Kreplin
Jerry D. Kreplin
Hugh W. Kring
Thomas Arthur Krittenbrink
Dennis D. Krivohlavek
Robert B. Kroeger
Billy E. Krouse
Eulyess G. Krouse
Norman F. Kroutil
William R. Kroutil
Walter Krumrei
Helen V. Krupnik
Harold E. Kubin
Don Kuebler, Jr.
Michael Kuehr
Gregory M. Kuester
G. Kuhn, Jr.
Larry Kuns
Ricardo A. Kurten
Albert Kushner
Robert W. Kuykendall
George H. Kyme
David Kyser
Kenneth Ray Labrum
Russell Anthony Labrum
William A. Lackey
Woodrow Lackey
Robert Lacombe
Dorothy Lacy
Karen M. Lacy
Linda G. Lacy
Ronald Lacy

Harry H. Ladd, Jr.
Edwin Ladlee
Joe LaFerry
Glen LaFiette
W. D. LaFolette
Michael A. LaFrance
John D. Lahmeyer
Howard Lain
George Lair
Michael G. Lakey
Ercle Lamar
Theodore R. LaMar
Harry S. Lamb
Mercy Lamb
George Lamberson
Don E. Lambert
Russuell Lambert
James W. Lamm
Lee Lampton
Maurice E. Lampton
Benjamin H. Lancaster
Jack Lancaster
Lucy Gayle Lancaster
Ray Lancaster
Robert Lancaster
Randy M. Lance
Gregory A. Land
Richard M. Land
Frank H. Lander
Larry S. Landers
Robert Landes
John B. Landes, Jr.
John Landess
Leon Landis
David L. Landman
Jimmie C. Landrith
Benson F. Landrum
Benny Lane
Darrell L. Lane
James W. Lane
Jerry Lane
John R. Lane
Marion A. Lane
Peter P. Lane
Robert C. Lane
Roger K. Lane
Roy Lane
Kenneth R. LaNear
Michael J. Lang
George Lange
Phil Lange
Guy Randolph Langley
James Langley

William J. Langmade
David P. Langston
Richard C. Langston
Robert M. Langston
Preston H. Langworthy
Hubert D. Lanier
Gary L. Lankister
Lawrence M. Lanman
William Lanning
Rodney Lansdowne
William L. Lanton
Lawrence Lantow
Roy Lantz
Roger F. LaPlante
Barry R. Larkin
Cheryl Lyn Larkin
Kenneth E. Larkin
Larry Larkin
Carl Jack J. Larsen
Bill A. Larson
Jack Larson
Jess Larson
K.P. Larson
Larry Larson
James S. Lasater
Eugene H. Lash
Nicholas L. Lassiter
Charles Laster
David Laster
William Laswell
Elmer D. Latham
Larry Latham
Robert J. Lathrop
Thomas Latta
Roger Laubach
Doug Laubhan
Frank J. Laumer
Sidney Laune
Daniel B. Lawhorn
Elbert C. Lawhorn
Alvin L. Lawrence
Deborah M. Lawrence
Franklin Michael Lawrence
Granville C. Lawrence
Mark D. Lawrence
Richard Lawrence
Roy A. Lawrence
Robert L. Lawrence III
Robert L. Lawrence, Jr.
Claude D. Lawson
Donald D. Lawson
Edward Lawson
Kenneth Lawson

Edgar Lawton
Gene J. Lawyer
Walter Lay
Owen P. Layden
George H. Leach
James D. Leach
Thomas B. Leahy
Randy Leathers
David W. Leavitt
Donald L. Leavitt
Gale Ledbetter
Homer Ledbetter
David Ledford
Robert G. Ledterman
Alice M. Lee
Betty J. Lee
Corey W. Lee
Edward D. Lee
Gary T. Lee
George O. Lee
James R. Lee
Joe S. Lee
Lynn A. Lee
Robert E. Lee
Robert K. Lee
Stephen Lee
Terry R. Lee
Wilbur P. Lee
Forest L. Leech
Bertram M. Leecraft
Abbie L. Leeds
Robert Henry Leeds
Charles Leedy
Hugh H. Leeper
Donald R. LeFan
David L. Leffel
Harold S. Leffel
Richmond Legate
Dan L. LeGrant
Wayne Legro
Clayton G. Lehmann
Larry Leibrock
Larry Leitner
Joseph M. LeMaster
Richard D. LeMay
Mary Lembcke
Robert Lembcke
David W. Lemmon
Ronnie E. Lemmon
Don Lemon
James D. Lemon
Thomas W. Lemon
Fred D. Lemons

Kay Lemons
Patti L. Lemons
Robert Lemons
Herman Lemons, Jr.
Joseph A. Lennox, Jr.
David G. Leon
Francisco A. Leon
Richard A. Leon
James M. Leonard
Roger Leonard
Thomas Leonard
Philip E. Leonhardt
James M. Lepree
Philip D. LePus
Richard David Lermy
Richard H. Lermy
John R. Leslie
Joseph B. Leslie
Wilbur J. Leslie
Hubert Lesperance
Millard Lessenger
George W. Lester
Hubert Lester
Mark C. Lester
Elmer C. Lette
LeRoy Lette
Kam F. Leung
Raymond E. Leverich
Larry Levern
Jerry W. Levin
Michael L. Levin
Alvin L. Levine
Robert F. Levine
Leroy G. Lewin
Allen L. Lewis
Arvle Lewis
Ben Lewis
Bill Lewis
Bobby Ben Lewis
Bobby S. Lewis
Charles Lewis
Dana Lewis
Donald Lewis
Frank G. Lewis
Gary N. Lewis
Haven M. Lewis
Herman D. Lewis
Jackie L. Lewis
James P. Lewis
Jaunez V. Lewis
John P. Lewis
Robert B. Lewis
Rodney M. Lewis

Ronald D. Lewis
Tommy W. Lewis
William J. Lewis
William T. Lewis
Willie N. Lewis
Yondel G. Lewis
Garland H. Lichty
Howard Liddell
James E. Lieberman
Robert C. Lienhardt
William J. Lierman
Dale Lightner
Richard R. Ligon
Henry M. Liibs
David J. Likes
Jay E. Lile
John Liles
Ronald D. Liles
John Lillard
Ross H. Lillard
Thomas Lillard
Kent R. Lillenberg
Thomas F. Lilly
Fred Limbaugh
George R. Lincoln
Steven B. Lindauer
John H. Lindensmith
Don Linder
Richard G. Lindholdt
John W. Lindley
James E. Lindsay
Ray G. Lindsay
Richard D. Liner
Jeanne M. Lingenfelter
John A. Lingenfelter
Paul B. Lingenfelter
Tom Lingenfelter
Virginia N. Linihan
Gary G. Link
John A. Link
Harold G. Linn
Kenneth Linson
William D. Linton
Clark C. Lipe
Arthur Lippa
Jay S. Lipshy
Carl F. Lister
Perry Litchfield
Ronal E. Litsey
David Little
Derrell C. Little
Jasper W. Little
Maj. Ron W. Little

R. E. "Gene" Little
Stephen Little
John M. Littlefield
Keaton R. Littlefield
I.B. Littleton
Jimmy D. Littrell
Ed M. Livermore
John T. Livingston
Richard L. Livingston
Harold C. Lloyd
Leon Lloyd
Ralph Lloyd
Walter D. Lloyd
Charles W. Locke
Victor Locke
Craig Lockett
G.L. Lockhard
Allen Lockhart
Richard G. Lockhart
Melvin N. Locklear
Jim Lockwood
Joe Lodies
John Lodies
John D. Loeb
Samuel H. Loeffler
Steven D. Loffer
Carl M. Loftis
Eugene E. Loftis
Roy Loftis
Tom D. Loftis
Cliff Logan
Joe D. Logan
John D. Logan
John L. Logan
Oscar Logan
J. M. Logsdon
Dan Logue
Phil M. Lohman
Ralph E. Lohnbakken
David R. Lohrke
Phillip W. Lomax
Charles G. Long
Darrell J. Long
David C. Long
Dorinda Sue Long
Douglas D. Long
Earl Long
Harold Long
James R. Long
Jerry Long
John E. Long
John G. Long
Jonathan K. Long

Joseph W. Long
Mary M. Long
Michael T. Long
Philis J. Long
Robert L. Long
Robert P. Long
Sam S. Long
Timothy Long
Houston W. Longino
Walton H. Longmire
Joe G. Longwith
Herman M. Lookout
Court E. Loomis
Cecil Looney
Fred L. Looney
Ned R. Looney
Armando R. Lopez
David Lopez
James L. Lopez
Mary G. Lopez
Michael D. Lopez
Victor D. Lopez
Charles C. Lord
Charles Lorenz
Kathie L. Loring
Marhsall D. Lory
Vernon Losey
Jared P. Lott
Stephen Loucks
Keith Louderback
Harry Loughmiller
J. K. Love
Jack Love
John Lovell
Ashley Lovett
Edwin Lovett
Robert W. Lowder II
Brice W. Lowell
Gregory J. Lowery
Linda R. Lowery
Max Lowery
Leon Lowrey
Wiley Lowrey
Gary W. Lowry
John R. Lowry
Richard R. Lowther
Laymond Loyd
Jack M. Lucas
William Lucas
Esther Ludlow
Margaret S. Ludlow
Charles Ludlum
Douglas J. Lugo

German Q. Lugo
Manuel C. Lujan
Corwin L. Lumly
Irl G. Lumm
David B. Lundy
David M. Lunsford
Holder L. Lunsford
Ben Luton
Richard Luttrell
Richard H. Lutz, Jr.
Eugene K. Lybarger
John Evans Lybrand
John Lybrand
Dick W. Lycan
Robert W. Lyday
Ronald S. Lyde
Roy N. Lykins
Clay Lynch
Clayton R. Lynch
Francis Lynch
Gerald Lynch
John T. Lynch
Robert R. Lynch
David A. Lynn
Ed Lynn
Leburn Lynn
Mitchell Lynn
James E. Lyon
Frank Lyons
Harry Lyons
Dolores E. Lytle
Herbert W. Maas III
Ronny Mabe
Vada Sharon Mabe
Joseph Mabee
Alden MacArthur
Douglas A. Mackay
Kay D. MacKenzie
Clabe C. Mackey
Jack Mackey
Joe Mackey
Thomas Mackey
Andrew Jay Mackie
Cleo A. Maddox
Henry A. Maddox
Ronnie Madera
Eddie K. Madewell
Ray L. Madewell
M. Madewell
Myrna C. Madsen
Gary E. Magid
Robert N. Magid
Richard F. Maginn

William Magoto
Edward C. Mahaffey
Frank Mahan
Perry R. Mahan
Robert D. Mahan
Wilmer Mahan
Jere L. Maher
Earl F. Mahlerbe
Harry R. Mahood
Marshall Mahurin
David A. Main
Joseph P. Main
William B. Mainwuring
Thomas A. Mairs
Jerald W. Major
Michael Majors
Edgar Maker
Harry Maker
Earl F. Malherbe
Mark S. Malinowsky
Timothy P. Malishenko
Bob Mallonee
Phillip E. Malney
James W. Malone
John Malone
Richard L. Malone
Alice Louise Maloy
Dan Maloy
James A. Malroney
Don L. Maly
George B. Manawa
Mary Ann Mancino
Rudolph S. Mancino
Stephen Rudolph Mancino
Thomas P. Mancino
Richard Manlove
Benny L. Mann
Billy Mann
Edwin Mann
Elbert R. Mann
Gregory L. Mann
Monty Mann, Jr.
Don L. Manning
Jane A. Manning
Mary E. Manning
Paul J. Manning
Walter T. Manning
Dalton K. Manson
Paul M. Mansur
Leroy Manuel
Larry G. Mapes
Roy Mapes
Harold J. Marcano

James E. Marcum
Ronald G. Marcum
James I. Marguardt
William J. Maril
David Marizon
James N. Marks
Loren P. Marks
Nathan Marks
Doris Marlar
Tom I. Marlin
Robert W. Marling
Leo Marlott
Clarence E. Marlow
Lee R. Marlow
Roger D. Marlow
Jack Maroney
Wayne Marple
James Marquardt
Kenneth W. Marquis
James W. Marrs
Timothy G. Marrs
Wayne W. Marrs
E. Marrs
Jack Marsee
Bill Marshall
Charles E. Marshall
Gene Marshall
J. W. Marshall
John B. Marshall
John E. Marshall
John T. Marshall
Juanetta P. Marshall
Leo Marshall
Stephen P. Marshall
Walter Marshall
Bill Marston
Arthur D. Martin
Barbara J. Martin
Clifford W. Martin
Curtis P. Martin
Donald R. Martin
Donald Ross Martin
Eugene Martin
J. B. Martin
Jack Martin
Jack E. Martin
James H. Martin
Jimmy L. Martin
John E. Martin
John H. Martin
John R. Martin
John R. Martin
John W. Martin

John Martin
Judy E. Martin
Ken Martin
Leonard Martin
Leroy Martin
Luther Martin
Max R. Martin
Oral R. Martin
Patricia R. Martin
Penny Kate Martin
Raymond E. Martin
Richard H. Martin
Roy T. Martin
Stephen C. Martin
Van J. Martin
William Martin
Thomas R. Martin Bueshier
Barbara J. Martin Malone
A. Martin, Jr.
Harold F. Martin, Jr.
Fred Marts
William Martz
William Mascho
Herbie Mashino
Reuben E. Mashunkashey
Archie L. Mason
Don R. Mason
John R. Mason
Kenneth L. Mason
Leo Mason
Michael R. Mason
P.S. Mason
Richard Z. Mason
Robert R. Mason
Terry Mason
William C. Mason
Philip Mason Jr.
Frank L. Masoner
Anthony M. Massad
Frank M. Massad
Michael L. Massad
Wayne A. Massad
Wade W. Massenburg
Lawrance D. Massey
R.W. Massey
Lonnie Massingale
Clayborne J. Masters
Sara K. Masters
Maurice Masterson
Florencio Mata
Michael L. Matheny
Marion Mathes
Gary S. Mathews

John G. Mathews
John G. Mathias
J. H. Mathis
Riley J. Mathis
Ed Matlock
Jerry Matthews
Oliver H. Matthews
Roger Matthews
Sam E. Matthews
Sam M. Matthews
Sandra Lynn Matthews
William L. Matthews
William R. Matthews
Michael M. Mattox
Arthur A. Mauldin
Homer E. Mauldin
Howard Mauldin
James H. Mauldin
John J. Maupin
Steven Maus
Ronald W. Maust
Benjamin A. Max
Charles Maxey
J.C. Maxey
Stephen L. Maxson
Conrad T. Maxwell
James D. Maxwell
James J. Maxwell
James S. Maxwell
Murray Maxwell
Ricky J. Maxwell
Sparky D. Maxwell
William R. Maxwell
Charles E. May
Charles May
Elbert May
Gary May
Phillip May
Edward W. Mayberry
Ernest Mayberry
Herbert S. Mayberry
Robert R. Mayberry
Robert E. Mayer
Charles Mayfield
David Mayfield
Mike D. Mayfield
Robert H. Mayfield
William Mayfield
Robert F. Maynard
Mable Crownover Maynes
Donald L. Mayor
Harold Mayor
Aquilla Mays

Fell Mays
Kendall S. Mays
Tommy E. Mays
Clausine Maytum
Scott W. McAfee
Reed McAlister
Donald B. McAllister
John McAllister
Max F. McAllister
Sterl McAllister
Mark McAnally
Darrell W. McArthur
Douglas E. McBeath
Wayne L. McBeath
Wm. W. McBeath
Walker C. McBee
Hugh McBirney
Carroll Dee McBride
David L. McBride
Dennis E. McBride
Joe McBride
John D. McBride
Paul McBride
Robert D. McBride
Robert McBrinn
Helen M. McBroom
John C. McBurnette
Walter C. McCabe
Jack J. McCafferty
Bill McCain
Carson N. McCain
Williston B. McCain
Jerome E. McCall
Sheila A. McCall
Garett H. McCallister
Robert A. McCalman
Robert L. McCalman
Richard McCalye
Thomas C. McCamey
Meredith G. McCandless
Norma G. McCarty
Owen H. McCarty
Robert McCarty
Henry J. McCasky
Monroe McCaughtry
Loren McCaw
Jack McCharin
Joe McClafferty
Arthur McClain
Donald G. McClain
James C. McClain
Ken D. McClain
Max A. McClain

Paul L. McClain
Nofle A. McClanahan
Carolyn J. McClellan
Thomas McClellan
William McClellan
Donald C. McClelland
John B. McClelland
Bessie O. McClendon
Clavin R. McClendon
Mark S. McClintic
Bill McClintick
Jeffrey W. McClure
Jessie D. McClure
Joe E. McClure
Oscar W. McClure
Virgil F. McClure
Tom McClurg
Harry McClusky
William J. McCollough
Bill McCollum
Bob McCollum
William McCollum
Jane McComb
William McComb
W. W. McCombs
Wayne McCombs
Bob McConnell
Carl E. McConnell
Damon McConnell
Emerson A. McConnell
James F. McConnell
Kenneth W. McConnell
Robert McCord
Jack D. McCorkle
Kenneth J. McCormick
Robert McCormick
Carmond V. McCoy
Carmond McCoy
Clarence McCoy
Craig W. McCoy
James McCoy
Marrilee L. McCoy
Paul M. McCoy
Phillip McCoy
Robert McCoy
Roy E. McCoy
Bobby G. McCrackin
Dennis Lindel McCrackin
Joe E. McCrary
Willis McCraw
J. L. McCrory
John M. McCrory
Mike McCrory

Dr. McCubbin
Herbert McCubbins
William McCubbins
Bob McCuistian
Robert A. McCulloch
Carl E. McCullough
Charles E. McCullough
Grant K. McCullough
Paton McCullough
Eddy A. McCurtain
Jack McCurtain
Stanley G. McCurtain
Bryce McDade
Alfred Randolph McDaniel
Catherine Ophella McDaniel
Demings McDaniel
Gary L. McDaniel
Johnny W. McDaniel
Larry M. McDaniel
Richard L. McDaniel
William E. McDaniel
Bill McDonald
Billie J. McDonald
Carl P. McDonald
David McDonald
G. McDonald
George S. McDonald
Gerald D. McDonald
Jess E. McDonald
John K. McDonald
John L. McDonald
John McDonald
Keith McDonald
Michael McDonald
Paul D. McDonald
Marvin J. McDonald
George W. McDonough
Steven W. McDorman
Douglas N. McDougall
Richard D. McDougall
David C. McDowell
Kevin R. McDowell
Everett McElreath
Argyle McElroy
Max E. McElroy
George V. McElvain
Paul E. McElvany
Jim A. McElwain
Thomas McEvers
Louis McEwen
Gary L. McFadden
George McFall
Charles E. McFarland

Wilford W. McFarland
Tom A. McFarlin
Clarence J. McFarron
Sarah Florence McGath
Ronald J. McGee
Terry G. Mcgehee
Thomas Samuel McGeisey
W. D. McGhee
Rex McGilberry
Ralph L. McGill
McGillest
James J. McGinnis
Robert W. McGinnis
Dean A. McGlasson
Raymond M. McGlone
Myron McGreagor
Mike McGregor
Deidra A. McGriff
William McGuire
James D. McHenry
Michael McHuin
Frank E. McIntire
Haskell McIntosh
Larry L. McIntosh
Lawrence Craig McIntosh
Charles A. McIver
William McIver
Donald McKay
Clark McKee
Hugh McKee
Jimmy F. McKee
John P. McKee
Ken McKee
Mary L. McKee
Michael E. McKee
Jack McKeehan
James McKeehan
Thomas L. McKeehan
Kay D. McKenzie
Wm. R. McKim
Henry J. McKinley
Michael S. McKinley
Bennie McKinney
Daniel W. McKinney
Donald B. McKinney
Durdell M. McKinney
Jimmy L. McKinney
William J. McKinney
Howard McKinnis
James T. McKnight
Jerry McKnight
Lantz P. McLain
Starr McLain

Virgil L. McLain
Alex McLane
Billie L. McLaughlin
Michael McLaughlin
Jenna L. McLean
William D. McLennon
Jim McLeod
Homer C. McLoughlin
Morris McMahan
Kenneth M. McMahon
Charles J. McMath
William McMath
Bobby R. McMeans
Curtis E. McMenamy
Bill McMichael
Jack W. McMichael
Jack W. McMichael, Jr.
Anthony H. McMillan
Ronald E. McMillan
Tod McMillan
Tony McMillan
Evelyn McMillian
Ray F. McMinn
Stuart F. McMinn
Phillip C. McMullen
Wayne McMullen
William P. McMullen
Elmer L. McNabb
Laura L. McNamara
Patrick McNamara
Harlin McNamee
Arthur A. McNatt
Steve D. McNaught
Veda G. McNaught
Trevor A. McNeal
Betina McNeill
Jerry L. McNeill
Jon M. McNerney
Boyd W. McNutt
Paul McPeters
Thomas F. McPeters
Larry Neil McPhail
Charles J. McPherran
John M. McPherren
Don C. McPherson
Albert M. McQueen
David McQuiston
Morgan T. McReynolds
Donna M. McSpadden
M. R. McSpadden
Sam McSpadden
Richard K. McWilliams
Charles Mead

David L. Mead
Fred Mead
Cecil Meade
Jeffrey R. Meade
R.K. Meaders
John Meadors
Joseph L. Meadors
Michael B. Meadors
Turner J. Meadors
Frank E. Meads
William Henry Meads
G. B. Mealy
Henry G. Measday
Herman W. Meason
Bruce A. Meckel
Wade E. Medbery
William D. Medford, Jr.
Edwin W. Medlin
Everett Medlin
Harold R. Medlin
Herschel S. Medlin
James C. Meehan
Harold Meek
Denise M. Meeker
Foster Meeker
Leo Megow
Charles Mehew
Glen H. Mehew
Michael J. Mehling
Winston B. Meidel
William H. Meissinger
Bill Melton
Michael G. Melton
Nancy S. Melton
Wendell Vaughn O. Melton
Jack R. Mendenhall
Michael E. Mendenhall
Robert L. Mendenhall
Joe F. Mendonca
Gerald Menees
Howard Meng
Johnnie H. Merchant
Bill Meredith
Leo Meredith
Maurice Meredith
Cora S. Merkle
Jerry D. Merkle
William S. Merliss
Charles T. Merrell
John H. Merrell
Robert F. Merrell
Ward Merrick Jr.
Paula S. Merriott

Charles J. Merritt
Timothy C. Merritt
Helen M. Mersch
William Kenneth Mersch, Jr.
Robert Merten
LeRoy Merveldt
Johnny R. Messimore
Richard T. Messimore
Thomas L. Metcalf
Tom C. Metcalfe
Nathan I. Metlitz
Fredric D. Metz
James C. Metz
Ed F. Meyer
Henry H. Meyer
Joe A. Meyer
Lorry R. Meyer
Mike D. Meyer
Stephen D. Meyer
Luther Meyers
Catherine L. Michael
Fred D. Michael
George P. Michael
Glenn E. Michael
James F. Michael
William H. Michael
Donald D. Mick
Joel S. Mick
Maurice Mickey
Fred L. Mickle
Howard Midkiff
John R. Midkiff
Ronald Keith Mieir
Jack I. Mikels
Carolyn J. Milam
Charles B. Milam
Phylis A. Milam
Robert Milam
Robert J. Milan
Jack M. Miles
Jeffery L. Milham
Stephen C. Milholland
Robert C. Millam
Aaron C. Miller
Allen Lee Miller
Ben F. Miller
Ben Miller
Bernard L. Miller
Bob R. Miller
Bruce E. Miller
Burns Miller
Cass H. Miller
Charles M. Miller

Charles R. Miller
Charles S. Miller
Clarence Miller
Clyde Miller
Congieta Delene Miller
Curtis W. Miller
Dan R. Miller
Davidson Miller
Emmett Miller
Everett A. Miller
Gary P. Miller
Hack N. Miller
Horace Miller
Hugh E. Miller
J. W. Miller
Jack Miller
James F. Miller
John A. Miller
John E. Miller
John M. Miller
John Miller
Johnny L. Miller
Judson F. Miller
Julian Miller
Kenton D. Miller
Lavora M. Miller
Louis A. Miller
M.H. Miller
Martin Miller
Millage C. Miller
O.H. Miller
Peter Miller
Richard A. Miller
Richard E. Miller
Richard L. Miller
Robert A. Miller
Robert H. Miller
Robert O. Miller
Roger C. Miller
Ronald I. Miller
Roscoe B. Miller
Sherry Lee Miller
Terry Don Miller
Thomas E. Miller
Thomas S. Miller
William Miller
Bernard Lee Miller, Jr.
Donald Herman Miller, Jr.
Irl D. Miller, Jr.
Edward A. Millican
Carlos E. Milligan
Don E. Milligan
Leon E. Millikin

Gaylan M. Million
Jeff J. Milliren
Bradley E. Mills
Gregory M. Mills
Michael V. Mills
Robert Carol Mills
Max B. Milner
James R. Milton
George B. Milum
Paul Miner
Gordon Minner
Arvil D. Minor
Jack C. Minor
Jack Minor
Patric A. Minor
Dirk C. Minson
George A. Minter
James E. Minter
Harold G. Minyard
Hugh Mitani
Robert T. Mitchel
Bob R. Mitchell
Bryan Mitchell
Charles Albert K. Mitchell
Darius F. Mitchell
Edwin R. Mitchell
Harry Mitchell
J. C. Mitchell
James O. Mitchell
James R. Mitchell
John L. Mitchell
John S. Mitchell
John S. Mitchell
Joseph D. Mitchell
Larry Mitchell
Lee Mitchell
Oscar R. Mitchell
Ralph H. Mitchell
Robert W. Mitchell
Robert W. Mitchell
Ronald H. Mitchell
Steve Mitchell
Horace Mize
James Mobley
Ann Renee C. Mobra
Mary C. Mobra
Robert Mocabee
Sherman J. Mocabee
Vincent P. Mocini
David Mock
Roy R. Moffeit
John C. Moguin
Michael G. Moguin

Rodney Mohon
Paul Mohr
Jack J. Momaz
Charles S. Mongrain
George Mongrain
Clifford Monroe
Jen F. Monroe
John F. Monroe
John P. Monroe
William J. Monroe
Willard C. Monsen
Hardman C. Montague
Lane Montaque
Charles A. Montgomery
Charles E. Montgomery
Harold D. Montgomery
Henry Montgomery
James E. Montgomery
John Montgomery
Kyle K. Montgomery
Pat L. Montgomery
Wendell E. Montgomery
Winston Montgomery
Gary J. Montin
Andy Moody
Diane E. Moody
James R. Moody
James Michael Moody
Paul J. Moody
Ronald H. Moody
Ryan M. Moon
Stanley J. Moon
Alvy J. Mooney
Bert Moore
Billy B. Moore
Billy J. Moore
Buddy C. Moore
Charles L. Moore
Curtis Moore
Dale Moore
Danny F. Moore
Dewey G. Moore
Dovel Moore
Dwayne Moore
Ellen L. Moore
Eugene Moore
Fred Moore
Gene E. Moore
Glen H. Moore
Gordon A. Moore
Harold D. Moore
Harold R. Moore
Harry C. Moore

Howard Moore
J. D. Moore
James P. Moore
James P. Moore
Jerry L. Moore
Jerry L. Moore
Jerry R. Moore
Jesse C. Moore
Joe F. Moore
John D. Moore
Larry E. Moore
Lee B. Moore
Leon Moore
Michael E. Moore
Michael W. Moore
Paul R. Moore
Phillip Darwin Moore
Raymond K. Moore
Robert E. Moore
Shelton G. Moore
Thomas H. Moore
Thomas H. Moore
William H. Moore
William R. Moore
Oscar J. Moore, Jr.
Ralph W. Moore, Jr.
Rex Moore, Jr.
William Curtis Moore, Jr.
Frances R. Moots
Marion Arch Mordecai III
Jerry L. Moree
Donald S. Morehead
Billy K. Moreland
J. P. Morelock
Jim Morey
Bruce Morgan
Craig P. Morgan
David L. Morgan
David Ralph Morgan
David Morgan
Douglas Morgan
Howard Morgan
Jack Morgan
James Morgan
Jeff Morgan
Michael S. Morgan
Robert T. Morgan
Sidney L. Morgan
William L. Morgan
Porter H. Morgan, Jr.
Eugene F. Moriarty
James W. Moritz
James D. Morrell

Buster Morris
Cecil Morris
Don Morris
Donald Morris
Gilbert Morris
Glenn O. Morris
James E. Morris
John Morris
Moran S. Morris
Paul C. Morris
Richard L. Morris
Ronald D. Morris
Russell Morris
William C. Morris
Albert Morrison
David J. Morrison
Jack Morrison
James H. Morrison
Larry R. Morrison
Max W. Morrison
Patrick J. Morrison
Thomas H. Morrison
Barbara C. Morrow
Fred A. Morrow
Guy S. Morrow
Samuel L. Morrow
George B. Morse
Clarence Morton
Timothy R. Morton
William R. Morton
Ralph L. Moseley
Edward Mosely
Eugene Moser
Ralph R. Moser
John F. Moses
Theodore Mosher
Thomas Mosier
Billy Moss
Stanley K. Moss
James L. Most
Maze Moton
James N. Mott
Robert Motter
Michael Mougin
James E. Mounce
Kenneth L. Mount
Donald R. Mountain
Cecil Mouser
Claud Moutray
Don Arlen Moyer
Linneaus Moyer
Neal R. Moyer
Vernon Mudd

Donald J. Mueller
Eric Mueller
Emaloyd G. Mulanax
Danny L. Mulbery
Kenneth Mulhausen
Carol Mullen
John B. Mullen
Orlin Mullen
John A. Mullendore
Charles A. Mullens
Jack Muller
Annetta J. Mullings
Jesse R. Mullinix
David C. Mullins
James M. Mullins
M.H. Mullins
Marilyn D. Mullins
Patricia J. Mullins
Jerry Mumford
Clarence Munch
Don Munday
John W. Munn
Fred Munroe
R. G. Munsey
William D. Munson
Donald E. Murdoch
Jon L. Murdock
Donald L. Murphy
Evelyn L. Murphy
Jack G. Murphy
James H. Murphy
Mary Murphy
Michael Thomas Murphy
Mike Murphy
Robert J. Murphy
Ronnie J. Murphy
William P. Murphy
A. G. Murray
G. Murray
Leonard Murray
Michael S. Murray
Thomas D. Murray
Thomas E. Murray
William P. Murray
Leonard E. Murray, Jr.
Carlos Murrell
Larry Murrell
George Musgrave
Edwin Musgrove
Jack L. Musgrove
John F. Musgrove
Charles L. Musick
Leland Musick

James F. Musser
Robert L. Muxlow
Carol R. Myers
Glenn E. Myers
Houston Myers
James A. Myers
John T. Myers
Warren D. Myers
Robert H. Myles
Miles H. Nabora
Richard V. Nafe
Robert Z. Naifeh
Raymond B. Nance
Thomas L. Naro
J.A. Nasey
Ralph M. Nash
Ruth Nash
Billy J. Nation
James M. Nation
Richard W. Nauman
Kenneth Nay
Walter Nayer
Arthur Naylor, Jr.
Elmer L. NcNabb
Lorene B. NcNames
Charles D. Neal
Eugene B. Neal
Larry J. Neal
Michael J. Neal
Olney R. Neal
Rick Neal
Robert R. Neal
Ross Neal
Willard Neal
Chester Nease
Louis E. Neatherlin
Richard A. Nedom
Aubrey D. Neece
John C. Neece
Paul U. Neece
Bill R. Needham
Tom Needham
Larry D. Neel
Renate E. Neel
David V. Neely
David Neely
Samuel Neely
Stephen P. Neely
Terrie Lyn Neely
Jerry W. Nees
Richard G. Nees
Frank L. Neidermeier
Marion Edward Neighbors

John L. Neill
Albert H. Neilson
James A. Neish
Clyde Nelms
Arthur B. Nelson
Belinda L. Nelson
Darrell M. Nelson
Douglas Nelson
Erin L. Nelson
Garth Nelson
Gilman H. Nelson
Jimmie R. Nelson
Joe Nelson
Steven C. Nelson
Wayne C. Nelson
Charles H. Nelson, Jr.
George Nesbitt
Michael E. Nesbitt
Neal Nesbitt
Burl W. Nethercutt
Robert B. Nettles
Ernest C. Neubert
Robert M. Neuffer
Robert Neumann
Emery Newbern
Ray Newbern
Robert Newberry
Sharon K. Newberry
Ben Newby
George F. Newell
Gregory Newell
Darryl E. Newkirk
Wallace Newkirk
James R. Newlon
Abney L. Newman
Donald Clifford Newman
Eddie Newman
Rita A. Newman
Purser E. Newman, Jr.
Robert C. Newman, Jr.
Melvin L. Newsom
Dean Newton
William G. Newton
Robert E. Ney
William I. Ney
LaRae G. Nichol
Markland G. Nicholl
Billy W. Nichols
Daniel L. Nichols
Duwayne L. Nichols
Harold O. Nichols
J.L. Nichols
James N. Nichols

John P. Nichols
John R. Nichols
Spencer E. Nichols
Steven W. Nichols
William H. Nichols
David G. Nicholson
James L. Nicholson
Robert M. Nicholson
Roger Nicholson
Franklin E. Nickell
Bonnie D. Nickerson
Burns Nickerson
Dempsey Nickerson
Raymond C. Nietert
James C. Nimmo
Bill Nipper
George T. Nipper
Truman Nipper
James W. Nix
Jimmy G. Nix
Rolan L. Nix
Loyd A. Nixon
Pat E. Nixon
Larry Nney
Roger Noakes
Jack A. Noble
Lemar C. Noble
William E. Noble
Billie Ray Noblin
T. Noe
Leon Nolan
Richard C. Nolan
Richard B. Noonan
Lawrence M. Noonkestor
Sanford H. Nord
Robert G. Norfleet
James Norick
Edward F. Norman
Jack Norman
Landy Norman
Lee Norman
Wesley D. Norman
Bill W. Norris
Randy A. Northcutt
Billy Norton
Veotta Norton
Marvin J. Norvell
Russel S. Norvell
William G. Norvell
Jack W. Nottigham
Spencer P. Nunley, Jr.
Lester A. Nutter
Bryan A. Oakes

Bill L. Oakley
Wm. S. Oates
Allen O'Bannon
Michael O'Bannon
William G. O'Bannon
Billy Obins
William O'Brien
Carey L. O'Bryan, Jr.
Andrew O'Connor
Michael W. O'Connor
Larry L. Odaffer
Betty L. O'Dell
Rodney Carl O'Dell
Sidney O'Dell
Charles J. Odend'hal-Sibel
Archibald D. Odom
Danny Odom
John S. Odom
Kenneth Odom
John A. O'Donnell
Michael J. O'Donnell
Burton Ogg
David M. Ogg
Joe D. Ogiela
John C. Ogle
Billy M. O'Hair
Patrick O'Hornett
David Oldaker
J. W. Oldham
Charles Olentine
Hildebrant C. Oleson
John Olin
P.T. Olinger
Paul Olinger
David L. Oliver
Larry Oliver
Lynn Oliver
Ray T. Oliver
William L. Oliver
David P. Oller
Michael D. Olliver
Earl O. Olmstead
Kenneth E. Olsen
Gordon R. Olson
Charles K. O'Neal
Clifford G. O'Neal
Harriet H. O'Neal
Shawn Clayton O'Neal
Steve O'Neal
Gregory O'Neill
Thomas L. O'Neill
Charles L. Oney
Carl M. Oquin

Jesse G. O'Quinn
George Orcutt
John Orcutt
Robert S. Orcutt
Noel C. Orcutt, Jr.
Charles D. Orindgreff
David Orndorff
Terry O. Orndorff
Thomas D. Orndorff
Andrew M. Orr
Don C. Orr
Jo A. Orr
Marvin L. Orr
Milton L. Orr
Thomas W. Orr
William Orr
Thad B. Orr, Jr.
Tommy Lee Orrick
Danny Lewis Ortega
David A. Ortenburger
Richard C. Ortloff
George S. Osborn
John R. Osborn
John T. Osborn
Joyce Osborn
Robert B. Osborn
Robert L. Osborn
Roll Osborn
Scott A. Osborn
Tommy L. Osborn
Joseph Osborne
Orin L. Osborne
Robert Osborne
Joseph Osborne III
Frantz Ostenberg
Morris E. Ott
Paul D. Overton
Robert C. Overton
Jack D. Owen
Marcia S. Owen
Phillip S. Owen
Raymond C. Owen
Robert L. Owen
Robert W. Owen
Roth Owen
Billy L. Owens
Edwin T. Owens
Ernest Lee Owens
Jerry Owens
Joel Owens
John C. Owens
John W. Owens
Marion K. Ownbey

Fletcher B. Ownby
Donald Frederick Oxford
Angela Lee Ozbun
James E. Ozbun
William Ozbun
Carolyn L. Pace
John T. Pace
Stephen R. Pace
James A. Pack
Vernon Pack
Billie R. Padgett
Douglas D. Padgett
Jesse L. Padgett
Thomas E. Pafford
Donald H. Page
Esthimes Page
Ethmer Page
George M. Page
Richard G. Page
John Painter
Jimmy G. Palmer
John Palmer
Mack Palmer
William D. Palmer
Jerry W. Palmour
William T. Pancoast
Richard D. Paniak
Kent Allen Pankey
Maurice Pappan
Harry M. Paramore
James R. Parcher
Ronald F. Paris
Ronald L. Paris
Donald G. Parish
James N. Park
Allen Wayne Parker
Bill J. Parker
Billy J. Parker
Bud Parker
D. M. Parker
Frank R. Parker
George B. Parker
Jerry T. Parker
Marvin R. Parker
Michael Parker
Nancy Parker
Richard G. Parker
Robert C. Parker
Robert F. Parker
Robert K. Parker
Roy F. Parker
Sidney Parker
Stephen B. Parker

Robert S. Parker, Jr.
Joe Parkhill
George F. Parks
Katherine N. Parks
Mike Parks
Thomas I. Parks
Audrey O. Parman
Kale G. Parman
Larry Parmeter
John B. Parnell
O. H. Parnell
Charles H. Parr
Rafael Parra-Alfonzo
Damon A. Parrett
Sharon L. Parrett
Joseph G. Parris
Feegeebee Parrish
Michael D. Parrish
William Lee Parrish
James A. Parrott
Theron S. Parrott
Albert Parsley
Robert Parsley
Ross H. Parsley
Alice Carolyn Parsons
Joe Parsons
John D. Parsons
Lionel E. Parsons
Woodrow Parsons
Craig Paschall
David J. Passmore
John B. Passmore
Jack L. Paton
Dana Patrick
Archie Bell Patterson
Billy M. Patterson
Harry A. Patterson
Joe P. Patterson
John T. Patterson
Joseph R. Patterson
Louis Patterson
Pat Patterson
Raymond E. Patterson
Richard A. Patterson
Robert A. Patterson
Robert Patterson
Ronald D. Patterson
William Pattison
James Patton
Caroline E. Paul
Jerome W. Paul
Thomas M. Paul
James L. Pauley

Malcom R. Pavey
Calvin Paxton
Charles E. Payne
Louis E. Payne
Pratt B. Payne
Solon R. Payne
Fred Payne, Jr.
Merle T. Paynter
Joe W. Payton
David H. Pearne
Fred B. Pearson
Ralph L. Pearson
Roger Pearson
Vance Pearson
Lawrence H. Pechacek
Lawrence Pechacek
Bob Peck
James T. Peck
Kathy Jean Peck
Robert C. Peck
Joseph S. Peddle
Victor Peden
Carl S. Pederson
George D. Peebles
Dorothy J. Peek
John E. Peek
Michael A. Peery
Billy Buck Pelts
Jack J. Pemberton
William F. Pemberton
Doyle V. Pendergraft
Maurice Pendroy
David Penn
Leon C. Penn
Michael S. Pennell
Gary L. Penney
Edward H. Pennington
Milt Pennington
Robert E. Pennington
Herbert D. Penny
John C. Penny
Don Penwell
Eddie Penwright
Leon Peper
Charles G. Perdue
Gerald D. Perdue
George Perkins
John R. Perkins
Kenneth Perkins
Michael E. Perkins
Norma C. Perkins
Ron Perkins
Donald Perram

Wayne P. Perrier
Jack C. Perritt
Arch Perry
John D. Perry
Joseph G. Perry
Michael Ray Perry
Cecil Perryman
Kenneth Perryman
F. B. Persels
Grover C. Peters
Joe Peters
Joseph J. Peters
Roy L. Peters
Cordie E. Peterson
Dale L. Peterson
Karen Jeanne Peterson
Steven J. Peterson
Robert C. Petit
Clark J. Petrie
R. B. Petrie
Arvil Pettet
Millard E. Pettey
Joan F. Pettigrove
Robert S. Petty
William V. Pfaff
Richard Pfeffer
David Eugene Pfeifer
Charles E. Phelps
Garnett R. Phelps
Raymond D. Phelps
William (Billy) G. Phelps
Marion Phiefer, Jr.
William J. Phifer
William C. Philley
Alan L. Phillips
C.R. Phillips
Dawson Phillips
Dennis Phillips
Elliott Phillips
Frank Phillips
Gary D. Phillips
George R. Phillips
Jack K. Phillips
Judy May Phillips
Milton Phillips
Norman J. Phillips
S. Phillips
Wayne K. Phillips
William D. Phillips
William O. Phillips
Walter James Philp
Norma J. Philpol
George Phinney

Chris A. Piccola
Jeff Piccone
Frank Pickell, Jr.
Harry A. Pickering
Marilyn S. Pickett
David D. Pickup
Jerry Pickup
Stanley Pieper
Allen R. Pierce
Hal N. Pierce
Harold F. Pierce
Jack L. Pierce
Owen R. Pierce
Jay R. Pierson
Robert D. Pierson
Catherine R. Pifer
Tesley O. Pifer
Floyd D. Piguet
Loretta M. Piguet
Rob J. Piguet
Harold F. Pilant
Selden H. Pile
James P. Pincham
Martin W. Ping
Mary Sue Ping
Clark G. Pinkerton
Rosezetta M. Pinkerton
Jerry D. Pinkston
Wiley O. Pinson
William Pintar
Gregory P. Pitcher
Robert Pitcock
Bill Pitcock, Jr.
F. Pittman
Forrest C. Pittman, Jr.
Everett H. Pitts
Jamie Pitts
Lehr Pitts
Terry G. Pitts
James B. Pitts III
Ann E. Pixley
Frances Warren Pixley
Paul R. Pixley
John D. Pizarro
Edward Charles Platow
John Pleasant
Robert W. Pleasant
Jack L. Pledger
James R. Plum
Elizabeth A. Plumer
Walter R. Plumer
Charles L. Plumlee
Denton Plumlee

John Plumlee
Chester C. Plummer
John D. Plunkett
Harry Poarch
Maurice J. Podder
John J. Podpechan
Jack Pointer
George Points
Kenneth G. Poivre
Thomas L. Police
Kenneth A. Pollard
Gregory M. Pollock
Donald L. Polson
John A. Pomeroy
David E. Ponder
Arvel R. Ponton
Bob Pool
Kenneth Pool
Michael Allen Pool
Michael W. Pool
Virgil G. Pool
Edward Poole
Maloy P. Poor
Bill Pope
Dennis H. Pope
Marvin LeDon Pope
Raymond Pope
Walter R. Pope
Robert Stanley Poreda
James Porta
Steve Porta
John W. Porter III
Jerry R. Porterfield
Larry Allen Porterfield
Phyllis A. Porterfield
George C. Porth
Bill Poteet
Bruce Poteet
James D. Poteet
John S. Potocki
Gary D. Potter
Harold Potter
James Potter
Melvin L. Potter
William O. Potter
James G. Potts
Joel W. Potts
Lloyd E. Potts
William E. Potts
Barrie A. Powell
Bob P. Powell
Dick W. Powell
Edward H. Powell

Fred Powell
Houston C. Powell
Jack G. Powell
Jack Powell
Jeffrey C. Powell
Jess H. Powell
Jess L. Powell
Louis R. Powell
Odis D. Powell
Shirley B. Powell
Walter Powell
William L. Powell
Charles Powell, Jr.
Roger M. Power
Hershal C. Powers
Paul B. Powers
Richard M. Powers
William E. Powers
William D. Prague
John R. Pranter
Lawrence J. Pranter
James Prather
Jerry W. Prather
Charles A. Pratt
Hal B. Pratt
LeMarr Pratt
Vernon C. Pratt
Phillip M. Preble
Louis Presbury
Ralph R. Presley
David Presnell
Floyd Prestage
Richard D. Prestage
Bill Preston
Don Prewitt
Mayne Anne Pribble-Rogers
Cleo M. Price
Duane C. Price
Jerry Price
John L. Price
Kevin K. Price
Prier L. Price
Walter Price
W. D. Priddy
Billy Clyde Pride
Darlas E. Prim
Jerry W. Primm
Larry D. Prince
Samuel E. Prince
Doyle Prince Jr.
Curtis A. Prins
Frank O. Prior
Tom G. Prior

George W. Pritchard
Russell L. Pritchett
Charles W. Procter
Richard A. Procter
Bob Proctor
Joe F. Proctor
Larry R. Proctor
William H. Proctor
Carl W. Propp
Lewis S. Prosser III
Bill B. Prothro
Bill Protiva
Michael Albert Protive
Patrick Protiva
Douglass H. Pruett
Babe Pruitt
Douglas E. Pruitt
Eugene E. Pruitt
Larry G. Pruitt
Wilson Pruitt
Eugene Prunkard
Anna L. Pryor
Charles Richard Pryor
Ella C. Pryor
Mary E. Psomas
Gerald K. Puchta
Frederick James Pugh
John W. Pugh
Roger Pugh
William Pugh
Harry H. Pullen
Clyde Pulse
George E. Pults
Anthony A. Puntillo
Clyde C. Purcell
John L. Purdum
Anita J. Purkey
Donald R. Purkey
Micheal Dean Purkey
Donald W. Purser
Michael G. Purser
Clarence H. Putnam
Dorothy M. Putnam
Marshall K. Putter
Roger Pyle
Harry Quails
Brooks Queen
Bobby G. Quier
Patrick H. Quinn
William Quintero
Felix A. Quinton
Franklin Quinton
Loyd E. Quisenberry

Lewis W. Quoss
Eugene S. Rabbitt
Glen Rabun
Terry Joe Rader
Charles E. Radford
John J. Rafferty
George Raffety
James Ragan
Kenneth R. Ragsdale
Mildred G. Ragsdale
George Rahhal
Elias S. Rahill
Harold C. Raine
Raymond Raines
Harold C. Rains
Roger Joseph Rainwater
Lee F. Rakestraw
James E. Raley
Michael Ralko
Marvin Rall
Robert H. Ralstin
Bill Ramsay
Ray D. Ramsay
Chester Ramsey
Clifford Ray Ramsey
Dale Kinard Ramsey
Danny R. Ramsey
Edwin P. Ramsey
Joe Ramsey
John Ramsey
Melton E. Ramsey
William S. Ramsey
John Ramsey, Jr.
James D. Rand
Rufus E. Randall
Thomas J. Randol
Floyd Randolph
Gary L. Randolph
Lavern Randolph
David G. Raney
Charles Rankin
Charles D. Raper
Homer E. Rapp
Jack E. Rapp
John R. Rapp
Richard L. Raskin
Billy Rasnic
Gary W. Rastelli
Jack J. Ratcliffe
Lagrange Ratcliffe
Emmett Rathburn
Jack M. Ratzlaff
Harvey A. Rau

Ervin Raus
Harry Ravitz
Steven E. Rawding
Wayne Rawley
Larry Rawlings
Dorthea Louetta Rawls
Fred W. Rawson
Allen C. Ray
Burton Ray
Clyde Ray
D. D. Ray
Gerald Ray
Jackie Ray Stanley
Leon R. Ray
Michael N. Ray
Robert L. Ray
Sherry L. Ray
Stanton L. Ray
William O. Ray
William Ray, Jr.
Glenn Raymond
Tom Raymond
Paul I. Razien
Gene Reader
Jon G. Reading
John R. Reagan
Keith A. Reagan
Tim Reasor
Harold Randolph Reavis
Leroy Reavis
Monica O. Reavis
Nancy Lou Reavis
Paul Reber
Wm. S. Rechardson
Edwin Recknagel
William A. Record
Clifford E. Red Elk
Elgin Red Elk
Harry L. Redak
Carroll Reddic Jr.
Kenneth Redding
Ronald Redding
Wayne Redding
David L. Reddout
Edward H. Reddy
Gary L. Reece
George M. Reece
William D. Reece
Arthur C. Reed
Browning Reed
Harold D. Reed
Harold W. Reed
Jack Reed

Keesko (Joe Frank) P. Reed
Larry N. Reed
M. Reed
Marvin Reed
Melvin E. Reed
Quinton M. Reed
Reginald Reed
Richard Reed
Robert Browning Reed
Robert M. Reed
Robert Stephen Reed
Robert Reed
Walker B. Reed
Welch E. Reed
Harry E. Reeder
Roy Reeder
Versie L. Reeder
B. A. Reedy
Carolyn R. Reedy
Herman L. Reedy
Richard Reel
Joe Rees
John T. Rees
Edgar G. Reese
Joe Reese
Paul C. Reese
Jon S. Reeves
Robert A. Reeves
Rawleigh Rehean
Bill R. Reichard
Charles R. Reichard
William Richard Reichard
James W. Reichert, Jr.
John L. Reid
William W. Reid
Robert J. Reid, Jr.
Ed Reif
Jack R. Reilly
Jack Reilly
Fred Reinauer, Jr.
William J. Reinhard
Arch Reinhardt
Bartley D. Reinhardt
Lawrence A. Reiter
Ferrell Remokluo
Donald N. Remund
Jack E. Renegar
James C. Renfro
Michael J. Renfro
Robert Renfrow
David A. Renick
Jack Renigar
Harry J. Renko

Patrick Renshaw
Raymond Lee Replogle
Wallace L. Rerick
Willis P. Rerick
Mary Katherine Reser
John T. Resler
John C. Reusch
Joseph Revard
Mark S. Revard
Craig A. Reynerson
Don W. Reynolds
George A. Reynolds
George C. Reynolds
Homer Reynolds
Jackie E. Reynolds
James A. Reynolds
Jimmy L. Reynolds
Omer Reynolds
R. D. Reynolds
Richard Reynolds
Robert H. Reynolds
Robert N. Reynolds
Ronald T. Reynolds
Timothy L. Reynolds
William D. Reynolds
Willis R. Reynolds
Wirt P. Rhea
Joseph Rhees
Danny V. Rhine
John L. Rhine
Gary R. Rhoades
Gordon Rhoades
Bruce M. Rhodes
Charles Rhodes
Philip B. Rhodes
Raymond Rhodes
Sammy Rhodes
Vern I. Rhodes
Volney H. Rhodes
Alice J. Ribbe
Byron C. Rice
Dale E. Rice
Donald Rice
Enoch R. Rice
John L. Rice
Robert James Rice
Sherry L. Rice
Carl Richard
B. Joan Richards
Barton F. Richards
Robert J. Richards
Ronald M. Richards
Thomas H. Richards

Tom Richards
William H. Richards
Edward R. Richardson
Jack C. Richardson
James E. Richardson
Larry D. Richardson
Leonard A. Richardson
Louis L. Richardson
Maclin E. Richardson
Patrick R. Richardson
Randel Richardson
Robert B. Richardson
Robert D. Richardson
Robert V. Richardson
William S. Richardson
Robert Richarz
Robert Richey
Clark S. Richie
Rodney J. Richmond
Peter G. Richter
Sallie A. Ricketts
Kent Ricks
Homer Riddle
Paul L. Riddle
Robert Riddle
Scott D. Riddle
William D. Riddle
Andrew B. Riddle III
Fred D. Riddle, Jr.
Johnny R. Riddles
Steven W. Riddles
Belissa Gayle Ridenour
Charles D. Ridenour
Linda F. Ridenour
Charles B. Rider
Pat A. Rider
Ralph F. Rider
Roscoe C. Rider
Donovan Ridgeway
Hoyt H. Ridings
Ronald Ridley
John C. Ridling
Gene P. Riesen
John E. Riesen
Ed Rife
Richard Homer Rigdon
Robert Rigg
W. C. Rigg
Clyde A. Riggs
Danny E. Riggs
Don R. Riggs
Joe V. Riggs
Samuel A. Riggs

Harry L. Riggs, Jr.
Paul Righter
Sam Righter
Robert Rigsby
Michael S. Riley
Warren H. Riley
Wilbur Riley
James Rimer
W. A. Rinehardt
Jim Rinehart
William R. Ripple
David P. Ristau
David Brian Ritchie
Eddie J. Ritter
Louis Ritzhaupt
George M. Rixey
H. F. Rixey
Charles Rixman
Charles Richard Roach
Loyal Roach
Ronald G. Roach
Jonathan G. Roark
David M. Robards
Don Robards
Dean W. Robb
Dempsey Robbins
George H. Robbins
John M. Robbins
Deborah K. Robedeaux
Ivan E. Roberdes
Brent T. Roberson
Max S. Roberson
Robert D. Roberson
Billy Ray Roberson, Jr.
Edward D. Robert
Bobby W. Roberts
Charles R. Roberts
Charles Raymon Roberts
David S. Roberts
David Eugene Roberts
Donald D. Roberts
Donald W. Roberts
Doyle Roberts
Grover C. Roberts
J. T. Roberts
Jack Roberts
James L. Roberts
James W. Roberts
Janice M. Roberts
Jim Roberts
John C. Roberts
John Roberts
Mark S. Roberts

Marvin M. Roberts
Melvin T. Roberts
Rayburn Roberts
Richard L. Roberts
Robert Roberts
Roy L. Roberts
Scott A. Roberts
W. Roberts
George Roberts III
J.C. Roberts, Jr.
Jack Lloyd Roberts, Jr.
Cecil L. Robertson
Dale Robertson
Davis Robertson
Gregory A. Robertson
James A. Robertson
Michael Douglas Robertson
Phillip Ray Robertson
Raymond D. Robertson
Terral L. Robertson
Andrew J. Robinson
Dale M. Robinson
Delmar Robinson
Donald E. Robinson
Flora Edora Robinson
George Robinson
Hubert Robinson
Hugh E. Robinson
Hugh Robinson
Ingrid C. Robinson
Jimmy G. Robinson
Kenneth C. Robinson
Larry Robinson
Leon Robinson
Macon Robinson
Marilyn S. Robinson
Maurice Ezel Robinson
Max R. Robinson
Michael J. Robinson
Roscoe Robinson
Teddy R. Robinson
Terry Wayne Robinson
Thomas M. Robinson
Ellis Irwin Robinson, Jr.
Donald G. Robison
Ronald Dwayne Robinson
Edward D. Robson
Frank C. Robson
Stanford Robson
John D. Roby
Michael Roby
James Rockhold
Howard R. Rockhold, Jr.

Joe S. Rockwood
Lewis Rockwood
Kenneth E. Roddy
Rodne Roden
Claude R. Rodgers
George L. Rodgers
Marvin F. Rodgers
Warren M. Rodgers
Dick Rodman
Jesse S. Rodman
Richard T. Rodman
Jack B. Rodman, Jr.
Stephen J. Rodolf
Julius C. Rodriguez
Steven Roff
Carl M. Rogdahn
Bobby M. Rogers
Carl E. Rogers
Charles (Buddy) T. Rogers
Don E. Rogers
Douglas W. Rogers
Ella A. Rogers
Guy A. Rogers
J. J. Rogers
Jerry L. Rogers
John L. Rogers
Loretta S. Rogers
Randall L. Rogers
Rick Rogers
Stanley K. Rogers
Thomas Rogers
Victor F. Rogers
W. O. Rogers
Guy A. Rogers II
Charles Rogers Jr
Leo Earl Rogsdale
Arlyn W. Rohr
Curtis L. Rohr
Joseph A. Rohr
Loren D. Rohr
Walter S. Rohr
Carl J. Rohsenberger
Kenneth H. Rojas
George E. Roland
Lee Roles
Joseph F. Rolette
Jerry D. Roll
Daniel M. Roller
Margaret Rollins
Terry Rollins
Richard L. Romans
David Romine
Alan H. Romm

John R. Rook
Paul W. Rooker
Robert H. Rooker
John P. Rosborough
Dale Rose
Elizabeth Ellen Rose
Everett L. Rose
Paul Rose
Rickie D. Rose
Joe Roselle
Alan D. Rosenbaum
Billie R. Ross
Charles B. Ross
David B. Ross
David K. Ross
Donald G. Ross
Douglas D. Ross
Edward Ross
Frank Ross
James Ross
John Ross
Ken Ross
Louis C. Ross
Marty Ross
Marvin G. Ross
Rex Ross
Rodney D. Ross
Michael G. Rosser
Bert Rosson
Vaughan Rotenbery
Dennis Roth
James A. Rothgeb
Foster D. Rotramel
Jay P. Rousek
David F. Roush
Donald K. Routh
Rob R. Routh
Bascom W. Routon
Cecil Rouwalk
Earl D. Rowden
Michael A. Rowe
Prentiss E. Rowe
John W. Roy
John Roy
Johnnie Lee M. Roy
Thomas Roy
W. H. Royce
Andy Roye
Jerry R. Ruark
Charles Rucker
R. H. Rucker
Wayne N. Rucker
Harold E. Ruckman

Larry J. Rucks
Mary C. Ruddle
Jack O. Rue
Eugene E. Ruffin
Donald Ruggles
Charles A. Rule
William D. Rule
Myra G. Rumbaugh
Ralph Rumbaugh
Robert G. Rumbaugh
Perry Rummage
Dwight Rumsey
Donald Runyan
David J. Ruppel
Jim Rush
Ralph L. Rush
Richard R. Rush
Robert Rush
William C. Rush
Wash Rushing
Michael H. Rushmore
Michael Rushton
David Russell
Douglas Russell
Garry B. Russell
Henry Russell
Jerrill Russell
Jodi L. Russell
John S. Russell
LaHugh Russell
Marion F. Russell
Patsy Ruth Russell
Willard T. Russell
William J. Russell
John W. Russell, Jr.
John Rust
S. M. Rutherford
Dewey H. Rutledge
Terry Rutledge
Claude W. Rutterford
Janice J. Ryan
Paul P. Ryan
Steven R. Ryan
Warren C. Ryan
Jeff R. Ryker
Robert H. Ryskamp
J.C. Sabine
Lawerence C. Sadler
Robert F. Sadler
Ronald Sadler
John S. Safe
Joe Safford
Thomas Safreed

John D. Sage
Lawanna Sue Sage
Charles E. Sala
Earl R. Salisbury
Roma Jo Sallee
Grant Salley
Paul G. Salter
John Saltzman
Joe M. Salyer
James A. Salzer
Betty L. Sam
Brent T. Sammer
Claude W. Sammons
Jeris L. Sample
John S. Sample
Brenda Kay Sampson
Gordon Lee Sams
David B. Samuel
Joel L. Samuel
Arville Sanders
Bill Ernest Sanders
Buddy Sanders
Burton Sanders
Connelly Sanders
DeWitt Sanders
Henry K. Sanders
Ralph Sanders
Robert Sanders
William Sanders
Henry K. Sanders II
Don Sands
John P. Sanford
Vernon T. Sanford
John G. Sanger
Terry G. Sanger
Alan D. Sanstra
Richard P. Sarachek
Margaret M. Sarfatis
Bruce L. Sargent
David K. Sargent
S.J. Sarkey
Donnie E. Sarratt
Timothy D. Sasewich
Robert K. Satterfield
Timothy L. Satterfield
William Satterfield
James Satterwhite
Jim Satterwhite
William P. Sauer
Eddie L. Saultzman
George M. Savage
Kenneth W. Savage
Kenneth Savage

Maurice E. Sawvel
Roger A. Sawvel
John W. Sawyer
Lowell T. Sawyer
Wesley Sawyer
Willam E. Sawyer
Lowell T. Sawyer Jr.
Ren G. Saxton, Jr.
Ben Saye
Deana Saylors
Ernest M. Scaggs
Thomas G. Scally
Michael T. Scanlon
Carolyn S. Scarth
Monte M. Schafer
William Donald Schafer
Steven C. Schale
Robert E. Schanafelt
John P. Schaubel
Daniel G. Schaul
Charles H. Scheller
Tom Scherer, Jr.
J. S. Schiff
Fred H. Schindler
William E. Schleuter
Charles O. Schlosser
Charles G. Schmidt
Lowell R. Schmidt
Terry Gene Schmidt
Walter J. Schmidt
Theodore E. Schmitz
Joseph G. Schmitz, Jr.
Earl L. Schnackenberg
Ralph Schneider
Palmer W. Schnepel
James Warren Schnorr
June C. Schoekecke
Major M. Schoenbrun
John E. Schoenecke
Bruce G. Schoggen
Bill Scholl
Jim B. Schonwald
Wally Edward Schott
Walter E. Schott
John M. Schreffler
James B. Schrepel
David E. Schroeder
Fred H. Schroeder
Terrance J. Schulte
Eugene W. Schultz
William Schultz
Edwin F. Schulz
Ron Schumacher

Charles Schuman
Campbell O. Schuster
Chris Schwab
Billy C. Schwartz
Clifton Schwebbe
Fred Schweikhurd
Joseph J. Schwemin
Geoffrey J. Schwende
Charles E. Sconyers
Allender Scott
Arthur Scott
Benjamin Scott
David L. Scott
Edward G. Scott
Fred R. Scott
Freddie Scott
Harry A. Scott
Homer C. Scott
J. Scott
Jerry Scott
John D. Scott
Leonard Scott
Mark R. Scott
Michael F. Scott
Percy Scott
Ronald K. Scott
Roy L. Scott
Shelby M. Scott
Terry E. Scott
Tommy R. Scott
Warren K. Scott
Raymond Scoufos
Harry Scoufos, Jr.
Herbert Scrines
Richard L. Scritchfield
Robert B. Scruggs
Bill Scudder
Billy H. Scyrkels
William A. Seabolt
Jake H. Seaborn
Joe M. Seabourne
Joe Madison Seabourne
Jack W. Seagraves
Arthur H. Seale
Thomas S. Seanland
John W. Searle
Charles D. Searoy
William D. Sears
Bobby D. Seat
Delbert Seay
Howard W. Seay
Carl T. Sebring
Mary A. Secrist

Tommy Nuke Seely
Michael O. Seem
James P. Seifried
John J. Seiler
A. Selby
Gene Selby
Gordon Selby
Leo Selby
Vera L. Self
Jack B. Sellers
James A. Sellers
John Sellers
Neal W. Sellers
Thomas Russell Sellers
William Sellers
James V. Sellman
Patrick R. Sells
James Selsor
Marlon Semke
James Senkel
A. L. Settle
J.H. Settle
Ward Settle
Jack J. Severns
Samuel J. Sevier
Reed Seward
Theresa A. Seward
James M. Sewell
Richard C. Sewell
Harry L. Shackelford
Jack S. Shackelford
Kenneth E. Shackelford
Robert E. Shackelford
Ronald B. Shafer
Vera M. Shafer
Frank Shaffer
George W. Shaffer
Lawrence T. Shaffer
Paul D. Shaffer
Paul G. Shaffer
Robert R. Shaffer
Vance Shaffer
William Shaffer, Jr.
Bruce E. Shamel
Gary Shamel
Gary D. Shand
John B. Shandy
Charlie Shane
Jack R. Shanklin
Bill M. Shanks
Don Shanks
Frances Shanks
Robert M. Shanks

Bill A. Sharp
Dick Sharp
George V. Sharp
James R. Sharp
Richard Sharp
Tommy E. Sharp
Vernon L. Sharp
James Sharpe
Jack Shastid
Duane D. Shaul
Franklin Shaw
Homer Shaw
Jack Shaw
John L. Shaw
Joseph Shaw
Norman Shaw
Patrick D. Shaw
Thomas P. Shaw
Joseph A. Shea
Denver Sheddy
Jess K. Shedrick
Geneva J. Sheehan
Leo L. Sheehan
Edwin H. Shelden
Eulys B. Shell
Sammy O. Shell
Stephen P. Shelley
Paul S. Shelor
Elmo Shelton
Fred Shelton
James Shelton
Michael Leroy Shelton
Weldon Shelton
John H. Shepard
Lorne Shepard
Richard L. Sherer
L. T. Sherrill
Everett Sherman
Arch W. Shero
Ernest L. Shero
Ancel Sherrard
Buddy F. Sherrill
Corliss Gary Sherrill
Lynn Lee Sherrow
Martin Sheward
Brawner Shi
Ronald M. Shideler
Ray I. Shields
Robert W. Shields
Welcome Shields
George G. Shimoon
Drew D. Shipley
Jerry D. Shipley

Howard Shirk
Mary G. Shirley
Steve D. Shirley
Billy Waitman T. Shock
F. L. Shock
Howard R. Shock
Thomas Shoemaker
Robert E. Shofstall
Golden V. Shook
Marvin M. Shook
Matthew Shope
Christian M. Shore
Carl M. Short
Jack Short
Phillip W. Short
Billy June Shoup
Robert Norman Shoup
Wayne Showalter
Quinten Shreck
Richard F. Shriner
Walter R. Shriver
Arno H. Shroyer
Glen William Shrum
Lloyd Shrum
Lance O. Shuler
Elvin F. Shultz II
Estel T. Shurden
Eugene H. Shure
Charles J. Sibel
Christine Sibley
Gary W. Sibley
Robert Sibley
Harold Sickler
Milton Siebert, Jr.
Lee Siegismund
Robert C. Siekman
William Siekman
Charles L. Sieminskie
Robert C. Sievert
Edgar Allen Siewart
William M. Siggins
Joseph L. Sigmon
Tommy J. Sills
Gary L. Silvis
Allison J. Simmons
Don Simmons
Donald R. Simmons
James L. Simmons
James R. Simmons
Jimmie D. Simmons
Lloyd N. Simmons
Sewell A. Simmons
Steven L. Simmons

James K. Simms
Mike L. Simms
Phil Simms
Dale Simms, Jr.
Kalman Simon
Leter E. Simon
Forest Simon, Jr.
James A. Simons
C.O. Simpson
Del J. Simpson
Gary L. Simpson
Harry Simpson
John D. Simpson
Robert C. Simpson
Robert Simpson
Sherry L. Simpson
Tom Simpson
Travis Simpson
William R. Simpson
Larry Sims
Scott A. Singer
Alfred T. Singletary
Tom Singletary
Michael L. Singleterry
George D. Singleton
James M. Singleton
David Ray Sink
Alan L. Sisemore
Michael Sisemore
Edgar Sisney
Harvey Sixkiller
Steve Sixkiller
Waite Sixkiller
Jerry L. Sizelove
Clyde S. Skeen
Walter Skeens
Thomas P. Skeeters
Robert L. Skelton
Arthur W. Skidmore
William P. Skipwith
Joe Skye
Eugene Slack
Ronald Slagle
David R. Slankard
John Slater
Claude Sledd
Beverly Sledge
Elmo M. Slemp
Robert Slepka
Thomas Randall Slimp
Nancy Sloan
Sam N. Sloan
Roy Slocomb

Mark W. Smalling
Bruce Smallwood
William Smallwood
Don Smart
Ernie Smart
Ernest L. Smart III
Alfred Smith
Andrew Smith
Barbara L. Smith
Billy G. Smith
Billy R. Smith
Buddy G. Smith
Charles B. Smith
Charles E. Smith
Claude S. Smith
Clayton E. Smith
Daniel C. Smith
Daniel Lee Smith
Davey A. Smith
David A. Smith
Don E. Smith
Donald L. Smith
Douglas G. Smith
Earle H. Smith
Edward Smith
Edwin Smith
Eugene C. Smith
Floyd H. Smith
Forrest B. Smith
Frank Smith
Gael Smith
Garland Smith
Gary L. Smith
Gary R. Smith
George H. Smith
Gordon A. Smith
Harry S. Smith
Howard S. Smith
Howard Smith
J. B. Smith
J. J. Smith
Jack R. Smith
James A. Smith
James H. Smith
James L. Smith
James O. Smith
James T. Smith
Jay Donald Smith
Jay H. Smith
Jerry A. Smith
Jimmie L. Smith
John F. Smith
John Smith

Johnnie P. Smith
Kenneth Smith
Larry G. Smith
Lee C. Smith
Leland W. Smith
Lloyd D. Smith
M. R. Smith
Michael E. Smith
Michael G. Smith
Morrell Smith
Nancy D. Smith
Norman J. Smith
Paul A. Smith
Paul D. Smith
Paul M. Smith
Phil L. Smith
Philip L. Smith
Phillip R. Smith
Ralph D. Smith
Randall Allen Smith
Randy Paul Smith
Raymond G. Smith
Richard E. Smith
Richard K. Smith
Richard Smith
Rickey L. Smith
Robert C. Smith
Robert H. Smith
Robert Smith
Robert Smith
Rodger B. Smith
Ronald D. Smith
Sam A. Smith
Shelby L. Smith
Sidney P. Smith
Stanley C. Smith
Steve Smith
Steven G. Smith
Sylvester Smith
Terry J. Smith
Thomas D. Smith
Thomas G. Smith
Troy J. Smith
Troy L. Smith
V. D. Smith
Vergil D. Smith
Vernon J. Smith
Walter S. Smith
Walter Smith
Wann Smith
Wes M. Smith
William Arthur Smith
William H. Smith

William L. Smith
William W. Smith
William Smith
Bill Smith
Floyd H. Smith, Jr.
Robert S. Smith, Jr.
Eugene C. Smith, Sr.
Ben Smittle
Robert Smock
John F. Smoller
Louisa C. Smoller
William Smoller
George R. Smoot
William Smreker
Alfred J. Smyser
Thomas D. Smyser
Jimmy H. Snavely
George Snedden
Jack R. Snedden
Mike Snedden
Paul Snediker
Henry Sneed
Jack F. Sneed
Robert Clyde D. Sneed
Billy Snell
Gene Snell
Jack Snell
James Snell
Curtis Snelling
Ella J. Snelling
J. V. Snelling
Jerry E. Snelling
Kenneth Snelling
John C. Snider
Johnny T. Snider
Alva W. Snodgrass
Lawrence R. Snow
Duane J. Snyder
Jack R. Snyder
Norman E. Snyder
Jerry S. Sochor
Richard E. Solsbery
Lee B. Somers
Ernest Leroy Son
Christopher W. Songer
Roger L. Soper
Beery L. Sorenson
James C. South
Michael A. Southard
Monroe C. Southard
Herbert C. Southern
Richard C. Sowers
Elmer Spain

Robert Spangler
Daniel E. Spargur
Furman Sparks
Harvey L. Sparks
Ronald L. Sparks
Steven Sparks
Tom C. Sparks
William Sparks
Streeter Speakman
John F. Spears
James S. Speck
John E. Speer, Jr.
Bryan D. Spencer
Charles D. Spencer
Gary G. Spencer
Harold M. Spencer
Jerry D. Spencer
Joe T. Spencer
Larry C. Spencer
Melvin Spencer
Michael C. Spencer
Mike Spencer
Jesse B. Spencer, Jr.
Gregory G. Spener
Billy Jean H. Spicer
Debbie K. Spicer
Victor G. Spielman
Willard F. Spiller, Jr.
John R. Spivey
Stephen A. Spivey
Tommy C. Spradlin
Virgil Spradlin
J.R. Spraker
Milus M. Spring
Charles Springer
Carma L. Sprow
Maurice Spurgin
Jack Nelson Spurlock
Steven R. Spurlock
Guy Spurrier
James Spurrier
Alger Srygley
Ronald N. St. Clair
Michael St. John
Van M. St. John
Glenn A. St.Clair
Michael St.John
Perry C. Stacy
Gary Stafford
J. Stafford
Jim R. Stafford
Roberta A. Stafford
Forest Albert Stagg

Jack Staggs
Rick M. Stahl
David Staires
Michael Staires
William J. Stalcup, Jr.
Esther M. Stallard
Travis B. Stallcup
Jon K. Stallings
Rex A. Standefer
Herbert Standeven
George E. Standing Bear
David Standsburg
Charles Stanfiel
Jimmie N. Stanfield
Delmar Lee Stanfill
James R. Stanfill
Bert Stanford
Harold E. Stanford, Jr.
Richard Wilson Stangland
Charles R. Stanley
Earl W. Stanley
Jerry William Stanley
LeRoy S. Stanley
Millard Stanley
Richard N. Stanley
Russell L. Stanley
William E. Stanley
Earle Stanley, Jr.
Ernest O. Stapler
Larry C. Stapleton
Richard G. Stapp
Donald K. Starbird
Howard J. Stark
James Stark
James Joseph Starkey
Ron Starnes
Blue Starr
Charlie Starr
James C. Starr
John B. Starr
Charles Staton
Lawrence W. Staton
Ronald A. Staton
James F. Stauss
John E. Stauter
Michael D. Stauter
Robert Stauter
James C. Staves
Kenneth R. Stavmen
Glenn Steady
Cecil N. Stebbins
Lawrence Stebbins
Andrew M. Stebler

Lin Stedman
Greg W. Steele
Leslie D. Steele
Michael A. Steele
Paul Steele
Robert D. Steele
William D. Steelman
William J. Steelman
Julian P. Stegall
Richard Stehr
Howard Steidley
Kenneth C. Steidley
Lloyd L. Steidley
Thomas C. Steidley
Charles L. Stein
Clifford Stein
Melvyn Stein
Marilyn V. Stellman
John Stemmens
Bill Stemmons
John Stemmons
John D. Stenhouse
Danny C. Stephens
Elmer Stephens
Gary C. Stephens
Grant Stephens
Guy Stephens
James E. Stephens
James K. Stephens
Randall L. Stephens
Sammie L. Stephens
W.B. Stephens
Roger L. Stephens, Jr.
James G. Stephenson
John L. Stephenson
Thomas E. Stephenson
Marvin E. Stepson
James B. Sterne
John R. Sterrett
John Sterritt
Lonnie K. Stevans
Vicky J. H. Stevans
Robert Stevens
Walter G. Stevens
Westley F. Stevens
C. R. Stevenson
Charles R. Stevenson
Donald G. Stevenson
John S. Stevenson
Alfred Stevenson, Jr.
James R. Steverson
James Steward
Patsy R. Steward

Phillip M. Steward
Charles E. Stewart
Charles P. Stewart
Donald M. Stewart
Everette D. Stewart
Frank W. Stewart
Jerry A. Stewart
John W. Stewart
Jon H. Stewart
Joseph E. Stewart
Lawrence Stewart
Marvin E. Stewart
William B. Stewart
Everett W. Stewart, Jr.
Jack H. Stewart, Jr.
Frank E. Stickle
Keith D. Stidman
Charles L. Stifflemire
George E. Stiler
Jay D. Stiles
William E. Stiles
Jay D. Stiles, Jr.
Homer Still
Wayne Stillabauer
Walter Stilley
Michael Stimson
Sue A. Stimson
Glen L. Stinchcomb
G. O. Stine
Jimmie Lou Stinson, Jr.
George W. Stipp
John V. Stirman
Roddic Stirman
Lloyd W. Stith
B. C. Stivers
Harold D. Stivers
John B. Stizza
Tom C. Stoalabarger
William R. Stoalabarger
John R. Stockdale
W. H. Stockett
Ronald L. Stocklos
Don P. Stockton
John Stockton
Michael W. Stockton
Jim Stoddard
Donald Stogsdill
Gary Stogsdill
James Stogsdill
John Stoker
Richard D. Stoker
Robert Stokes
James G. Stolbe

Casey E. Stone
Charles Thomas Stone
Dexter Stone
James R. Stone
Paul Stone
William R. Stone
Gary L. Stonebarger
Larry D. Stonebarger
Howard L. Stoner
W.R. Stonum
Bill Stookey
Lloyd D. Stoops
Richard G. Storch
Bill M. Story
Jack Story
John Story
Martin Story
Terry Story
Martin V. Story, Jr.
Charles E. Stosberg
Gordon R. Stotts
Bert W. Stout
Bill W. Stout
Edward L. Stout
Elden L. Stout
Gary G. Stout
George Stout
Glenn Stout
Mark E. Stout
Raymond Stout
Timothy Sheffield Stout
Cynthia Lea Stover
Howard E. Stover
Robert M. Stover
Stewart Stover
Urna L. Stover
Dan W. Stowers
Richard Stowers
Leara L. Strain
Lewis S. Strain
Marvin J. Strain
Richard D. Strait
Charles E. Strange
Gary D. Strate
Louis Straus
Jim Stravlo
Grover Street
John G. Street
Ralph Street
Eltinge Streeter
Tom Strickel
Vernon Strickel
Barbara Alicia Strickland

Harold Strickland
William A. Strickland
Joe Strickler
Larry D. Stringer
Nancy Jane B. Stringer
Olive W. Stringer
Thomas H. Stringer
Frank Strom
Gregory R. Strong
James D. Stroup
Kenneth W. Stroup
Clark Strubar
James W. Strubar
John C. Stuart
Scott R. Stuart
J. C. Stubbs
Karen Sue Stubbs
Willie G. Stubbs
Chester D. Stuckey
Samuel S. Stunkard
Ted R. Stunkard
Robert Stuntz
George Henry D. Sturdevant
James P. Sturdevant
W.R. Sturdevant
Marion C. Sturdivant
George M. Sturgell
Lloyd Sturgeon
Tony L. Sturgeon
Glenn W. Sturm
Phillip M. Suchan
Vance Suffield
Chris Sugar, Jr
Wendell B. Sugg
Jerry C. Suggs
Larry R. Suggs
Harold Franklin Sullivan
Steven Leroy Sullivan
Tommy Erwin Sullivan
George M. Sullivan, Jr.
Herschel E. Sullivan, Jr.
Steve Summar
David L. Summers
James L. Summers
Jean Summers
Norman L. Summers
Stephen C. Summy
Steven D. Summy
Neal Sumner
Robert Sumner
Donald R. Sumter
James E. Sumter
Monroe A. Sumter

Larry D. Sunby
Randolph D. Sunday
Rodney J. Sunderland
Lester K. Sundstrom
Harold R. Sundvahl
Charles Supernaw
George B. Suppes
Jerry L. Surber
Jim Sussex
Donald L. Sutherland
Robbie Gay Sutherland
Kenneth Sutley
Kurtis Sutley
Don Sutlieff
David L. Suttle
Betty J. Sutton
Bob Sutton
Donald Sutton
Jack Sutton
Jeffrey L. Swafford
John J. Swaim
Robert D. Swaim
Johnnie T. Swais
George F. Swan
Sandra E. Swan
Bill Swanson
Don Swarner
Gary L. Swartz
Mary E. Swartz
Richard E. Swartz
Dennis R. Sweet
Paul G. Sweet
Richard L. Sweet
Phillip B. Sweeting
Dwight Swift
Harvey A. Swift
Kenneth Swindler
Robert B. Sympson
Joe M. Synar
Patrick L. Synar
Connie L. Tacker
Fernando Tagle
William D. Tait
Alvin R. Talbert
Kelly E. Taliferro
Edward C. Talley
Maxine Talley
Danny W. Tammen
Cecil Tangner
Carl Arthur Tangner, Jr.
Louis H. Tannehill
Billy B. Tanner
Clyde Tanner

Dan Tanner
David V. Tanner
Elmer Tanner
Elmo Tanner
James Tanner
Janie M. Tanner
Jean A. Tanner
Jean Tanner
Joan Tanner
Wahnee M. Tanner
Warren G. Tanquart
Rhodes E. Tardy
Patty D. Tarpley
Gary Leon Tarrant
Fred Tarver
Oscar B. Tate
Walter Tatge
Jack L. Taton
John Tatroe
Paul R. Tatroe
John B. Tatum
Preston Taulbee
Fred Tayar
Robert Tayar
Beverly J. Taylor
Charles W. Taylor
Clark B. Taylor
Dan L. Taylor
David G. Taylor
Donald E. Taylor
Douglas L. Taylor
Ed Taylor
Gary A. Taylor
Gary G. Taylor
Gary W. Taylor
Howard Taylor
Jimmy Taylor
Joel W. Taylor
John I. Taylor
Maurice Taylor
Oscar L. Taylor
Peter C. Taylor
Phillip Taylor
Q. M. Taylor
Randolph W. Taylor
Sam Taylor
Thomas E. Taylor
Thomas Taylor
William C. Taylor
William D. Taylor
William E. Taylor
Willis Taylor
John E. Taylor III

Richard D. Tayrien
Robert C. Tayrien
Chuck Teague
D.B. Teague
David Teague
Jack Teague
James Teague
Janice N. Teague
Ricky L. Teague
Dwight Teakell
Billy L. Tedlock
James Deloss Teel
Charles Teenor
William H. Telford
Edward A. Temple
George L. Temple
Lynn D. Temple
Michael L. Templeton
Robert L. Templeton
Kenneth C. Templeton, Jr.
Cleo F. Templin
Michael W. Tennant
Thomas Tennery
W. E. Tennery
Charles C. Terrell
Clifford Terrell
James A. Terrell
Roger B. Terrell
Stephen G. Terrell
James K. Terry
William Teter
Jack Teusink
Robert D. Teverbaugh
John S. Tevis
Gladys V. Thatcher
Ben D. Thedford
Bobby R. Thedford
Frank E. Theimer
Luke J. Theodore
James C. Thibodaux
Robert Thibus
Stephen W. Thicksten
James V. Thiessen
Andrew Thomas
Bette Jeanne Thomas
Betty L. Thomas
Dana Eric Thomas
Hanna Thomas
Homa Thomas
J. C. Thomas
John C. Thomas
John G. Thomas
Keith H. Thomas

Paul C. Thomas
Phil Thomas
Philip Daryl Thomas
Robert E. Thomas
Robert L. Thomas
Robert R. Thomas
Robert Thomas
Roger L. Thomas
Warren W. Thomas
William M. Thomas
William P. Thomas
Tom Thomas III
William Thomas III
Richard G. Thomas, Jr.
William M. Thomas, Jr.
Herman H. Thomason
Joyce G. Thomason
Martha E. Thomason
Roy L. Thomason
Fred D. Thomasson
Arthur R. Thompson
Benny Thompson
Bob Thompson
Charles E. Thompson
Clark Thompson
Cleve W. Thompson
Clifford Thompson
Curtis B. Thompson
Dale G. Thompson
Eugene Thompson
Eulys L. Thompson
Howard W. Thompson
Howard Thompson
Isom P. Thompson
J.S. Thompson
Jack W. Thompson
Joe C. Thompson
John K. Thompson
John Thompson
Karen S. Thompson
Kenneth E. Thompson
Lester Thompson
Mattie Gail Thompson
Neal W. Thompson
Phillip Thompson
Ralph J. Thompson
Robert R. Thompson
Robert W. Thompson
Robert Thompson
Robert Thompson
Roger D. Thompson
Ruby Jean Thompson
Temple Thompson

Terry L. Thompson
Tim Dale Thompson
Wayland G. Thompson
Glenn C. Thompson, Jr.
Lynn Thompson, Jr.
Robert E. Thompson, Jr.
Ronald Thomson
Billy Thoreson
John R. Thorman
Tandy Thornton
William H. Thornton
Bill Thorpe
Charles Thorpe
Christopher Thorpe
Johnnie R. Thorpe
William J. Thorpe, Jr.
Billie Thorson
Gregory Moore Thrasher
Floyd Thurlow
Jack E. Thurman
John A. Thurman
Marion E. Thurman
William D. Thurman
Frank Thurmon
Paul Tibbens
Larry D. Tibbetts
Becky E. Tice
James Tice
Travis Tice
Ralph E. Tidwell
John W. Tiger
John Tiger
Johnnie Tiger
Eddie O. Tilford
Dan Tillman
Virgil Tilly, Jr.
Richard F. Timmons
Eugene P. Tims
James Tindell
Marshall Tindell
Clarence Tinker
William Tinker
William H. Tinker, Jr.
David N. Tinney
Scott P. Tinney
Tray Tinney
Alfred I. Tinsley
Jerry Tinsley
Dale M. Tipton
James P. Tipton
William T. Tipton
James Barrow Tisdale
Thomas L. Tisdale

Doyle E. Toby
Alfred G. Todd
Larry D. Todd
Charles F. Toegel, Jr.
William M. Tolleson
Ernest M. Toma
Schaff Toma
John C. Tomlin
Chuck B. Tomlins
Phyllis Toon
Benjamin A. Tootle
Robert L. Tow
Michael P. Towers
Johnny G. Towne
John M. Townley
Charles W. Townsend
Irvin H. Townsend
James E. Townsend
James Townsend
Guy M. Townsend, Jr.
Humphrey C. Townsley
Richard Tracy
Thomas J. Traglin
Herman H. Trammel
Gary D. Trammell
Jarrett W. Trammell
Robbie Trammell
Robert W. Trammell
Robert M. Travis
Durell Treadway
Hal A. Treadwell
Gary A. Trede
Michael Edward Treen
Frank Trelaroney
Bonnie R. Tremble
Richard Trent
Arthur Tribbey
Joe Tribble
Wiltz B. Tribble
James S. Trimble, Jr.
Claude Trindle, Jr.
Richard P. Trippet
Sam R. Trizza, Jr.
John Trompeter
Leonard E. Trost
Delbert Trotter
John Trotter
Mitchell H. Trotter, Jr.
Keith A. Trout
Larry E. Trout
Leroy D. Trout
Michael Trout
Deborah Jean Trower

Michael Trower
Lawrence Trowes
Jesse C. Truax
Larry Z. Truax
Marvin L. Truby
James R. Trudgeon
William S. Trudgeon
Bob Trumbly
Pat Trumbly
Patrick M. Trumbly, Jr.
Lawrence L. Trumbull
Allison C. Tryon
Robert L. Tscherne
Joseph J. Tucci
Charles G. Tuck
Allan R. Tucker
Barran E. Tucker
David E. Tucker
David L. Tucker
Donel G. Tucker
Eugene Tucker
James D. Tucker
Marshall A. Tucker
W.R. Tucker
Steven J. Tucker III
Jack O. Tuggle
David T. Tuley
John Tunder
John W. Tunstall
Lewis Turck
Harry L. Turk
Kenneth C. Turk
Wayne Turk
Burl Turman
Paul Turnbull
Charles M. Turner
Chas H. Turner
Clark G. Turner
David H. Turner
Donald M. Turner
Frank Turner
Fred Turner
George H. Turner
George S. Turner
Jack Turner
Joe Turner
John C. Turner
John Turner
Lewis Turner
Martin Turner
Michael Dale Turner
Roger Turner
Rosalie Turner

Sammy C. Turner
Tim Turner
Avista Turnipseed
William G. Turpen
William L. Turpen
Wayne L. Turpin, Jr.
Danny Turrel
Gregory J. Turrel
Raymond C. Turrell
Frank H. Tuscany
Alvin Tuter
Larry Tuttle
Guy I. Tutwiler III
Dennis C. Twist
Wendell Twist
Burt Tyler
Edward O. Tyler
Joe Tyler
William S. Tyler
Stanley Tyrone
Pete B. Tyson
Jon A. Udden
Richard Uhr
Jerry R. Ulmer
Donnie Undernehr
Bobby D. Underwood
Donald Underwood
Max D. Underwood
Bob F. Unverferth
Michael C. Upkide
Ross M. Upson
George Upton
Marlo M. Uzcategui
Christopher R. Vail
Richard J. Valdes
Arthur T. Vallier
George A. Van Antwerp
Ronald R. Van Dyke
Donald G. Van Horn
R C. Van Nostrand
Everett Van Patten
Charles Van Pelt
H. B. Van Pelt III
Lowell M. Van Tassel
Gerald E. Van Valkenburg
James W. Van Velzer
Virginia M. Van Velzer
Jerry C. Van Winkle
Cyrus Vance
Leland S. Vance
Peter C. Vandaveer
Laeman L. Vanderburg
Bruce A. Vandergriff

Charles R. Vandergriff
Milbert V. Vandergriff
Gary Y. Vandever
Ronald Vann
Gary V. Vantine
Mary H. Vanvelzer
Justin VanWie
Jackie Vanya
William M. Vardeman
Dick W. Varley
Joe Varva, Jr.
Frank C. Vassour
Edward M. Vaughan
Gary J. Vaughan
Walton Vaughan
Frank Vaughn
Dale Vaught
Frederick L. Vaught
Richard Loyd Vaught
Tommy E. Vaught
Gary G. Veach
Donald D. Veatch
Austin E. Veatch, Jr.
Rollo E. Venn
Richard E. Vensel
James C. Vernon
Johnny H. Vestal
Donald Vick
Herman L. Vickers
Ira C. Vickers, Jr.
James M. Vickrey
Michael A. Vickrey
James Viefhaus
Randy Vierling
Ralph Viersen
William G. Vilott
Charles Vincent
Joseph Vincent
Earl H. Vincent, Jr.
Jesse L. Vint
William M. Vint
Jeffie Virginia
Barbara Jean Vitt
Jon Voelker
James E. Von Tungeln
Charles Vonhees
Leland E. Vosburgh
Charles Edward G. Voss
Leslie Voss
Edward C. Voss II
Charles C. Waddle, Jr.
Billy D. Wade
Christopher V. Wade

Jonathan Blake Wade
Maurice W. Wade
Neal J. Wade, Jr.
Bob L. Wadley
Nickolas C. Wadman
Haskel Waggoner
Homer H. Waggoner
John Waggoner
Robert M. Waggoner
Ronald L. Waggoner
William G. Waggoner
Bill Wagner
Carl Wagner
Carlton L. Wagner
Lawrence G. Wagner
Roy J. Wagner
William Wilson Wagner
Alton H. Wagnon
Robert W. Wagoner
Thomas A. Wagoshe
Elmer H. Wahl
W. L. Waid
James Waits
Oden J. Waits
Don R. Walden
Johnny D. Waldo
George D. Waldrop
Robert E. Waldrop
Robert Max L. Waldrop
Arthur Walker
Charles F. Walker
Clyde Allen Walker
Curtis Walker
David Walker
Debbie Kehler Walker
Don J. Walker
Dustin L. Walker
Foster L. Walker
George R. Walker
J. R. Walker
Jim Walker
Joella C. Walker
John Lewis Walker
Johnny M. Walker
Kenneth M. Walker
Kenneth S. Walker
Larry D. Walker
Mickey F. Walker
Philip M. Walker
Raymond G. Walker
Richard Walker
Robert L. Walker
Robert W. Walker

Ronald R. Walker
Ronnie Gale Walker
Sammy J. Walker
Steve E. Walker
Tommy L. Walker
Vernon A. Walker
Joseph F. Walker, Jr.
Gerald D. Walkingstick
Charles E. Wall
J. Z. Wall
Cecil L. Wallace
Darrel R. Wallace
Jimmy D. Wallace
John Harrison Wallace
Lewis Wallace
Michael J. Wallace
Micheal Ray Wallace
Patricia A. Wallace
Stuart Wallace
Thomas J. Wallace
Wayne C. Wallace
William M. Wallace
Robert D. Wallack
Gary A. Waller
John L. Wallis
Karen Faye Wallis
Peggy S. Wallis
Ronald R. Wallis
John F. Wallmork
Clarence W. Walls
Garland Walls, Jr.
Marjorie M. Wallsmith
Dennis P. Walsh
Thomas Walsh
Robert N. Walter
William L. Walter
C. C. Walters
Dale E. Walters
Donald Eugene Walters
Harold G. Walters
J. H. Walters
Jerry Walters
Rex Walters
William W. Walters
John Walthour
David Scott Walron
David Walton
Deborah J. Walton
Gary T. Walton
James R. Walton
Richard A. Walton
William G. Walton
David Hoyt Walworth

Larry Wayne Walworth
Burkett Wamsley
Ralph H. Wantland
Brenda Kay Ward
Carl Ward
Charles R. Ward
David Ward
Diana Lee Ward
Fred Ward
James P. Ward
Joel F. Ward
Kent Ward
Lew Ward
Michael N. Ward
Michelle A.. Ward
Richard D. Ward
Robert N. Ward
Sammy Richard Ward
Shirley M. Ward
Sidney J. Ward
Theodore D. Ward
Thomas E. Ward
Wilbur Ward
William H. Ward
William R. Ward
Charles G. Ward, Jr.
Bill L. Warden
H. E. Wardlow
Charles F. Ware
Michael J. Ware
Gary H. Warmack
Gurney Warnberg
Clyde G. Warr
David B. Warren
Dennis L. Warren
Leonard Warren
Lloyd C. Warren
Mark T. Warren
Richard L. Warren
Robert F. Warren
Robert G. Warren
Floyd E. Warterfield III
Allen W. Warwick
Richard Douglas Washam
Glenn E. Wasson
Orville H. Wasson
Charles W. Waters
Charles R. Watkins
Charles R. Watkins
David M. Watkins
Gordon E. Watkins
Larry G. Watkins
Mark W. Watkins

Raymond Louis Watkins
Wayne Wilson Watkins
Billy J. Watson
Bryan J. Watson
Donald K. Watson
John A. Watson
John E. Watson
John W. Watson
Mary J. Watson
Maurice Watson
R. P. Watson
Robert L. Watson
Tom Watson
William E. Watson
Delbert D. Watson II
Jeff R. Watts
John Watts
Ronald D. Watts
Thomas R. Watts
Tipp Watts
Wayne E. Watts
Cheryl Lea Way
Harvie D. Way
Phillip Way
Jerry Waymire
Jack Wayne
James L. Wayne
Stephen C. Wayne
Norma L. Weaklay
Charles Wear
Jack L. Wear
Marvin Weatherford
Buck Weathers
Bryon R. Weaver
Charles J. Weaver
Charles M. Weaver
Frank William Weaver
J. H. Weaver
Jack Weaver
James E. Weaver
Jim Weaver
John F. Weaver
Larry W. Weaver
Richard D. Weaver
Rodney K. Weaver
Bradley W. Webb
Clark D. Webb
Dennis Michael Webb
Franklin R. Webb
James Webb
Jeff Webb
Jerry D. Webb
Joe M. Webb

Lawrence G. Webb
Marion Webb
Robert Webb
Roy L. Webb
Theta J. Webb
William J. Webb
William M. Webb
Willie E. Webb
Cyrus E. Webb III
Charles D. Webber
Chery Weber
Judy B. Weber
Virginia Weber
Walter Weber
Calvin Webster
Chester D. Webster
Donald L. Webster
E. J. J. Webster
Steven L. Webster
Charles J. Weddington
Joseph L. Weddington
Troy Nelson Weddle
Ervin J. Wedel
Randall Eugene Wedin
Randy Wedin
Roger D. Weedn
Noel Weeks
Ronald C. Weeks
Ray Weems
Richard Weems
Paul Weidenheimer
William E. Weidman
John S. Weil
Charles M. Weill
Elmer Weinrich
Thomas F. Weiss
Thomas F. Weiss
Alvin L. Weitz
Don Welch
Edgar R. Welch
Eugene C. Welch
Joan E. Welch
Rowland W. Welch
Rupert Welch
Wentworth Welch
Wlliam D. Welch
Gordon Welcher
Harold D. Welcher
James E. Weldon
Lawrence Theodore Welker
Richard B. Weller
Marvin E. Wellman
Betty J. Wells

C. G. Wells
Carolyn S. Wells
Henry C. Wells
James L. Wells
James M. Wells
Lloyd K. Wells
Patricia Delora Wells
Ralph S. Wells
Donald P. Welty
Charles D. Wendorff
Dale Wensell, Jr.
Larry W. Wescott, Jr.
Dail West
George West
Harold G. West
James L. West
Leron West
Stanford L. West
Victor T. West
Gary S. Westbrook
Lee Westbrook
Lee Westbrook
Wilton Westbrook
Robert Donald Westenhaver
Frank E. Westerman
James W. Weston
Michael E. Weston
William B. Weston
Victor D. Westphall
Paul Wetherell
Jerry Wetmore
Ray G. Wettengel
William F. Wetzel
William S. Wetzel
Charles D. Weyland
Robert M. Wharry
Kenneth F. Whatley
Michael E. Whatley
John J. Whattoff
Jerry F. Wheatcraft
Frederick Wheeler
Harry Wheeler
Jack Wheeler
James Wheeler
John Wheeler
Judy K. Wheeler
Levell Wheeler
Clel Wheeling
Steve Wherenberg
Robert Whetstine
Stephen M. Whetstone
William T. Whiddon
Keith Whightsil

Donald J. Whinery
Nancy L. Whisenhunt
David Whisnant
Charles Whistler
Jere Whitaker
Kimbrough W. Whitaker
Lynn E. Whitaker
Nicholas B. Whitaker
Archie F. White
Arthur L. White
Bill White
Carl Junior White
Clarence W. White
Dennis G. White
Dewey D. White
Don White
Donald R. White
Ewers White
Garland White
Gary C. White
Gary E. White
Gary L. White
Herbert White
Jack W. White
James D. White
Jerry L. White
Joe D. White
Joe White
John A. White
John F. White
John M. White
Joyce A. White
Larry A. White
Malcolm M. White
Maury M. White
Melvin White
Michael A. White
Neeley T. White
Percy A. White
Phil J. White
Randolph S. White
Richard E. White
Richard Wendell White
Robert White
Rufmill W. White
Samuel D. White
Tilden R. White
Watson R. White
Wayne White
Roy R. White II
Mayo Sidney Whitecrow
Sam Whitehill
Edgar Whitehorn

Stanley D. Whitehurst
Bobby Whitekiller
Robert H. Whiteley
Jack Whitelock
Chance F. Whiteman
James Whiteneck
Robert Whitfield
Roger Harold Whitfield
William C. Whitford
Billy R. Whitington
Charles Whitman
Elmer Whitman
Clyde P. Whitmire
David Lyman Whitney
Susan Beth Whitney
Merle L. Whitney II
John Whitsel
William Whitsel
John Whitt
Dale C. Whittaker
Jere Whittaker
Leil L. Whittemore
Clay Foster Whitten
Eugene C. Whitten
Grover E. Whitten
John W. Whitten
William P. Whittenburg
Bert A. Whittington
Jo E. Whitworth
Roy Whitworth
Barney Whorton
James H. Wickemeyer
William B. Wicker
George G. Wickliffe
John Wickstrom
Richard Widdows
Ernest W. Wiemann
Sharon Kay Wigginton
Glenn L. Wigton, Jr.
Rodney W. Wiiest
Vernon L. Wikor
Kenneth O. Wilbanks
Stark H. Wilbor
John M. Wilcox
Michael W. Wilcox
Philip M. Wilcox
Robert D. Wilcox
Stacey W. Wilcox
Jeffie V. Wilde
Mike Wilde
Pamela J. Wilde
Patrick N. Wilde
Paul K. Wilde

Donovan L. Wilder
Grant Wilder
Charlotte Wilderman
Lester L. Wiles
Raymond H. Wiles
William T. Wiles
Lester L. Wiles, Jr.
Dyke Wiley
Nicholas D. Wiley
Robert L. Wiley
Frankie Wilhite
Gerald Wilhite
Phil Wilhite
John Wilhoite
Gerald Wilhour
Edward V. Wilkerson
Edwin Wilkerson, Jr.
Jack Wilkes
Bill H. Wilkins
Galyn S. Wilkins
James Ray Wilkins
Robert C. Wilkins
E. B. Wilkinson
Eugene Wilkinson
Fredrick Wilkinson
Glen E. Wilkinson
J. B. Wilkinson
Jack M. Wilkinson
Jack Wilkinson
Samuel Wilkinson
Ted A. Wilkinson
Larry F. Wilks
Oran H. Willbanks
Orion M. Willbanks
Burr L. Willcox
Sara Kay Willey
Phil Willhite
Brenda Louisa Willhoite
Charles Willhoite
John D. Willhoite
Mary Leota Willhoite
Robert R. Willhoite
Wendell Wayne Willhoite
John C. William
Albert L. Williams
Arthur B. Williams
Arthur D. Williams
Billie G. Williams
Billy L. Williams
Bobby D. Williams
Charles E. Williams
Clifford Williams
Dale Williams

David M. Williams
David W. Williams
Dean Williams
Dennis E. Williams
Don C. Williams
Earl Williams
Fred D. Williams
Fred O. Williams
Gene T. Williams
Guy Allen Williams
Harold Williams
Harry T. Williams
Howard E. Williams
J.D. Williams
Jack P. Williams
Jack Williams
James M. Williams
Jay T. Williams
Jim D. Williams
John T. Williams
Jon Williams
Judy E. Williams
Kenneth H. Williams
Lana Joy Williams
Larry D. Williams
Lee E. Williams
Matthew B. Williams
Michael J. Williams
Phillip Williams
Richard Williams
Rick Williams
Robert C. Williams
Robert Williams
Ronald N. Williams
Roy B. Williams
Roy Williams
Russell Edwin Williams
Steve A. Williams
Theodore R. Williams
Thomas E. Williams
Tom Williams
Virgil H. Williams
Walter L. Williams
Wendell Williams
Paul C. Williams III
Bill Williams Jr
Jack A. Williams, Jr.
Louis B. Williams, Jr.
Charles H. Williamson
Gene Williamson
John Williamson
Lyndall C. Williamson
Robert T. Williamson

Rodger O. Williamson
Bucky Willis
Herbert B. Willis
Ken Willis
Orlie Willis
Rebecca J. Willis
F.C. Wills
Dan Willson
Doug Willson
Allen Wilson
Arthur B. Wilson
Carol L. Wilson
Charles E. Wilson
Charles H. Wilson
Charles L. Wilson
Charles M. Wilson
Clarence E. Wilson
Dave Wilson
Don E. Wilson
Donald A. Wilson
Douglas H. Wilson
Floyd M. Wilson
Frank Wilson
Gene Wilson
H. J. Wilson
Harrold J. Wilson
Homer F. Wilson
Jack Wilson
Jackie W. Wilson
James L. Wilson
James T. Wilson
James T. Wilson
Jerome Wilson
Jerry Wilson
Jimmy Wilson
Joe W. Wilson
John D. Wilson
John E. Wilson
John J. Wilson
John P. Wilson
John W. Wilson
John Wilson
Joseph E. Wilson
Judson Wilson
K.C. Wilson
Larry G. Wilson
Mary L. Wilson
Mary Avalene P. Wilson
Michael D. Wilson
Miles D. Wilson
Noble Wilson
R. C. Wilson
Roland A. Wilson

Ron Wilson
Ronaldeen Wilson
Ronnie W. Wilson
Skip Wilson
Tom L. Wilson
Wayne Wilson
William A. Wilson
William R. Wilson
Wilma Lee Wilson
Woodrow H. Wilson
Wrey W. Wilson
Joe E. Wilson III
Dewey F. Wilson, Jr.
Paris Wilson, Jr.
John R. Wilver
Paul S. Wimmer
John T. Winchell
Lemard J. Winchester
Ollie Winders
Jerry W. Windham
John B. Windom
James O. Windsor
Marvin D. Windsor
Mitchel E. Winegeart
George Winfield
Monroe V. Wingate
Harry Wingfield III
Allan Winkler
George Winkler
David R. Winn
F. B. Winn
Harold L. Winn
Melvin W. Winn
Robert D. Winn
Valeria E. Winn
Elbert V. Winningham
Warren T. Winsett, Jr.
Neil C. Winston
Richard P. Winterroth
Kenneth York Winters
Ralph L. Winters
Ralph Winters
Tom Wintle
Charles Wisdom
Philip C. Wise
Robert E. Wise
Robert G. Wiseman
Robert M. Wissman
Bobby Witt
Bruce F. Witt
Jerry A. Wittels
William R. Wittmeyer
Fred Witty

Edward L. Wodraska
Charles E. Wofford
Darold W. Wofford
Donald Wofford
Dorothy I. Wofford
Frank Wofford
Thomas S. Wojcik
Thomas F. Wolfe
William J. Wolfe
Larry E. Wolverton
Carolyn L. Womac
Fabian Gregory Womac
Clyde Wood
Dale D. Wood
Donald F. Wood
Fenton Wood
Frank V. Wood
Fred Wood
Harold D. Wood
Henry S. Wood
James W. Wood
Jerry D. Wood
Jerry D. Wood
Michael G. Wood
Miles M. Wood
Phyllis O. Wood
Rhame P. Wood
Sandra J. Wood
Seth Wood
Steven H. Wood
Virgil W. Wood
Walter Wood
Woody Wood
Fred Wood, Jr.
Lawrence G. Wood, Jr.
Noah P. Wood, Jr.
William D. Wood, Jr.
Stewart Albert Woodard
Bobby V. Woodmansee
Robert J. Woodring
Preston Woodruff
Herman Woodruff, Jr.
Anson T. Woods
Fred W. Woods
Howard Woods
James F. Woods
Jerry Woods
Paul Woods
Ricky Woods
Shirley Woods
Charles Woodson
Dan Woodson
Donnie L. Woodson

Joe B. Woodson
Larry D. Woodson
Francis R. Woodward
Frank Woodward
Leon Woodward
Mony P. Woody
Michael J. Woolley
Denny L. Woolman
Johnny R. Woolman
Larry Woolsey
Steve Woolsey
Ricky C. Woosley
Charles G. Wooster
Charles Wooster
Darrell W. Wooster
George Wooten
Howlett C. Word
Kenneth Wayne Workman
Philip P. Workman
James D. Worrell
Wesley D. Worrell
Paddy J. Worthington
Ervin Wortman
William Wortman
Larry Woverton
Mark A. Wray
Billie Jean Wright
Billy Wright
Bob K. Wright
Bradley L. Wright
Duff R. Wright
Earl Wright
Emerson Wright
George K. Wright
George W. Wright
Glenn A. Wright
Harold B. Wright
Harold T. Wright
Howard W. Wright
James C. Wright
James F. Wright
James Wright
James Malcolm Wright
Lamar Wright
Philip Wright
Richard Wright
Robert A. Wright
Robert L. Wright
Robert Wright
Roger D. Wright
S. C. Wright
Ted Wright
Thomas G. Wright

W. C. Wright
Wilfred C. Wright
Clarence Wright, Jr.
Clarence J. Wurtz
Harvey R. Wyant
Bryan Harned Wyatt
Burke Wyatt
E. M. Wyatt
Tom Wyche
McMein Wyckoff
Robert D. Wycoff
William R. Wylder
Ralph J. Wymer
Nelda R. Wynne
Vance Wyrick
William E. Wyrick
William V. Wyrick
Sidney Yaffee
Ray A. Yagher, Jr.
Craig M. Yancey
Joel E. Yarborough
Dan W. Yarbrough
James F. Yarbrough
John F. Yarbrough
David A. Yates
Jack Yates
Lawrence Yates
Marshall Yates
Rex Yates
Sharon Lee Brown Yates
Lawrence Yates, Jr.
David Yauck, Jr.
Steven L. Yeager
Bobby J. Yeatts
John Yellow Bull
Edward Yelton
Emory O. Yelton, Jr.
Bill Yenny
Donald E. Yeokum
William R. Yetter
James Yingling
William Yingling
Harold J. Yoakum

Jerry Yoakum
Ralph Edward Yocham
Billy York
Calvin York
Daniel W. York
Marvin B. York
Norma June York
Richard D. York
Ron Yost
Clifford W. Young
Dean Young
Dennis Young
Ernest N. Young
Glenn E. Young
Herbert E. Young
James Young
Jefferson H. Young
Leon Doug Young
Nancy J. Young
Noland K. Young
Richard M. Young
Rick C. Young
Terry Young
Thomas H. Youngblood
Marvin D. Younger
Frank Yount
Frederick J. Yount
Clifford W. Youts
Theodore J. Yustak
Homer L. Zacharias
Richard Zajic
Curtis E. Zell
Frank Zetko
Herbert J. Ziegenfuss
Betty Marie H. Zimmerman
Jackie H. Zimmerman
Kathryn S. Zimmerman
John Zoellner, Jr.
John P. Zook
Gregory L. Zorn
Karl Goodwing Zschach
Sam Zumwalt
Jack I. Zweifel